THE REVELS PL.

Former general editors
Clifford Leech
F. David Hoeniger
E. A. J. Honigmann
J. R. Mulryne
Eugene M. Waith

General editors
David Bevington, Richard Dutton, Alison Findlay,
Helen Ostovich, and Martin White

DAVID AND BATHSHEBA

MANCHESTER
1824

Manchester University Press

THE REVELS PLAYS

ANON *Thomas of Woodstock*
or King Richard the Second, Part One

BEAUMONT *The Knight of the Burning Pestle*

BEAUMONT AND FLETCHER *A King and No King*
The Maid's Tragedy Philaster, or Love Lies a-Bleeding

CHAPMAN *All Fools*

CHAPMAN *Bussy d'Ambois An Humorous Day's Mirth*

CHAPMAN, JONSON, MARSTON *Eastward Ho*

DEKKER *The Shoemaker's Holiday*

FORD *Love's Sacrifice The Lady's Trial*

HEYWOOD *The First and Second Parts of King Edward IV*

JONSON *The Alchemist The Devil Is an Ass*
Epicene, or The Silent Woman Every Man In His Humour
Every Man Out of His Humour The Magnetic Lady
The New Inn Poetaster Sejanus: His Fall
The Staple of News Volpone

LYLY *Campaspe* and *Sappho and Phao Endymion*
Galatea and Midas Love's Metamorphosis
Mother Bombie The Woman in the Moon

MARLOWE *Doctor Faustus Edward the Second*
The Jew of Malta Tamburlaine the Great

MARSTON *Antonio and Mellida*
Antonio's Revenge The Malcontent

MASSINGER *The Roman Actor*

MIDDLETON *A Game at Chess Michaelmas Term A Trick to*
Catch the Old One

MIDDLETON AND DEKKER *The Roaring Girl*

MUNDAY AND OTHERS *Sir Thomas More*

PEELE *The Troublesome Reign of John, King of England*

WEBSTER *The Duchess of Malfi*

THE REVELS PLAYS

DAVID AND BATHSHEBA

GEORGE PEELE

edited by Mathew R. Martin

MANCHESTER
UNIVERSITY PRESS

Introduction, critical apparatus, etc.
© Mathew R. Martin 2018

The right of Mathew R. Martin to be identified as the editor of
this work has been asserted by him in accordance with the
Copyright, Designs and Patents Act 1988.

This edition published by Manchester University Press
Oxford Road, Manchester M13 9PL

www.manchesteruniversitypress.co.uk

British Library Cataloguing-in-Publication Data
A catalogue record for this book is available from the
British Library

ISBN   978 1 7849 9303 0   hardback
ISBN   978 1 5261 6398 1   paperback

First published 2018
Paperback published 2022

The publisher has no responsibility for the persistence or accuracy
of URLs for any external or third-party internet websites referred
to in this book, and does not guarantee that any content on such
websites is, or will remain, accurate or appropriate.

Typeset
by Toppan Best-set Premedia Limited

Om

General Editors' Preface

Clifford Leech conceived of the Revels Plays as a series in the mid-1950s, modelling the project on the New Arden Shakespeare. The aim, as he wrote in 1958, was 'to apply to Shakespeare's predecessors, contemporaries, and successors the methods that are now used in Shakespeare's editing'. The plays chosen were to include well-known works from the early Tudor period to about 1700, as well as others less familiar but of literary and theatrical merit. 'The plays included', Leech wrote, 'should be such as to deserve and indeed demand performance'. We owe it to Clifford Leech that the idea became reality. He set the high standards of the series, ensuring that editors of individual volumes produced work of lasting merit, equally useful for teachers and students, theatre directors and actors. Clifford Leech remained General Editor until 1971, and was succeeded by F. David Hoeniger, who retired in 1985.

Ever since then, the Revels Plays have been under the direction of four or five general editors: initially David Bevington, E.A.J. Honigmann, J.R. Mulryne, and E.M. Waith. E.A.J. Honigmann retired in 2000 and was succeeded by Richard Dutton. E.M. Waith retired in 2003 and was succeeded by Alison Findlay and Helen Ostovich. J.R. Mulryne retired in 2010. Published originally by Methuen, the series is now published by the Manchester University Press, embodying essentially the same format, scholarly character, and high editorial standards of the series as first conceived. The series now concentrates on plays from the period 1558–1642. Some slight changes have been made: for example, starting in 1996 each index lists proper names and topics in the introduction and commentary, whereas earlier indexes focused only on words and phrases for which the commentary provided a gloss. Notes to the introduction are now placed together at the end, not at the foot of, the page. Collation and commentary notes continue, however, to appear on the relevant pages.

The introduction to each Revels play undertakes to offer, among other matters, a critical appraisal of the play's significant themes and images, its poetic and verbal fascinations, its historical context, its characteristics as a piece for the theatre, and its uses of the stage for which it was designed. Stage history is an important part of the story. In addition, the introduction presents as lucidly as possible the criteria for choice of copy-text and the editorial methods employed in presenting the play to a modern reader. The introduction also considers the play's date and, where relevant, its sources, together with its place in the work of the author and in the theatre of its time. If the play is by an author not previously represented in the series, a brief biography is provided.

The text of each Revels play, in accordance with established practice in the series, is edited afresh from the original text of best authority (in a few instances, texts), in modern spelling and punctuation and with speech headings that are consistent throughout. Elisions in the original are also silently regularised, except where metre would be affected by the change. Emendations, as distinguished from modernized spellings and punctuation, are introduced only in instances where error is patent or at least very probable, and where the corrected reading is persuasive. Act divisions are given only if they appear in the original, or if the structure of the play clearly points to them. Those act and scene divisions not in the original are provided in small type. Square brackets are also used for any other additions to, or changes in, the stage directions of the original.

Rather than provide a comprehensive and historical variorum collation, Revels Plays editions focus on those variants which require the critical attention of serious textual students. All departures of substance from the copy-text are listed, including any significant relineation and those changes in punctuation which involve to any degree a decision between alternative interpretations. The collation notes do not include such accidentals as turned letters or changes in the font. Additions to stage directions are not noted in the collations, since those additions are already made clear by the use of brackets. On the other hand, press corrections in the copy-text are duly collated, as based on a careful consultation of as many copies of the original edition or editions as are needed to ensure that the printing history of those originals is accurately reported. Of later emendations of the text by subsequent editors, only those are reported which still deserve attention as alternative readings.

One of the hallmarks of the Revels Plays is the thoroughness of their annotations. Besides explaining the meanings of difficult words and passages, the annotations provide commentary on customs or usage, on the text, on stage business – indeed, on anything that can be pertinent and helpful. On occasion, when long notes are required and are too lengthy to fit comfortably at the foot of the page below the text, they are printed at the end of the complete text.

Appendices are used to present any commendatory poems on the dramatist and play in question, documents about the play's reception and contemporary history, classical sources, casting analyses, music, and any other relevant material.

Each volume contains an index to the commentary, in which particular attention is drawn to meanings for words not listed in the *OED*, and (starting in 1996, as indicated above) an indexing of proper names and topics in the introduction and commentary.

Our hope is that plays edited in this fashion will promote further scholarly and theatrical investigation of one of the richest periods in theatrical history.

DAVID BEVINGTON
RICHARD DUTTON
ALISON FINDLAY
HELEN OSTOVICH

Acknowledgements

I would like to thank David Bevington, this edition's supervisory editor, for his guidance at every stage of the preparation of this edition. My thanks also go to the staff at the libraries that house copies of the 1599 quarto edition of *David and Bathsheba* for facilitating the digital reproduction of those copies. I would like to acknowledge the support of Brock University's Humanities Research Institute for funding the digital reproduction. Lastly, thank you to Editions Slatkine for permission to reprint the Du Bartas verse in the commentary notes and appendix. It is taken from Guilliaume de Salluste Sieur du Bartas, *The Works of Guilliaume De Salluste Sieur Du Bartas*, ed. Urban Tigner Holmes, Jr, John Coriden Lyons, and Robert White Linker, 3 vols (1940; rpt Geneva: Slatkine Reprints, 1977).

Abbreviations and References

EARLY EDITIONS OF *DAVID AND BATHSHEBA*

Q George Peele, *The Love of King David and Fair Bethsabe. With the Tragedie of Absalon* (London: Adam Islip, 1599) [quarto]. STC 19540.

QBod Copy of Q at the Bodleian Library, Oxford.

QBL 1 Copy of Q at the British Library, London, shelf mark 162.d.52.

QBL 2 Copy of Q at the British Library, London, shelf mark C.34.d.54.

QFol Copy of Q at the Folger Library, Washington, DC.

QH Copy of Q at the Huntington Library, San Marino, CA.

QHv Copy of Q at Harvard University, Cambridge, MA.

QHC Copy of Q at Haverford College, PA.

QIl Copy of Q at the University of Illinois, Urbana-Champaign.

QM Copy of Q at Magdalene College, Cambridge.

QNLS Copy of Q at the National Library of Scotland, Edinburgh.

QP Copy of Q at the National Trust Collections, Petworth House, Petworth, West Sussex.

QTex Copy of Q at the Harry Ransom Center, University of Texas at Austin.

QVAM Copy of Q at the Victoria and Albert Museum, Dyce Collection, London.

QWC Copy of Q at Worcester College, Oxford.

MODERN EDITIONS OF *DAVID AND BATHSHEBA*

Blistein *David and Bethsabe*, ed. Elmer M. Blistein, in vol. 3 of *The Life and Works of George Peele*, ed. Charles T. Prouty, 3 vols (New Haven: Yale University Press, 1970).

Bullen *David and Bethsabe*, ed. A.H. Bullen, in vol. 2 of *The Works of George Peele*, 2 vols (London: Nimmo, 1888).

Dyce 2   *David and Bethsabe*, ed. Alexander Dyce, in vol. 2 of *The Works of George Peele*, 3 vols (London: Pickering, 1829–39).

Dyce 3   *David and Bethsabe* in *The Dramatic and Poetical Works of Robert Greene & George Peele*, ed. Alexander Dyce (London: Routledge, Warne, and Routledge, 1861).

Greg   *The Love of King David and Fair Bethsabe*, ed. W.W. Greg (Oxford: Malone Society Reprints, 1912 [1913]).

Hawkins   *The Love of King David and Fair Bethsabe: With the Tragedy of Absalon* in vol. 2 of *The Origin of the English Drama*, ed. Thomas Hawkins, 2 vols (Oxford: Clarendon, 1773).

Keltie   *The Love of King David and Fair Bethsabe, With the Tragedy of Absalon* in *The Works of the British Dramatists*, ed. John Scott Keltie (Edinburgh: Nimmo, 1873).

Manly   *The Love of King David and Fair Bethsabe With the Tragedie of Absalon* in vol. 2 of *Specimens of the Pre-Shaksperean Drama*, ed. John Matthews Manly, 2 vols (Boston: Athenaeum Press, 1897).

Morley   *The Love of David and Fair Bethsabe, With the Tragedy of Absalon* in *Plays and Poems by George Peele*, ed. Henry Morley (London: Routledge, 1887).

Rabkin   *David and Bethsabe*, ed. Norman Rabkin, in vol. 1 of *Drama in the English Renaissance*, ed. Russell A. Fraser and Norman Rabkin, 2 vols (Upper Saddle River, NJ: Prentice Hall, 1976).

Thorndike   *David and Bethsabe* in *The Minor Elizabethan Drama: I. Pre-Shakespearean Tragedies*, ed. Ashley Thorndike (London: Dent, 1910).

OTHER REFERENCES

Allott   Robert Allott, ed., *England's Parnassus* (London: N.L.C.B and T.H., 1600). STC 378.

Antony of Padua   St Antony of Padua, 'The Saints Compared to Eagles' in *Mediaeval Preachers and Mediaeval Preaching*, ed. J.M. Neale (London: Mozley, 1856).

Ashley, *Authorship*   Leonard Ashley, *Authorship and Evidence: A Study of Attribution and the*

	Renaissance Drama Illustrated by the Case of George Peele (1556–1596) (Geneva: Librairie Droz, 1968).
Ashley, *Peele*	Leonard R.N. Ashley, *George Peele* (New York: Twayne, 1970).
Auger	Peter Auger, 'The *Semaines*' Dissemination in England and Scotland until 1641', *Renaissance Studies* 26.5 (November 2012), 625–40.
Baines	Barbara J. Baines, *Representing Rape in the English Early Modern Period* (Lewiston, NY: Mellon, 2003).
Bamford	Karen Bamford, *Sexual Violence on the Jacobean Stage* (New York: St Martin's, 2000).
Berek	Peter Berek, 'Tamburlaine's Weak Sons: Imitation as Interpretation before 1593', *Renaissance Drama* 13 (1982), 55–82.
Bevington	David Bevington, *Tudor Drama and Politics: A Critical Approach to Topical Meaning* (Cambridge, MA: Harvard University Press, 1968).
Birch	Bruce C. Birch, 'The First and Second Books of Samuel: Introduction, Commentary and Reflections,' in vol. 2 of *The New Interpreter's Bible*, 12 vols (Nashville: Abingdon Press, 1994), 947–1383.
Bishops'	*The Holy Bible, Containing the Old Testament and the New: Authorised and Appointed to be Read in Churches* (London: Christopher Barker, 1588). STC 2149.
Blackburn	Ruth H. Blackburn, *Biblical Drama under the Tudors* (The Hague: Mouton, 1971).
Boehrer	Bruce Thomas Boehrer, *Monarchy and Incest in Renaissance England* (Philadelphia: University of Philadelphia Press, 1992).
Bourne	William Bourne, *An Almanac and Prognostication for X. Years, Beginning at the*

	Year of our Lord 1581 (London: Richard Watkins and James Robertes, 1581). STC 418.
Braunmuller	A.R. Braunmuller, *George Peele* (Boston: Twayne, 1983).
Browning	W.R.F. Browning, *Oxford Dictionary of the Bible*, 2nd ed. (Oxford University Press, 2009).
Bunny	Edmund Bunny, *The Coronation of David* (London: Thomas Gubbin, 1588). STC 4090.
Bushnell	Rebecca W. Bushnell, *Tragedies of Tyrants: Political Thought and Theater in the English Renaissance* (Ithaca and London: Cornell University Press, 1990).
Calvin	Jean Calvin, *The Institution of Christian Religion*, trans. Thomas Norton (London: Thomas Vautrollier, 1578). STC 4418.
Campbell	Lily B. Campbell, *Divine Poetry and Drama in Sixteenth-Century England* (Cambridge University Press, 1961).
Catty	Jocelyn Catty, *Writing Rape, Writing Women in Early Modern England: Unbridled Speech* (Houndmills, Basingstoke: Macmillan, 1999).
Cheffaud	P.H. Cheffaud, *George Peele* (Paris: Librairie Felix Alcan, 1913).
Clemen	Wolfgang Clemen, *English Tragedy Before Shakespeare: The Development of Dramatic Speech*, trans. T.S. Dorsch (London: Methuen, 1961).
Compost	Anon., *The Compost of Ptholomeus Prince of Astronomy: Very Necessary, Utile, and Profitable for All Such as Desire the Knowledge of the Science of Astronomy* (London: Thomas Colwell, n.d.). STC 20481.7.
Connolly	Annaliese Connolly, 'Peele's *David and Bethsabe*: Reconsidering Biblical Drama of the Long 1590s', *Early Modern Literary*

	Studies Special Issue 16 (October 2007), 9.1–20, <URL: http://purl.oclc.org/ emls/si-16/conpeel.htm>.
Costley	Clare L. Costley. 'David, Bathsheba, and the Penitential Psalms', *Renaissance Quarterly* 57.4 (Winter 2004), 1235–77.
Craik	T.W. Craik, 'The Reconstruction of Stage Action from Early Dramatic Texts', *Elizabethan Theatre V*, ed. George Richard Hibbard (Toronto: Archon, 1975), 76–91.
Cummings	Robert Cummings, 'Reading Du Bartas', in *Tudor Translation*, ed. Fred Schurink (New York: Palgrave Macmillan, 2011), 175–96.
De Worde	Wynkyn de Worde trans., *The Golden Legend*, by Jacobus de Voragine (Westminster: De Worde, 1498).
Deighton	Kenneth Deighton, *The Old Dramatists: Conjectural Readings on the Texts of Marston, Beaumont and Fletcher, Peele, Marlowe, Chapman, Heywood, Greene, Middleton, Dekker, Webster* (Westminster: Archibald Constable, 1896).
Dekker	Thomas Dekker, *A Knight's Conjuring, Done in Earnest, Discovered in Jest* (London: William Barley, 1607).
Doctor Faustus	Christopher Marlowe, *Doctor Faustus, A- and B-texts (1604, 1616)* (The Revels Plays), ed. David Bevington and Eric Rasmussen (Manchester University Press, 1993).
Drayton	Michael Drayton, *The Muses' Elizium* (London: John Waterson, 1630). STC 7210.
Du Bartas	Guilliaume de Salluste Sieur du Bartas, *The Works of Guilliaume De Salluste Sieur Du Bartas*, ed. Urban Tigner Holmes, Jr, John Coriden Lyons, and Robert White Linker, 3 vols (1940; rpt Geneva: Slatkine Reprints, 1977).

Edelman   Charles Edelman, ed., *The Battle of Alcazar*, by George Peele, in *The Stukeley Plays* (Manchester: Manchester University Press, 2005).

Edward II   Christopher Marlowe, *Edward the Second* (The Revels Plays), ed. Charles R. Forker (Manchester University Press, 1994).

Ephraim   Michelle Ephraim, *Reading the Jewish Woman on the Elizabethan Stage* (Aldershot, VT: Ashgate, 2008).

Ewbank, 'House'   Inga-Stina Ewbank, 'The House of David in Renaissance Drama: A Comparative Study', *Renaissance Drama* 8 (1965), 3–40.

Ewbank, 'Love'   Inga-Stina Ewbank, 'The Love of King David and Fair Bethsabe', *English Studies* 39 (1958), 57–62.

Famous Victories   *The Famous Victories of Henry V* in *The Oldcastle Controversy: Sir John Oldcastle, Part 1 and The Famous Victories of Henry V* (The Revels Plays), ed. Peter Corbin and Douglas Sedge (Manchester University Press, 1991).

Farmer and Lesser   Alan B. Farmer and Zachary Lesser, *Database of Early English Playbooks*. http://deep.sas.upenn.edu. Accessed 3 August 2016.

Firth   Katherine R. Firth, *The Apocalyptic Tradition in Reformation Britain 1530–1645* (Oxford University Press, 1979).

Foakes   R.A. Foakes, ed., *Henslowe's Diary*, 2nd ed. (Cambridge University Press, 2002).

Forker   Charles R. Forker, ed., *The Troublesome Reign of John, King of England* (The Revels Plays), by George Peele (Manchester: Manchester University Press, 2011).

Frontain and Wojcik   Raymond-Jean Frontain and Jan Wojcik, eds, *The David Myth in Western Literature* (West Lafayette, IN: Purdue University Press, 1980).

Geneva	*The Bible: That is, the Holy Scriptures Contained in the Old and New Testament* (London: Christopher Barker, 1590). STC 2153.
Gray	Dionis Gray, *The Storehouse of Brevity in Works of Arithmetic* (London: William Norton and John Harison, 1577). STC 12201.
Greg	W.W. Greg, *A Bibliography of the English Printed Drama to the Restoration*, 4 vols, Illustrated Monographs 24, 1–4 (London: Bibliographical Society, 1939–59).
Grimal	Pierre Grimal, *The Dictionary of Classical Mythology*, trans. A.R. Maxwell-Hyslop (Oxford: Blackwell, 1996).
Gurr	Andrew Gurr, *The Shakespearean Stage 1574–1642*, 3rd ed. (Cambridge University Press, 1992).
Guy-Bray	Stephen Guy-Bray, 'The Shame of Siblings in *David and Bethsabe*', in *Sibling Relations and Gender in the Early Modern World: Sisters, Brothers and Others*, ed. Naomi J. Miller and Naomi Yavneh (Aldershot: Ashgate, 2006), 140–9.
Hall	Kim Hall, *Things of Darkness: Economies of Race and Gender in Early Modern England* (Ithaca and London: Cornell University Press, 1995).
Holland	Henry Holland, *David's Faith and Repentance* (London: R. Field, 1589). STC 135865.
Homer	Homer, *Iliad*, trans. Richmond Lattimore (University of Chicago Press, 1951).
Homilies	Anon., *The Second Tome of Homilies* (London: Edward Allde, 1595). STC 13674.
'Homily'	'An Homily against Disobedience and Wilful Rebellion' in *The Second Tome of Homilies* (London: Edward Allde, 1595). STC 13674.

Hook	Frank S. Hook, ed., *Edward I*, by George Peele, in vol. 2 of *The Life and Works of George Peele*, gen. ed. C.T. Prouty, 3 vols (New Haven: Yale University Press, 1952–70).
Horne	David H. Horne, *The Life and Minor Works of George Peele*, vol. 1 of *The Life and Works of George Peele*, gen. ed. C.T. Prouty, 3 vols (New Haven: Yale University Press, 1952–70).
Huttar	Charles A. Huttar, 'Frail Grass and Firm Tree: David as Model of Repentance in the Middle Ages and Early Renaissance', in Raymond-Jean Frontain and Jan Wojcik, ed., *The David Myth in Western Literature* (West Lafayette, IN: Purdue University Press, 1980), 39–54.
Jew of Malta	Christopher Marlowe, *The Jew of Malta* (The Revels Plays), ed. N.W. Bawcutt (Manchester University Press, 1978).
Keenan	Siobhan Keenan, *Travelling Players in Shakespeare's England* (New York: Palgrave Macmillan, 2002).
Kilgore, 'Mixing'	Robert Kilgore, 'Mixing Genres in George Peele's *David and Bethsabe*', *Renaissance Papers* (2010), 11–22.
Kilgore, 'Politics'	Robert Kilgore, 'The Politics of King David in Early Modern Verse', *Studies in Philology* 111.3 (Spring 2014), 411–41.
Knutson	Roslyn L. Knutson, 'Marlowe Reruns: Repertorial Commerce and Marlowe's Plays in Revival', in *Marlowe's Empery: Expanding His Critical Contexts*, ed. Sara Munson Deats and Robert A. Logan (London: Associated University Presses, 2002), 25–42.
LEME	*Lexicons of Early Modern English*, ed. Ian Lancashire (Toronto: University of Toronto Press, 2013), <http://leme.library.utoronto.ca/index.cfm>.

Lindberg   David C. Lindberg, *The Beginnings of
                            Western Science* (University of Chicago
                            Press, 1992).
Lloyd   Richard Lloyd, *A Brief Discourse of the
                            Most Renowned Acts and Right Valiant
                            Conquests of Those Puissant Princes Called
                            the Nine Worthies* (London: R. Warde,
                            1584). STC 16634.
Locrine   W.S., *The Lamentable Tragedy of Locrine*
                            (London: Thomas Creede, 1595). STC
                            21528.
Logan   Robert A. Logan, *Shakespeare's Marlowe:
                            The Influence of Christopher Marlowe
                            on Shakespeare's Artistry* (Aldershot:
                            Ashgate, 2007).
McMillin and MacLean   Scott McMillin and Sally-Beth MacLean,
                            The Queen's Men and Their Plays (Cam-
                            bridge University Press, 1998).
Merry Conceited Jests   *Merry Conceited Jests of George Peele Gen-
                            tleman, Sometimes a Student in Oxford*
                            (London: Francis Faulkner, 1607). STC
                            19541.
Middleton   Thomas Middleton, *The Triumphs of
                            Integrity. A Noble Solemnity, Performed
                            through the City, at the Sole Cost and
                            Charges of the Honorable Fraternity of
                            Drapers, at the Confirmation and Estab-
                            lishment of Their Most Worthy Brother the
                            Right Honorable, Martin Lumley, in the
                            High Office of his Majesty's Lieutenant,
                            Lord Mayor and Chancellor of the Famous
                            City of London* (London: Nicholas Okes,
                            1623). STC 17901.
Milton   John Milton, *Paradise Lost* in *Complete
                            Poems and Major Prose*, ed. Merritt
                            Y. Hughes (New York: Macmillan,
                            1957).
Montrose   Louis Adrian Montrose, 'Gifts and
                            Reasons: The Contexts of Peele's *Arayg-
                            nement of Paris*', *English Literary History*
                            47.3 (Autumn 1980), 433–61.

Munday   Anthony Munday, *The Mirror of Muta-*
                            bility (London: John Allde, 1579). STC
                            18276.
New King James   *Holy Bible: The New King James Version.*
                            New York: Thomas Nelson, 1982.
OED   *Oxford English Dictionary Online* (Oxford:
                            Oxford University Press, 2013), <http://
                            www.oed.com>.
Peele   *The Life and Works of George Peele*, gen.
                            ed. C.T. Prouty, 3 vols (New Haven:
                            Yale University Press, 1952–70).
Petrarch   Francesco Petrarcha, *Rime sparse* in
                            Petrarch's Lyric Poems, trans. and ed.
                            Robert M. Durling (Cambridge, MA:
                            Harvard University Press, 1976).
Pliny   Pliny, *The History of the World. Commonly*
                            called, The Natural History of C. Plinius
                            Secundus, trans. Philemon Holland, 2 vols
                            (London: Adam Islip, 1603). STC 20029.
Prescott, *French Poets*   Anne Lake Prescott, *French Poets and*
                            the English Renaissance: Studies in Fame
                            and Transformation (New Haven: Yale
                            University Press, 1978).
Prescott, 'Reception'   Anne Lake Prescott, 'The Reception of
                            Du Bartas in England', *Studies in the*
                            Renaissance 15 (1968), 144–73.
Prime   John Prime, *The Consolations of David*
                            Briefly Applied to Queen Elizabeth (Oxford:
                            Joseph Barnes, 1588). STC 20368.
Roston   Murray Roston, *Biblical Drama in*
                            England from the Middle Ages to the
                            Present Day (Evanston: Northwestern
                            University Press, 1968).
Rutter   Tom Rutter, 'Marlovian Echoes in the
                            Admiral's Men Repertory: *Alcazar*,
                            Stukeley, Patient Grissil', *Shakespeare*
                            Bulletin 27.1 (Spring 2009), 27–38.
Sampley, 'Text'   Arthur M. Sampley, 'The Text of Peele's
                            David and Bethsabe', *PMLA* 46.3 (Sep-
                            tember 1931), 659–71.
Sampley, 'Version'   Arthur M. Sampley, 'The Version of the
                            Bible Used by Peele in the Composition

of "David and Bethsabe"', *Studies in English* 8 (1928), 79–87.

Schoenbaum
: Samuel Schoenbaum, *Internal Evidence and Elizabethan Dramatic Authorship* (Evanston, IL: Northwestern University Press, 1966).

'Sermon'
: 'The Second Part of the Sermon on Obedience', in *Certain Sermons appointed by the Queen's Majesty* (London, 1559). STC 13648.5.

Shakespeare
: William Shakespeare, *The Complete Works of Shakespeare*, ed. David Bevington, 7th ed. (Boston: Pearson, 2014).

Shapiro
: James Shapiro, *Rival Playwrights: Marlowe, Jonson, Shakespeare* (New York: Columbia University Press, 1991).

Sidney
: Philip Sidney, *The Defence of Poesy* in *The Major Works*, ed. Katherine Duncan-Jones, revised edition (Oxford University Press, 2002).

Smith, *Dictionary*
: William Smith, *Smith's Bible Dictionary* (Old Tappan, NJ: Spire Books, 1982).

Smith, *Humanist's*
: John Hazel Smith, *A Humanist's 'Trew Imitation': Thomas Watson's* Absalom (Urbana: University of Illinois Press, 1964).

Solga
: Kim Solga, *Violence Against Women in Early Modern Performance: Invisible Acts* (New York: Palgrave Macmillan, 2009).

The Spanish Tragedy
: Thomas Kyd, *The Spanish Tragedy*, ed. J.R. Mulryne, with introduction and notes by Andrew Gurr, 2nd ed. (London: A. & C. Black, 1989).

Speaight
: Robert Speaight, *William Poel and the Elizabethan Revival* (London: Heinemann, 1954).

Spenser
: Edmund Spenser, *The Faerie Queene*, ed. Thomas P. Roche (London: Penguin, 1978).

Sykes
: H. Dugdale Sykes, 'Peele's Borrowings from Du Bartas', *Notes and Queries* 147 (November 1924), 349–51, 368–9.

1 Tamburlaine   Christopher Marlowe, *Tamburlaine the Great, Part One* (The Revels Plays), ed. J.S. Cunningham (Manchester University Press, 1981).

2 Tamburlaine   Christopher Marlowe, *Tamburlaine the Great, Part Two* (The Revels Plays), ed. J.S. Cunningham (Manchester University Press, 1981).

Troublesome Reign   George Peele, *The Troublesome Reign of John, King of England* (The Revels Plays), ed. Charles R. Forker (Manchester: Manchester University Press, 2011).

Vaughan   Robert Vaughan, *The Portraitures at Large of Nine Modern Worthies of the World* (London, 1622), STC 24602.

Vickers   Brian Vickers, *Shakespeare, Co-Author: A Historical Study of Five Collaborative Plays* (Oxford University Press, 2002).

Weil   Judith Weil, 'George Peele's Singing School: *David and Bethsabe* and the Elizabethan History Play', *Themes in Drama* 8 (1986), 51–66.

Wentworth   Peter Wentworth, *A Pithy Exhortation to Her Majesty for Establishing Her Successor to the Crown* (n.p., 1598). STC 25245.

Werstine   Paul Werstine, 'Provenance and Printing History in Two Revels Editions', *Medieval and Renaissance Drama in England* 1 (1984), 243–62.

Whitney   Geffrey Whitney, *A Choice of Emblems* (Leyden: Christopher Plantyn for Francis Raphelengius, 1586). STC 25438.

Whitney-Brown   Carolyn Whitney-Brown, ' "A Farre More Worthy Wombe": Reproductive Anxiety in Peele's *David and Bethsabe*', in *In Another Country: Feminist Perspectives on Renaissance Drama*, ed. Dorothea Kehler and Susan Baker (London: Scarecrow Press, 1991), 181–204.

All biblical quotations are from the Geneva version unless otherwise specified.

Introduction

GEORGE PEELE

The author of *David and Bathsheba* was born in London in 1556; forty years later, in 1596, in London he died (Horne, 3, 108). Peele was born into the middle classes of London citizenry. James Peele, George's father, was an accountant (he published two books on double-entry accounting), clerk, teacher, and writer and producer of Lord Mayor pageants. Liveryman of the Salters' Company, in 1562 James became Clerk of Christ's Hospital, an institution established by the City to provide relief for the City's 'impotent poor', the aged and orphans. He held this position until his death in 1585. His annual salary, including the value of free rent, his teaching, and his clerkship, amounted to £65. The average clerkship ran between £10 and £20 (Horne, 4–16). Yet James died in debt, perhaps, David Horne speculates, because of the costs of George's university education (Horne, 17).

George was James's eldest child. He had three sisters, Anne, Isabel, and Judith, and a younger brother, James (Horne, 18–19). George would have commenced his education in Christ's Hospital's 'pettie school' upon his father's acceptance of the position of Clerk. After learning the basics of reading and writing there for three years, George attended the Hospital's grammar school for the next six before leaving in 1571 at the age of fourteen for Christ Church, Oxford. He was awarded his BA in 1577 and his MA two years later, in 1579 (Horne, 32, 37). In 1580 Peele married Ann Cooke, whose father died shortly thereafter, leaving Ann a good inheritance of around £250. Gaining control over that inheritance seems to have been problematic, however, and for the next four years Peele was involved in constant litigation over the property on which the inheritance was based (Horne, 49–56). During this period Peele shuttled back and forth between London and Oxford, where in June 1583 he managed the stage, scenery, costuming, and special effects of the university's production of two plays by William Gager, *Rivales* and *Dido*, to honour its visiting guest Albertus Alasco, Count Palatine of Siridia, Poland (Horne, 57–64). In spite of his wife's inheritance, however, Peele's financial position was not secure, and he spent the remainder of his life in London seeking, like many of his fellow university graduates such as Robert Greene, Thomas Watson, Thomas Lodge, Christopher Marlowe, and Thomas Nashe, to eke out an existence through his pen, writing court plays, patronage-seeking verses, City pageants, and plays for the professional stage, and dying in poverty in 1596 (Horne, 65–109). A number of contemporary allusions to Peele indicate that he was well known as a poet during his life, and he figures as the hero of an anonymous jestbook, *The Merry Conceited Jests of George Peele Gentleman* (1607), published a decade after his death.

Peele's earliest known work is a lost translation of Euripides's *Iphigenia*, for which survive two commendatory verses by William Gager, who was Peele's contemporary at Oxford. The verses place Peele's translation of the classical Greek tragedy among the accomplishments of his Oxford days and declare that 'Viueret Euripides, tibi se debere putaret, / Ipsa tibi grates Iphigenia daret [Were Euripides to be alive, he would consider himself indebted to you; Iphigenia herself would give you thanks]' (Horne, 43). Throughout his literary career, Peele penned and published a variety of non-dramatic verse. In 1589 he published *The Tale of Troy* together with *A Farewell. Entitled to the Famous and Fortunate Generals of Our English Forces, Sir John Norris and Sir Francis Drake Knights and All Their Brave and Resolute Followers*. *The Tale of Troy* is a 493-line epitome of the Trojan War that concludes when 'The good Aneas' (478), for whom the gods have 'Reserv'd some better future' (479), 'Arives at Lavine land' (482). The work with which this display of Peele's classical learning was coupled by the printers, *A Farewell*, praises two other seafaring heroes, Norris and Drake, who 'bid statelie Troynovant adiewe' (4) in order to 'fight for Christ and Englands peereles Queene, / Elizabeth, the wonder of the worlde' (66–7) against the Spanish. Norris and Drake set sail from Plymouth on 18 April 1589 as part of England's counter-attack against Spain's failed Armada (Horne, 161–2).

Before the return of the English ships several months later in failure, the events sparked another opportunity for Peele's versifying: the Earl of Essex had joined the expedition against Elizabeth's prohibition, and upon his return to England's shores Peele praised the valiant earl in *An Eclogue Gratulatory. Entitled: To the Right Honourable and Renowned Shepherd of Albion's Arcadia, Robert Earl of Essex and Ewe for his Welcome into England from Portugal*. This dialogue between the two shepherds Piers and Palinode imitates Spenser's *The Shepherd's Calendar* and observes a pastoral decorum: 'Of Armes to sing, I have not lust nor skill, / Enough is me, to blazon my good will' (32–3), declares Piers, 'To welcome home that long hath lacked beene, / One of the jolliest Shepherds of our Greene' (34–5). Peele published another occasional poem in 1590, *Polyhymnia*, in honour of Sir Henry Lee's last performance as the Queen's champion in the Accession Day tilts on 17 November 1590 (Horne, 165–6). He wrote two other occasional pieces before his death: *The Honour of the Garter*, published in an undated quarto in 1593 to celebrate the Earl of Northumberland's entrance into the Order of the Garter (Horne, 173), and *Anglorum Feriae*, which survives only in manuscript and celebrates Elizabeth's 1595 Accession Day (Horne, 178). To Peele is also attributed *The Praise of Chastity*, a 111-line poem in a collection of poetry by Oxford poets, *The Phoenix Nest*, published in 1593.

Along with this varied mass of largely occasional verse Peele also wrote three Lord Mayor's pageants: *The Device of the Pageant Borne before Woolstone Dixi, Lord Mayor of the City of London* (1585), *The Device of the Pageant Borne before the Right Honourable Martin Calthrop Lord Mayor of the City of London* (1588), and *Descensus Astraeae: The Device of a Pageant borne Before M. William Web, Lord Mayor of the City of London* (1591). The second of these three civic pageants is no longer extant (Horne, 155–6), but in the other two Peele deploys his classical education to present the spectacle of a London in rapturous harmony with the 'peerless mistresse soveraigne of my [London's] peace' (*Woolstone Dixi*, 64) and 'Astraea daughter of the immortall Jove, / Great Jove defender of this antient towne, / Descended of the Trojan Brutus line' (*Descensus Astraeae*, 14–16).

During his time in London from 1581 until his death in 1596 Peele also wrote a considerable amount of dramatic verse. A.R. Braunmuller wryly remarks that 'with the possible exception of Robert Greene', Peele 'has the dubious distinction of being claimed as the true father of more dramatic foundlings than any other Elizabethan dramatist' (9), and Samuel Schoenbaum lists twelve plays besides the ones currently accepted in the Peele canon that have been attributed to Peele at one time or another (xvii–xviii). Modern scholarship, however, has narrowed Peele's dramatic oeuvre down to seven plays that survive in whole or in part. The following five are attributed to Peele in Alan B. Farmer and Zachary

Lesser's *Database of Early English Playbooks*: *The Arraignment of Paris, The Battle of Alcazar, Edward I, The Old Wives' Tale*, and *David and Bathsheba*. Charles Forker has made a compelling case for adding *The Troublesome Reign of John, King of England* to these five in his recent Revels edition of the play. There also survive portions of a seventh play by Peele, *The Hunting of Cupid*. To place this in some context, the canon of Marlowe's plays, written in the slightly shorter period between 1587 and 1593, also contains seven plays.

Peele wrote *The Arraignment of Paris*, performed at court by the Children of the Chapel, between 1581 and its publication in 1584. The play returns to the incident that might be said to be the immediate cause of the Trojan War, Paris's giving the golden ball to Venus rather than Juno or Minerva, and rewrites it so that the play concludes with a tribunal of the gods reassigning the role of judge from Paris to Queen Elizabeth. '*The Araygnement of Paris* is typical of royal entertainments in its hyperbolic treatment of its royal spectator and her fictional personae', Louis Montrose observes, 'But it differs from many of the entertainments of the previous two decades in that it fully acknowledges and celebrates the Queen's own choice, her complex transcendence of the simplistic oppositions contrived by her courtiers' (444). Peele seems to have written another courtly pastoral drama, *The Hunting of Cupid*, of which only fragments have survived in a manuscript transcription by William Drummond (1609) and excerpts in *England's Helicon* (1600) and *England's Parnassus* (1600) (Horne, 153).

Peele's other five plays were written for the professional London stage or, more precisely, for the professional adult acting companies for whom the London stages were major venues if not home. *The Battle of Alcazar*, the title page of whose first, 1594 quarto assigns it to the repertoire of the Admiral's Men, dramatises the life of the notorious English adventurer Thomas Stukeley in the hyperbolic style of Marlowe's *Tamburlaine* plays, first performed 1587–88, and the play's composition is usually dated slightly after Marlowe's plays, 1587–89 (Edelman, 15-16). *Edward I* is one of two of Peele's forays into the genre of the history play. First published in 1593 and written as early as 1590 (Hook, 5), the play is a romantic dramatisation of Edward I's engagement with the rebellious Welsh. The play's title page does not assign the play to any company, but, if the play entitled *Longshanks* in Henslowe's diary is the same as *Edward I*, then by 1595 the play was in the Admiral's Men's repertoire (Hook,

8). The title page of the 1595 quarto of Peele's romance comedy, *The Old Wives' Tale*, states that this play was performed by the Queen's Men; *The Troublesome Reign of John, King of England*, for which the play's most recent editor suggests a date of composition between 1589 and 1590, was also performed by the Queen's Men (Forker, 31). Elmer Blistein has suggested that *David and Bathsheba* (1587–94) also might have at one point belonged to the Queen's Men (153 n.1), although more recently Annaliese Connolly has cogently argued that it belonged to the Admiral's Men.

On the basis of an allusion in *The Merry Conceited Jests*, Leonard Ashley speculates that in addition to these seven plays Peele also wrote a play, now lost, entitled *The Turkish Mahomet and Irene the Fair Greek* (*Authorship*, 89). Many scholars now also consider Peele to be co-author, along with Shakespeare, of *Titus Andronicus* (Vickers, 243). Given the diversity of Peele's literary output, both non-dramatic and dramatic, A.R. Braunmuller has concluded that 'The single unifying element [in Peele's oeuvre] appears to be an economic one: Peele wrote to earn money' (10). Braunmuller's conclusion may be true, but it belies the intellectual and creative intensity and dramatic and poetic craftsmanship that can be found throughout Peele's work, especially Peele's biblical drama *David and Bathsheba*.

DAVID AND BATHSHEBA

On its title page, the 1599 quarto of *David and Bathsheba* advertises Peele's play as 'The Love of King David and Fair Bethsabe. With the Tragedie of Absalon'. The terseness of the title belies the complexity with which the play treats its topics, the Israelite King David's adulterous relationship with the beautiful Bathsheba and his son Absalom's rebellion against him. Early modern readers of the quarto, arguably more familiar with biblical history than modern readers, would have readily bridged the title's period and connected the two topics as central events in David's long reign, and to stress their interconnectedness Peele's play inventively rearranges the chronology of its biblical sources even if at times individual passages in the play appear to be mere paraphrases of the Bible. The Bible, church sermons, and other cultural sources would have given ambivalent resonance to the title's key words: 'love', 'fair', and 'tragedy'. As early modern readers would know, David's love for Bathsheba is sinful, David is tempted by Bathsheba because she

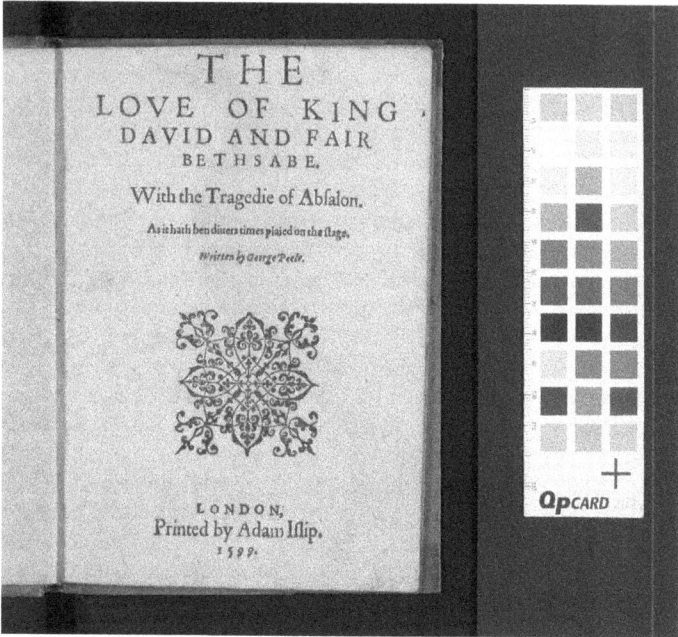

Title page of the 1599 Quarto, reproduced by permission of the
National Library of Scotland

is fair, and, according to Elizabethan homilies, Absalom's tragedy
expresses God's punishment of wicked rebels.

The play itself extends the title's connotative richness and ambivalence. Dramatising at length David's initial sight of Bathsheba and
his immediate sexual solicitation of her, the play's first scene jux-
taposes the splendidly erotic lyrical poetry of Bathsheba's opening
song and speech and David's breathless appreciation of her beauty
to multiple unvarnished and frequently ironic acknowledgements
that the sexual affair that will spring from this eroticism is morally
wrong and coercive. David's later penitence for his sins, staged
repeatedly throughout the rest of the play with melodramatic flair,
increases rather than closing down the ambivalence of the play's
treatment of this theme. However weak and sinful David might
be, his penitence and his status as God's anointed king ensure that

he ultimately escapes the potentially tragic consequences of his actions. The play displaces the tragic consequences of David's actions on to his son Absalom, whose rebellion is represented not unsympathetically as a response to David's moral laxity and political ineptitude generally and specifically to David's failure to punish a sexual crime that resembles his own, his eldest son Amnon's rape of Absalom's sister Tamar. Even so, the play's second chorus calls Absalom's fate the 'dreadful precedent of His just doom' (1). The complexity of Peele's drama is demonstrated not only by its refusal to simplify these entanglements of the sexual, political, and theological but also by the prominence it gives to the voices of the female characters who are caught up in and traumatised by them. Through Bathsheba, Tamar, and David's concubines the play exposes the role of sexual violence against women in the establishment and maintenance of patriarchal sovereignty. In the play, rape is paradoxically both criminal and sanctified. The play's treatment of this paradox is enriched by its engagement with other, non-biblical intertexts. The play's often ironic treatment of Guilliaume Du Bartas's *Divine Weeks* and Marlowe's *Tamburlaine* plays deepens its development of the themes discussed above and extends their resonance into the literary and dramatic worlds of Elizabethan England in the 1580s and 1590s, a resonance further extended by David's popularity as a figure across a range of Elizabethan cultural discourses, from poetic to political.

DAVID IN MEDIEVAL AND RENAISSANCE LITERATURE AND CULTURE

David's popularity in Elizabethan cultural discourses was a legacy of his prominence in Western culture generally. As Raymond-Jean Frontain and Jan Wojcik observe in their introduction to *The David Myth*, that prominence was the result of his exemplarity as much as his historical significance. 'For the pre-Renaissance world – from the time of the earliest religious interpretations through the European Middle Ages – David's significance was as a type', they write: 'For the Jews, he satisfied the type of the Old Testament hero: an improbable choice for a ruler by human standards, yet selected by the inscrutable Yahweh and raised over more likely candidates' and '[h]is career reflects the development of the Israelites themselves: enjoyment of God's favor is interrupted by a fall from grace through

sin; repentance and sincere contrition effect a reconciliation with
the Lord' (3), while '[f]or Christian audiences David is a type of
Christ' (3). In the same essay collection, Charles Huttar elaborates
upon the Christian significance of David. In *The Golden Legend*,
Huttar notes, David is an example of the penitent sinner (39), and
'From the beginning to the end of the Middle Ages and on into
the seventeenth century, if the evidence of English sermons is any
indication, the role of David as a model of repentance was most
prominent in the portrayal of this hero' (40). After charting some
narrative variations in the medieval tradition of stories about David's
sin and repentance, Huttar concludes that 'through all the changes
remains the constant theme that the repentant and restored David,
now spiritually stronger than ever, stands as an encouragement and
guide to ordinary sin-prone men and women' (54).

As the tradition of David as penitent grew, David's adultery
with Bathsheba was often singled out as his most grievous sin, a
fact reflected in Books of Hours. In her study of the illustrations
accompanying Books of Hours, Clare Costley observes that, while
medieval Books of Hours use a variety of images to illustrate the
Penitential Psalms, in the sixteenth century the image that predomi-
nates is the image of David watching Bathsheba bathe in a fountain: 'Most sixteenth-century *Horae* use a single image [to illustrate
the Penitential Psalms,] and that image typically represents David
observing a naked, or nearly-naked, Bathsheba' (1261). This is, of
course, the dramatic scenario with which the action of *David and
Bathsheba* commences.

David as a model repentant sinner can be found in a broad spec-
trum of early modern English texts, from pamphlets and sermons to
plays and poems. In the 'History of David' in Wynkyn De Worde's
translation of *The Golden Legend* (1498), David's status as model
penitent is confirmed by the story that David composed Psalm
51, the first Penitential Psalm, as a form of penance after having
been confronted by Nathan. David buried himself in the earth up
to the neck and remained interred until he could feel the worms
eating his flesh, at which point he had himself disinterred, composed a verse of the psalm (there are twenty), then had himself
buried again (fol. xxxviii–xxxix). In Antony Munday's *The Mirror
of Mutability* (1579), David exemplifies the sin of lechery but in
his complaint offers himself to the reader as an example of both
spiritual overconfidence and genuine repentance: 'Be warned by
me', David exhorts the reader, and '[s]ee how I fell that never

thought to fall; / God's mercy yet received me at last, / And sorrowing tears did make amends for all' (sig. C2v). In *David's Faith and Repentance* (1589), Henry Holland divides David's life into three parts: 'The first before his fall: the second in his fall: the third after his fall' (6). His great fall, of course, is Bathsheba, with whom he commits adultery and for whom he commits murder (36). Adapting David to the Protestant context of Elizabethan England, Holland contends that 'It was not in David's power to prescribe unto himself a time of repentance' (48). None the less, David's exemplary status remains: 'And thus by God's good assistance', Holland writes, 'I will lay open unto thee (good Reader) by David's example, what constant faith, what unfeigned repentance, what pure religion, what grievous temptations, what great frailty God's children have, and how notwithstanding by God's good providence they are upholden unto their lives' end' (7). 'David's example', Holland asserts, 'is a perfect precedent unto all good Christians of true repentance' (45).

David and Bathsheba would seem to concur with Holland's assessment of David's exemplarity. The play presents David as the model penitent, both in his words and his actions. Immediately after Nathan has applied his parable to David, turning David's guilty verdict upon the rich man back on to David, David exclaims

> Nathan, I have against the Lord, I have
> Sinned, oh, sinned grievously, and, lo,
> From heaven's throne doth David throw himself
> And groan and grovel to the gates of hell!
>
> (6.55–8)

The stage directions state that '*He* [David] *falls down*' (6.59 SD). David displays similar gestures of self-humiliation throughout the play. In scene 10, driven from Jerusalem by Absalom's rebellion, David declares the rebellion 'a plague on David's sin' (11) and several lines later '*lies down, and all the rest after him*' (19 SD). Even as one by one his companions rise, he lies prostrate for the rest of the lengthy scene, telling those gathered round him that 'Here lie I armed with a humble heart / T'embrace the pains that anger shall impose / And kiss the sword my Lord shall kill me with' (91–3). Only at the scene's conclusion, after Hushai has urged David to 'rise, referring the success to heaven' (132), does David stand.

Two scenes later David passively acquiesces to Shimei's verbal abuse and stone-throwing 'Because the Lord hath sent him to reprove / The sins of David' (12.42–3), refusing to allow Abishai 'to take away his head' (38) or Joab to 'Send hence the dog with sorrow to his grave' (66). Like the guilt-ridden Redcross Knight's tempter Despair in Book I of *The Faerie Queene*, Shimei urges David to commit suicide:

> If, then, thy conscience tell thee thou hast sinned
> And that thy life is odious to the world,
> Command thy followers to shun thy face,
> And by thyself here make away thy soul,
> That I may stand and glory in thy shame.
>
> (46–50)

As model penitent, however, David needs no Una to help him formulate the appropriate response:

> I am not desperate, Shimei, like thyself,
> But trust unto the covenant of my God,
> Founded on mercy, with repentance built,
> And finished with the glory of my soul.
>
> (51–4)

Unlike Marlowe's Doctor Faustus, David does not give in to the unpardonable sin of despair and consequently provides an example of true penitence for the play's Protestant Elizabethan audience. Chorus 1 signals this exemplarity to the audience with its question, 'If Holy David so shook hands with sin, / What shall our baser spirits glory in?' (15–16).

The moralising commentary of the play's choruses does not wholly capture the complexity of the play's representation of David and his sexual engagement with Bathsheba, however. In its representation of the affair, the play is significantly influenced by the classical as well as the biblical tradition. Demonstrating 'the close connection of *David and Bathsheba*, not only in *language*, but also in *situation* and *theme*, with the poetry of the Elizabethan Ovidian tradition' ('Love', 58), Inga-Stina Ewbank argues that in *David and Bathsheba* 'Peele explores, and fuses with his biblical stuff, the Ovidian-mythological tradition' (58–9). Ewbank concludes that 'Peele is not merely out to give us a *de casibus* play on David's sins of the flesh and the divine punishment for them, nor just to chronicle a Bible story' (61–2) but 'is also out, in the Ovidian fashion, to show us the beauty of the flesh and of the senses' (62).

The scene of David watching Bathsheba bathe is the point at which the Ovidian influence on the biblical tradition is registered most intensely. In European and English Renaissance literature the scene could evoke two responses, Ewbank argues in a later article, one biblical and the other classicising: Bathsheba as Eve; Bathsheba as Venus. Peele avoids the classicism of transforming Bathsheba into Venus: 'though his bathing scene is steeped in beauty, his imagery is taken from the Bible, especially from the Song of Songs, rather than from classical myth' ('House', 12). None the less, the scene's classical emphasis on sensuous beauty remains, even if it is later placed within the framework of the biblical tradition's moralising: 'Like the illustrators of the Penitential Psalms, Peele is having his cake and eating it too', Ewbank concludes, 'for, after using the first scene to celebrate the beauties of the flesh and the senses, he moves on to a strictly moral structure for the rest of the scenes dealing with the love story' (14). Recently, Michelle Ephraim has argued that the play's fusion of sensuousness and salvation is much more intimate than the serial progression that Ewbank posits. 'Bethsabe guides' David, Ephraim argues, 'to read her body correctly and to reject his voyeuristic ways: she directs him away from his rebellious son Absolom and towards their second child, Solomon, a symbol of David's inward illumination' (70). The positive force of Bathsheba's sensuousness is arguably more powerful in the play's final scene than in the first scene. It is the 'sweet sight' (17) of Bathsheba that acts as a 'sacred balm / To cheer' David 'past all earthly joys' (18), the joys of his reign and the joys he found in his beautiful but rebellious son Absalom, and to prompt him to tutor his son and new heir Solomon in the transcendental joys of divine contemplation and to accept Absalom's death. In Peele's complex representation of David as an exemplary penitent, then, Bathsheba's sensuousness may, as Holland insists, be the cause of David's great fall. More significantly, though, that sensuousness works throughout the play to redeem David.

The play's refusal to reduce David to a two-dimensional figure of sin and repentance is registered more widely in its incorporation of two other common early modern figurations of David: David as poet, and David as prophet. David was frequently invoked as a divine poet. In *The Defence of Poesy*, Philip Sidney bolsters his argument for poetry by noting that 'the holy David's Psalms are a divine poem' (133) which 'imitate the unconceivable excellencies of God'

(224–5). In the opening eight lines of 'David and Goliah' in *The Muses' Elizium* (1630), Michael Drayton figures David as a divine poet, musician, and prophet:

> Our sacred Muse of Israel's singer sings,
> That heavenly harper whose harmonious strings
> Expelled that evil spirit which Saul possessed
> And of his torments often him released;
> That princely prophet David whose high lays,
> Immortal God, are trumpets of thy praise,
> Thou Lord of Hosts be helping then to me,
> To sing of him who hath so sung of thee.

Finding its echo in the lines from Drayton quoted above, *David and Bathsheba*'s Prologue introduces David not as a penitent but as a poet, as 'Israel's sweetest singer' (1), 'Whose muse was dipped in that inspiring dew / Archangels stillèd from the breath of Jove' (3–4). Arguably, it is David's poetic sensibility that permits Bathsheba's physical beauty to be such a transformative force in David's spiritual journey over the course of the play.

David figures equally prominently as a prophet in early modern English literature. 'No prophet ever reigned on earth more greater than was I' (sig. C2v), David himself declares in Richard Lloyd's *A Brief Discourse of the Most Renowned Acts and Right Valiant Conquests of Those Puissant Princes Called the Nine Worthies* (1584). Chorus 1 of Peele's play adds this role to its characterisation of David by explicitly calling him 'the prophet' (23). At the play's conclusion, David fully assumes the role of prophet as he educates his son Solomon, advising him to depend not on 'frail conjectures of inferior signs' (17.95) or 'the figures of some hidden art' (97) for his divine knowledge but rather to implore God to

> ⠀⠀⠀⠀⠀⠀⠀ravish my earthly sprite,
> That for the time a more than human skill
> May feed the organons of all my sense,
> That, when I think, Thy thoughts may be my guide
> And, when I speak, I may be made by choice
> The perfect echo of Thy heavenly voice.

(110–15)

In these lines David adopts the Christlike role of mediator between God and Solomon, teaching his son how to pray. The projected prophetic ecstasy will shortly become Solomon's, but as David speaks these lines it is his 'sprite' that is ravished as he fuses the roles of poet and prophet and becomes 'The perfect echo of Thy heavenly voice'.

DAVID AND BATHSHEBA, ELIZABETHAN POLITICS, AND MARLOWE

In the early modern period David was used not only as a religious and poetic example, however. From the reign of Henry VIII to the Civil War and the Restoration, David was commonly used to support various political arguments (Frontain and Wojcik, 5–6). As Robert Kilgore has recently observed, discussion of 'the tyranny of kings' ('Politics', 419) was one such sphere of political discourse in which the figure of David was employed. Focusing on David's refusal to kill King Saul even when he had the opportunity, the Elizabethan government in 'The Second Part of the Sermon on Obedience' and 'An Homily against Disobedience and Wilful Rebellion' cites David in support of its argument that even tyrants should not be resisted by their subjects. It is not lawful to rebel against the authorities, the writers of the 'Second Part of the Sermon on Obedience' assert: 'David also teaches us a good lesson in this behalf, who was many times most cruelly and wrongfully persecuted of King Saul, and many times also put in jeopardy and danger of his life by King Saul and his people, yet he neither withstood, neither used any force or violence against King Saul his mortal and deadly enemy, but did ever to his liege and master King Saul most true, most diligent, and most faithful service' (sig. S3r).

The 'Homily against Disobedience and Wilful Rebellion' elaborates upon this lesson by quoting David: 'The Lord keep me (saith David) from doing that thing, and from laying hands upon my Lord God's anointed, for who can lay his hand upon the Lord's anointed and be guiltless?' (sig. Mm4v). Conversely, David's son Absalom becomes the paradigmatic rebel whose end exemplifies God's judgement upon all who attempt to lay hands on the Lord's anointed. 'The example of Absalom is notable', states the writer of the 'Homily', and his fate 'give[s] an eternal document that neither comeliness of personage, neither nobility, nor favour of the people, no nor the favour of the king himself, can save a rebel from due punishment' (sig. Oo1r). Peele's play echoes even if it does not fully endorse the homily's representation of Absalom: 'Oh, dreadful precedent of His just doom' (1), Chorus 2 declaims immediately following the scene of Absalom's defeat and death at the hands of David's brutal general Joab.

The play's representation of David is also in keeping with Elizabethan political orthodoxy in so far as from beginning to end it insists on David's sacred status as the Lord's anointed King of Israel. David is 'Elected to the heart of Israel's God' (1.80) and 'the Lord's anointed' (4.122). When He rebukes David through Nathan, God reminds him that 'I thee anointed king in Israel / And saved thee from the tyranny of Saul' (6.35–6). In the play's final scene we witness the smooth transfer of power from father to son as David affirms as heir his son Solomon, 'Whom God in naming hath anointed king' (17.49). Yet the play's insistence upon the rhetoric of divine anointment paradoxically calls it into question. As Kilgore observes, 'What becomes painfully clear throughout Peele's play is that David has lost control personally, domestically, and politically in the manner that kings often lose control in tragic-historical plays' ('Politics', 420). Before he became king David may have offered the supreme example of the subject's proper response to tyranny, but as the play represents him in all his weakness he himself conforms to the pattern of the tyrant as set by Saul. David Bevington argues that 'Superficially orthodox in its depiction of David's suppression of the revolt of his son, and in its use of truisms about divine right, the play nevertheless offers comfort to the disaffected by its disparaging view of kingship' (219), adding that 'David's human frailty strikes at the divinity of monarchs. Whether or not Peele condones rebellion, he is at least sympathetic to its motives. The question of what to do about an inadequate monarch remains unanswered. Absalom's rebellion cannot succeed, yet David is unfit to govern' (220).

The ambivalence that Bevington perceives in the play's representation of David as a monarch can fully be seen when the play is compared to one of its major intertexts, Marlowe's *Tamburlaine* plays. Although Marlowe's influence on Peele's drama has often been noted, critical discussion of Marlowe's influence on the drama of his contemporaries and successors has most frequently focused on the complex and generative relationships among Marlowe's plays and those of Shakespeare and Jonson. In the literary critical narratives that emerge out of such studies as James Shapiro's *Rival Playwrights: Marlowe, Jonson, Shakespeare* (1991) and Robert Logan's *Shakespeare's Marlowe: The Influence of Christopher Marlowe on Shakespeare's Artistry* (2007), Marlowe's plays provide Shakespeare and Jonson with both obstacles that must be creatively overcome and strikingly new patterns upon which they can exercise their own dramatic genius.

When discussion has turned to the dramatic works of Marlowe's lesser known contemporaries, however, such as Robert Greene and George Peele, Marlowe's influence has typically been considered to be dominating, even stifling. This is especially so in regard to the influence of what were perhaps Marlowe's two most popular plays, *Tamburlaine the Great Part One and Part Two*. As Peter Berek (1982) observes, the *Tamburlaine* plays spawned a multitude of imitations, such as Greene's *Selimus* and Peele's *Battle of Alcazar* and *The Troublesome Reign of John, King of England*, featuring martial heroes modelled on Tamburlaine and declaiming Tamburlainian 'high astounding terms' (*1 Tamburlaine*, Prologue 5) at every available opportunity. Indeed, Peele's *Troublesome Reign* explicitly positions itself in competition with Marlowe's *Tamburlaine* plays. As Scott McMillin and Sally-Beth MacLean observe, the play's first printing as a two-part play in 1591 'was obviously intended to do battle with *Tamburlaine* on the bookstalls' (156). Moreover, the play's Prologue invites its audience, who 'Have entertained the Scythian Tamburlaine, / And given applause unto an infidel' (2–3), to 'Vouchsafe to welcome with the like courtesy / A warlike Christian and your countryman' (4–5) who 'For Christ's true faith endured ... many a storm' (6). Berek labels these plays the 'weak sons' of *Tamburlaine*, arguing that 'the early imitations of *Tamburlaine* suggest that Marlowe's audience, and therefore his imitators, wanted to be entertained by his splendid rhetoric and glamorous stage effects without having to yield to the discomfort of unconventional ideas' (59). Wolfgang Clemen (1961) concludes that 'The various derivatives of *Tamburlaine* that appeared within the next few years show how ill the highly original genius manifested in Marlowe's dramatic first-fruits lent itself to imitation' (130; qtd Rutter 27).

Recent criticism, however, has modified this conclusion, at least in relation to Peele. Tom Rutter, for example, contends that Peele's use of Marlowe in the *Battle of Alcazar* is often, though not always, 'inventive and original' (30); according to Judith Weil, *David and Bathsheba* is 'one of the most thorough-going and serious' (63) dramatic responses to the *Tamburlaine* plays. However derivative Peele's *Battle of Alcazar* may be, *David and Bathsheba* represents an intelligent but far from comforting Protestant humanist response to Marlowe. As Annaliese Connolly has detailed, the influence of the *Tamburlaine* plays on *David and Bathsheba* is obvious and pervasive: 'Peele deliberately replicates aspects of stage spectacle from Marlowe's *Tamburlaine*, including scenes of siege warfare with vaunting between characters upon city walls, together with the hanging of characters either from walls or, in the case of Absalon, from a tree'; moreover, 'Peele's king shares a surprising number of qualities with Marlowe's Scythian, and David's status as God's anointed warrior allows the play to recall Tamburlaine's epithet as "The Scourge of God" with its Old Testament origins' (10). But David is pointedly not Tamburlaine. In almost every respect David is weak where Tamburlaine is strong, and Peele's play is a sustained, consistent examination of this weakness as a Protestant alternative or answer to the bloody, hypermasculine ethos of the *Tamburlaine* plays. David's weakness leads initially to humiliation and doubt but ultimately to a confident assertion of divine election even more powerful than Tamburlaine's precisely because it is rooted in human weakness.

Peele's response is not an intellectual retreat into orthodoxy, though. David's weakness is every bit as disturbing as Tamburlaine's brutal strength. Indeed, David's weakness is crucial to Peele's critique of Marlowe's Tamburlainian aesthetics. If, as Weil contends, the play 'denies the *Tamburlaine* hypothesis' (63), it does so most forcefully by confronting the audience or reader with the paradox of election as it plays itself out in the realm of the political, a paradox that brings to light a submerged but necessary connection between David's tyranny and his penitence. Kilgore argues that 'English writers turned to this [the regal] David to talk either of the tyranny of kings or of how even such a man as David can sin, and yet through poetry and penance, be restored' ('Politics', 419). No one, according to Protestant theology, not even David, can be worthy of or merit being chosen or elected by God and given His grace, whether that be the private grace of the individual believer or the political grace bestowed upon the divinely appointed ruler. Unlike Tamburlaine, Peele's David is obviously unworthy of his election, and the consequences of David's unworthiness are adultery, murder, and civil war. Yet because of his unworthiness David is also the model penitent; his penitence only confirms his status as God's chosen king. *David and Bathsheba* does not resolve this uncomfortable disjunction between election and worth, unlike the *Tamburlaine* plays, which to the extent that they glorify Tamburlaine embody a fantasy avoidance of the problem. From Peele's perspective, for all its high astounding terms, the *Tamburlaine* aesthetic is intellectual cowardice. *David and Bathsheba*, then, demonstrates

that even among his lesser contemporaries Marlowe's influence
could be generative and, conversely, that even such lesser figures as
Peele could respond to Marlowe's innovative drama in thoughtful
and creative ways that warrant serious critical attention.

Peele's juxtaposition of the biblical king David with the late medieval Central Asian conqueror Tamburlaine is not in itself surprising. Early modern English culture placed the two figures in similar
categories. Both were considered to be 'Worthies', historical figures
whose outstanding military accomplishments made them exemplars
of heroic virtue. Lloyd defines the Worthies as 'the greatest and
mightiest conquerors and Worthies of the world, / As well for their
courageousness as magnanimities, / Their valiantness, their wisdoms
rare, and princely policies' (sig. A2v), and he intends to narrate
'How God exalted them on high to earthly dignity, / And gave them
kings and kingdoms by triumphant victory, / Appointing them to
be his scourge, the wicked to confound / And their unrighteous
seed unroot with sword from of the ground' (sig. A2v). David was
one of Lloyd's three Old Testament Worthies, along with Joshua
and Judas Maccabeus. Lloyd's representation of David highlights
another of David's major attributes, his status as a figure of social
mobility. '[D]oughty David, in whom God did delight', Lloyd tells
us, 'From shepherd being made a King, was righteous in God's
sight' (sig. A2v). David was 'Promoted up to regal room, though
come but of mean race' (sig. C2v). Echoing Lloyd in the context of
a Jacobean Lord Mayor's pageant, *The Triumphs of Integrity* (1623),
Thomas Middleton calls David 'The Prince of Prophets' who 'being
a King anointed, did not scorn, / To be a shepherd after' (sig. A4v).

Later writers offered updated lists of modern figures. Thus, Robert
Vaughan's *The Portraitures at Large of Nine Modern Worthies of the
World* (1622) begins with an engraving of Tamburlaine, followed by
images of Ottoman Emperors Mehmed II and Suleiman the Great,
then Holy Roman Emperor Charles V, George Scanderbeg, the
Black Prince, Henry V, Henri IV, and, rounding out the list, William
of Orange. As well as being Worthies, both David and Tamburlaine
are shepherds who become kings (Connolly, 13). Middleton combines the idea of worthiness and the upward social trajectory in
The Triumphs of Integrity when he links the two figures as Worthies
who 'were born / Shepherds and rise to kings, took their ascending
/ From the strong hand of Virtue, never ending' (28–30).

Marlowe and Peele both emphasise the shepherd origins of their
protagonists. In 1.2 of *1 Tamburlaine*, for example, Tamburlaine

declares to the captured Zenocrate that 'I am a lord, for so my deeds shall prove, / And yet a shepherd by my parentage' (34–5). In the second scene of *David and Bathsheba*, Hanun king of the Ammonites dismisses the Israelite army that is besieging his city Rabbah with the contemptuous question, 'What would the shepherd's dogs of Israel / Snatch from the mighty issue of King Ammon?' (31–2). Indeed, both Tamburlaine and David are repeatedly taunted with their ignoble origins by enemies they later defeat. David, then, might seem to be the ideal character through which Peele could accomplish the goal at which he aimed in *The Troublesome Reign of John, King of England*: offering his audience a Christian, or Christianised, version of Tamburlaine that will out-Tamburlaine Tamburlaine.

David and Bathsheba reproduces Tamburlainian rhetoric and echoes the *Tamburlaine* plays at various points in its staging, however, only in order to foreground the differences between David and Tamburlaine. As David parades in triumph after conquering Rabbah, for example, his generals Joab and Abishai glorify him in the hyperbolic terms that saturate descriptions of Tamburlaine. 'Beauteous and bright is he among the tribes' (9.11), declaims Joab,

> As when the sun attired in glist'ring robe
> Comes dancing from his oriental gate
> And bridegroom-like hurls through the gloomy air
> His radiant beams, such doth King David show,
> Crowned with the honour of his enemy's town.
> Shining in riches like the firmament,
> The starry vault that overhangs the earth,
> So looketh David King of Israel.
>
> (12–19)

'Joab, why doth not David mount his throne' (20), Abishai continues, 'Whom heaven hath beautified with Hanun's crown?' (21). If David follows Abishai's suggestion at this point, the scene would recall 4.2 of *1 Tamburlaine*, in which Tamburlaine steps to his throne on the back of the defeated Bajazeth and then proclaims:

> Now clear the triple region of the air
> And let the majesty of heaven behold
> Their scourge and terror tread on emperors.
> Smile, stars that reigned at my nativity,
> And dim the brightness of their neighbour lamps.
>
> (30–4)

Significantly, however, it is Joab and Abishai, and not David himself, who produce the Tamburlainian description.

Moreover, Peele undercuts the Tamburlainian pomposity of the stage echo: immediately after David has mounted his throne, Jonadab enters to announce that Absalom has murdered David's first-born son, Amnon. David then laments,

> Ay me, how soon are David's triumphs dashed,
> How suddenly declineth David's pride!
> As doth the daylight settle in the west,
> So dim is David's glory and his gite.
>
> (9.32–5)

This moment typifies Peele's redeployment of the elements of Marlowe's Tamburlaine aesthetics. Throughout *David and Bathsheba*, characters other than David use Tamburlainian rhetoric because they want David to be a Tamburlainian figure, but the play, and David, continually disappoint. It is Absalom, with his desire to 'glut his longing soul / With sole fruition of his father's crown' (11.139–40), who most closely self-identifies with Tamburlaine, and even at the end of the play, after Joab has defeated Absalom's rebel forces for him, David refuses to be Tamburlaine. Instead, broken by the news of Absalom's death, he sulks in his pavilion and must be threatened by Joab before he assumes the comportment appropriate to a conqueror:

> Advance thee from thy melancholy den,
> And deck thy body with thy blissful robes,
> Or by the Lord that sways the heaven I swear
> I'll lead thine armies to another king.
>
> (17.238–41)

After further threats David does leave his tent, but the play tellingly concludes not with a rousing speech from David but with Joab's verbal slap on David's back, 'Bravely resolved, and spoken like a king! / Now may old Israel and his daughters sing' (279–80).

David and Bathsheba's ironic deployment of Tamburlainian rhetoric is not accompanied by a representation of David as a more positive political leader than Tamburlaine. On the contrary, like Tamburlaine, David becomes a tyrant, and his tyranny is not a new form of hypermasculine virtue but effeminising sin. Both Tamburlaine and David are usurpers, but Marlowe represents Tamburlaine's various usurpations as victories of the deserving hero over effeminate, pompous, and weak opponents. 'Your births shall be no blemish to your fame' (4.4.125), Tamburlaine tells his companions during the banquet of crowns in 4.4 of *1 Tamburlaine*, 'For virtue is the fount whence honour springs, / And they are worthy she investeth kings' (126–7). In contrast, although the play for the most part is silent about David's usurpation of the throne of Israel from Saul, when the matter does surface in Shimei's accusations in scene 12, David does not attempt to refute the charge. Shimei calls David 'The man of Israel that hath ruled as king / Or rather as the tyrant of the land, / Bolstering his hateful head upon the throne / That God unworthily hath blessed him with' (1–4), asserting that 'The Lord hath brought upon thy cursèd head / The guiltless blood of Saul and all his sons, / Whose royal throne thy baseness hath usurped' (26–8). When Abishai responds to Shimei's outburst by asking David to 'Let me alone to take away his head' (38), David surprisingly replies:

> Why meddleth thus the son of Zeruiah
> To interrupt the action of our God?
> Shimei useth me with this reproach
> Because the Lord hath sent him to reprove
> The sins of David, printed in his brows.

> (39–43)

David's sins include, of course, not merely usurpation but other crimes characteristic of tyrants, such as the violation of the sexual and property rights of his subjects and murder. In the play's first scene, David observes Bathsheba bathing and immediately commands her sexual compliance to his desire through his intermediary Hushai; when Bathsheba becomes pregnant, he sends her husband Uriah off to the front lines of his war against the Ammonites in order to be killed, thus allowing him to claim Bathsheba as his own wife. In unequivocal terms the play's first chorus condemns David's tyrannous actions as the 'proud revolt of a presumptuous man' (1) and an example of unbridled 'lust' (17) whose 'sequel' (18) will be 'greater ill' (18): the death of Bathsheba's child, the rape of Tamar, the murder of Amnon, and, finally, Absalom's rebellion. The play's opening scenario and its consequences stand in marked contrast to the opening scenario of *1 Tamburlaine*: Tamburlaine captures Zenocrate in 1.2, but this rape only becomes Tamburlaine's opportunity to demonstrate his masculine virtue and self-control by, on the one hand, preserving Zenocrate from 'all blot of foul unchastity' (5.2.422) and, on the other, resisting the emotional assault of her pleas for her native Damascus. By 'thus conceiving and subduing' (5.2.120) the 'thoughts effeminate and faint' (114) about Zenocrate that would, were they to conquer him, lead to his own effeminisation, Tamburlaine 'Shall give the world to note, for all my birth, / That virtue solely is the sum of glory / And fashions men with true nobility' (125–7). David, in contrast, is subdued by his own lust (this is the Platonic definition of a tyrant (Bushnell, 9)) and consequently destroys his glory with his sins.

The contrast between the two leaders extends to their use of the rhetoric of divine election. Tamburlaine frequently invokes the rhetoric of divine election. In 1.2, for example, he tells Theridamas that 'sooner shall the sun fall from his sphere / Than Tamburlaine be slain or overcome' (176–7), that, should Theridamas attempt to assault him, 'Jove himself will stretch his hand from heaven / To ward the blow' (180–1), and that 'as a sure and grounded argument / That I shall be the monarch of the East, / He sends this Sultan's daughter', Zenocrate, 'To be my queen' (184–7). In 3.3 he calls himself 'the Scourge and Wrath of God' (44), a phrase he repeats in *2 Tamburlaine* after murdering his son Calyphas for cowardice. The captive Natolian king Orcanes denounces the murder as 'this thy barbarous, damnèd tyranny' (4.1.137), to which Tamburlaine replies:

> Villains, these terrors and these tyrannies,
> If tyrannies war's justice ye repute,
> I execute, enjoined me from above,
> To scourge the pride of such as heaven abhors.
>
>   (144–7)

Since 'I exercise a greater name, / The Scourge of God and Terror of the World, / I must apply myself to fit those terms' (151–3), Tamburlaine asserts. Significantly, Tamburlaine here declares his status as God's chosen but also asserts that he must be (and, presumably, is) worthy of such election.

With its emphasis on David's sinfulness, however, *David and Bathsheba* makes it clear that David is not worthy his election, and the play highlights the ways in which various characters manipulate the rhetoric of election for ends that are less than godly. Juxtaposed with its emphasis on David's tyranny and sinfulness, the play's equally emphatic insistence on David's status as God's anointed or chosen ruler often appears to be highly cynical. The rhetoric of election is the tool by which Hushai enforces Bathsheba's compliance to David's sexual demands in the play's opening scene: 'David, thou

knowst, fair dame, is wise and just, / Elected to the heart of Israel's
God' (79–80), he tells Bathsheba to silence her protests, 'Then do
not thou expostulate with him / For any action that contents his
soul' (81–2). It is the rhetoric that fuels the religious fanaticism
of Joab and his army: 'Ye fight the holy battles of Jehovah, / King
David's God, and ours and Jacob's God' (2.7–8), Joab tells his
troops at the siege of Rabbah. It is the rhetoric that Joab will invoke
to defeat Absalom's rebel army ideologically after he has defeated
them in battle: 'Error hath masked your much too forward minds'
(16.12), he tells the defeated rebels, 'And you have sinned against
the chosen state, / Against his life for whom your lives are blessed'
(13–14), but

> Joab pities your disordered souls
> And therefore offers pardon, peace, and love
> To all that will be friendly reconciled
> To Israel's weal, to David, and to heaven.
>
> (17–20)

Throughout the play, David and those around him exploit the rhetoric of election to further David's tyranny and warfare, only further
supporting Shimei's accusation that 'God unworthily hath blessed'
(12.4) David with the throne of Israel.

David's unworthiness, however, is essential to the play's characterisation of David as the model penitential sinner, a characterisation that does not subvert but disturbingly reaffirms the rhetoric
of election that David's followers seem so cynically to manipulate.
As was outlined earlier in the introduction, in medieval and early
modern Christianity David was the paradigmatic biblical penitent,
and Peele's play similarly frames David as the exemplary sinner. 'If
holy David so shook hands with sin, / What shall our baser spirits
glory in?' (15–16), Chorus 1 asks, making the basic theological point
that 'all have sinned and are deprived of the glory of God' (Rom.,
3:23). Through David's unworthiness and penitence, however, the
play also insists upon the point made by the verse that follows and
completes Romans. 3:23, 'and are justified freely by his grace'.

Over the course of the play David ostentatiously repents of his
sins numerous times – and is forgiven. The most revealing example
occurs in the middle of Absalom's rebellion, when Shimei tempts
David to despair over his sins. 'If then thy conscience tell thee thou
hast sinned, / And that thy life is odious to the world' (12.46–7),
Shimei tells David, 'Command thy followers to shun thy face, / And

by thy self here make away thy soul' (48–9). For Shimei, David's unworthiness should be grounds for his spiritual and political rejection by God. David's reply, however, turns his sinfulness into the foundation of his spiritual and political strength. He has shaken hands with sin and is stronger for it: 'I am not desperate' (51), he tells Shimei, 'But trust unto the covenant of my God, / Founded on mercy, with repentance built, / And finished with the glory of my soul' (52–3). David's penitence does not cancel out his unworthiness; indeed, it depends upon it. Were David, like Tamburlaine, worthy of his divine election, that election would not be the result of God's grace. God is not an 'accepter of persons' (*Institution* fol. 397r), Jean Calvin writes. God elects some and rejects others for no inherent quality or virtue. Here we can locate the overarching difference between Marlowe's *Tamburlaine* plays and Peele's response. By foregrounding David's unworthiness, Peele's play directly confronts its audience with the disturbing political consequences of the logic of the Protestant doctrine of election rather than attempting to construct a fantasy figure in whom election and worth coincide. David is indeed, in Shimei's words, 'murderer, thou shame to Israel, / Foul lecher, drunkard, plague to heaven and earth' (60–1). But he is also God's penitent anointed king, and consequently quite literally gets away with murder fully confident that 'my God is spotless in His vows / And that these hairs shall greet my grave in peace' (10.51–2).

DAVID AND BATHSHEBA, QUEEN ELIZABETH, AND SEXUAL VIOLENCE

The impact of the play's critique of the orthodox political position David was commonly conscripted to serve was no doubt heightened by the extensive links constructed in the period between David and the reigning monarch, Queen Elizabeth. Many Elizabethan writers compared Elizabeth to David and Elizabethan England to Davidic Israel. Speaking in the immediate aftermath of the defeat of the Spanish Armada and thirty years after Elizabeth's accession to the throne, for example, John Prime in his 1588 Accession Day sermon *The Consolations of David, Briefly Applied to Queen Elizabeth* declares that '[T]he happy 17. Day of November, 1558 cometh, and God maketh it manifest to all the world, that himself was with her in all these tempests, and then the platform was broken up and the snare taken away, and a daughter of David had as great deliverances as ever David had' (sig. B2v). Prime later asserts God's providential

protection of Elizabeth and England: 'Truly, the deliverances of
David were but a taste of those which we feed on' (sig. C1r).
Peele draws the comparison himself in *Anglorum Feriae*, a poem
written to celebrate the 1595 Accession Day. 'London's shepherd'
(108), presumably Peele, 'Praiseth the Mighty One of Israel, / And
with the strings of his unfeigned heart / Tunes his true joy for all
those days of peace' (109–11) that the English have enjoyed under
Elizabeth, 'Whom Jacob's God hath many ways preserved / ... /
From Pharaoh's rod and from the sword of Saul' (149, 152).

The general comparison between the two figures led to application
to specific historical details of Elizabeth's reign, such as Elizabeth's
relationship with Mary Queen of Scots, who was figured as Absalom
to Elizabeth's David (Bevington, 219), and the succession crisis as
it became apparent that Elizabeth would not leave behind her any
natural heirs. Imprisoned in the Tower for his refusal to be silent
on the issue of Elizabeth's succession, for example, the combative
member of parliament Peter Wentworth wrote *A Pithy Exhortation
to Her Majesty for Establishing her Successor to the Crown* (1598),
which uses David as an example of a monarch who appointed his
successor during his lifetime and thereby ensured his kingdom's
stability: 'Wherefore as the state of Israel then moved David to make
his successor known, so now the state of England ought to move
you' (14). Although unlike Wentworth's treatise it avoids making
the comparison between David and Elizabeth explicit, *David and
Bathsheba*, according to Carolyn Whitney-Brown, none the less
addresses the fears involved in the succession crisis: the death of
David and Bathsheba's first son, followed by the false news of the
slaughter of all of David's sons, 'raises the anxiety of no succession,
the anxiety of the monarch's, and indeed society's, dependence
upon the worthy female womb' (190).

David and Bathsheba directs attention to the female womb, and to
female sexuality generally, not only through its representation of the
anxieties of succession but also through its representations of sexual
violence, which have received less attention than they deserve in the
literary criticism on the play. The representation of rape in early
modern English literature has been the subject of a number of recent
full-length scholarly studies, such as Jocelyn Catty's *Writing Rape,
Writing Women in Early Modern England* (1999), Karen Bamford's
Sexual Violence on the Jacobean Stage (2000), Barbara Baines's
Representing Rape in the English Early Modern Period (2003), and
Kim Solga's *Violence Against Women in Early Modern Performance*

(2009). Curiously, however, in their discussions of early modern English drama these studies largely ignore *David and Bathsheba*, although it contains more instances of sexual coercion and rape than any other Elizabethan drama of which I am aware. In fact, as Catty observes, among Elizabethan plays only *Titus Andronicus* (now held to have been co-authored by Peele and Shakespeare) and *David and Bathsheba* 'actually present violent rapes' (91). *Titus Andronicus* presents the shocking single instance of Lavinia's appalling rape and mutilation. Peele's play begins with the sexual coercion of Bathsheba, which is followed shortly thereafter by Amnon's rape of his half-sister Tamar; later in the play, Absalom attempts to secure his grip on his father's throne by publicly raping his father's concubines; the stated goal of David's final assault on the Philistine city Rabbah is to '[s]ubdue the daughters of the gentiles' tribes' (8.13).

 David and Bathsheba dramatises the tumultuous history of David's reign as a history driven by sexual violence and its consequences. Yet Peele's play has had little impact on modern critical investigations of the development of representations of sexual violence in the drama. Catty, for example, merely mentions the play, and Baines, although she discusses at length the rape of Tamar as it is found in the Old Testament narrative (34–48), does not mention the play at all. This lacuna, which might be the result of the absence of a readily available modernised edition of the play, is unfortunate, for *David and Bathsheba*'s representations of rape problematise in a number of ways the classical and Old Testament rape paradigm upon which critics argue dramatists from Shakespeare to Fletcher based their representations of rape. *David and Bathsheba* critiques sexual violence against women through its representation of rape not only as criminal but also as the sanctified mode by which unlimited patriarchal sovereignty reproduces itself.

 In the classical and Old Testament rape paradigm generally, the male violation of the female body is sharply distinguished from the female body's lawful possession by the appropriate male. Rape is a criminal act committed against a male or group of males through the female body. When the perpetrator possesses sovereign authority, the act renders him a tyrant whose deposition is lawful and necessary for justice to be restored. 'The rape or attempted rape is exploited in the interests of political action' (21), Catty states, and 'the idea of sexual violence as a woman's traumatic experience is written out of the narrative in favour of its "greater" political significance' (21). The rape of Lucretia is, according to Catty, the paradigmatic classical rape narrative and 'exemplifies the attitudes of early modern writers towards rape and its victims' (12). The Argument with which Shakespeare's 'Rape of Lucrece' begins provides a condensed version of the paradigm. Having been raped by Tarquinius Superbus, Lucretia convokes a council of her male relations, in which her rape is transformed from an act of violence against Lucretia (Tarquin 'violently ravished her' (31–2) in the privacy of her 'chamber' (31)) into the grounds for revolutionary political action, the abolition of the Roman monarchy, and the establishment of the Roman Republic:

> She, first taking an oath of them for her revenge, revealed the actor and whole manner of his dealing, and withal suddenly stabbed herself. Which done, with one consent they [Lucretia's male relations] all vowed to root out the whole hated family of the Tarquins; and bearing the dead body to Rome, Brutus acquainted the people with the doer and manner of the vile deed, with a bitter invective against the tyranny of the King, wherewith the people were so moved that with one consent and a general acclamation the Tarquins were all exiled and the state government changed from kings to consuls. (39–52)

This pattern is repeated in Shakespeare and Peele's *Titus Andronicus*, already noted as the only Elizabethan play other than *David and Bathsheba* to stage violent rape. In 3.1 Marcus presents the raped and mutilated Lavinia to her father Titus as a 'deer' (89) found 'straying in the park, / Seeking to hide herself' (88–9), to which Titus replies 'It was my dear, and he that wounded her / Hath hurt me more than had he killed me dead' (91–2). The violence committed against her by her rapists, the sons of the former Queen of the Goths and now the reigning Roman Emperor's consort, silences Lavinia. She, like Lucretia, then becomes the grounds for political action by her male relations, Marcus, Titus, and Lucius. After bidding 'Farewell' to 'proud Rome' (290) at the end of the scene, Lucius bids 'Farewell, Lavinia' (292) and vows to her that

> If Lucius live, he will requite your wrongs
> And make proud Saturnine and his empress
> Beg at the gates, like Tarquin and his queen.
> Now will I to the Goths and raise a power
> To be revenged on Rome and Saturnine.
>
> (296–300)

The complete subordination of Lavinia's trauma to her male relations' concerns ultimately demands Lavinia's silencing through further violence against her. In the play's final scene Titus kills Lavinia while proclaiming, 'Die, die Lavinia, and thy shame with thee, / And with thy shame thy father's sorrow die!' (5.3.46–7), thus simultaneously asserting his ownership of his daughter and attempting to efface her traumatic experience, her 'shame'.

As Baines observes, Old Testament rape narratives, including the narrative of Tamar's rape in 2 Samuel, adhere to a similar pattern. 'The Old Testament, like the classical texts of Ovid and Livy, contributed to an ideology of rape as a means of founding nations and governments; both the classical and biblical traditions reveal a patriarchal structure that necessitated the containment and objectification of women' (8), Baines writes, adding that in Old Testament rape narratives 'power relations and rivalry among men are as important or more important than lust in defining the motives of the rapists, and revenge is the consequence of rape' (35). In the case of Tamar's rape, the revenge takes the form of Absalom's murder of the rapist, Amnon, who is King David's heir, and Absalom's subsequent rebellion against David. Baines quotes theologian Bruce Birch's verdict that 'Tamar's rape sets in motion a course of events that eventually eliminates the two leading contenders for the Davidic throne. Tamar is an event rather than a person in history' (qtd Baines 35). In the classical and Old Testament paradigm, then, rape and the response to rape delimit the bounds of sovereignty and lead to its redistribution among male subjects as the right to the exclusive possession of the bodies of women, playing out in the realm of secular political history Freud's Darwinian myth of the primal horde.

In contrast, *David and Bathsheba* represents rape as the mode by which sovereignty reproduces itself as unlimited. The play dramatises rape as self-contradictorily criminal and sanctified, the instantiation of a divinely appointed sovereignty above the law and ultimately beyond the reach of the political consequences of that law's violation. The play's dramatisation of Tamar's rape falls in line with the biblical narrative, placing the emphasis on the criminal aspect of the rape and its function as grounds for subsequent political action. Amnon is explicitly represented as a type of tyrant, a 'prince, whose power may command' (3.38) but who cannot quell 'the rebel passions of his love' (39) for Tamar. Lacking self-control, he rapes his half-sister and then abandons her, acts which delegitimate his status as a political figure and as a man. As she is being thrust out of Amnon's house, Tamar denounces him as 'Unkind, unprincely, and unmanly Amnon, / To force and then refuse thy sister's love' (4.3), labelling the rape an 'offence' (5). Vowing revenge for his sister's rape, Absalom calls Amnon a 'Traitor to heaven, traitor to David's throne, / Traitor to Absalom and Israel' (43–4). Upon hearing of the rape from Absalom, David consolidates the process of delegitimation by disinheriting Amnon: 'I'll thrust the flattering tyrant from his throne' (85), he decrees. David then transforms Tamar's rape into an issue of the legitimate exercise of sovereign power: 'revenge not thou this sin' (88), he admonishes Absalom, 'Leave it to me, and I will chasten him' (89). 'To God alone belongs revenge' (9.98), the Widow of Tekoa tells David later in the play, but David here is making clear to Absalom that he, David, as God's appointed king alone has the right to punish Amnon's infringement of his sovereignty.

David fails to follow through on his promise to punish Amnon, however, and Absalom sees this failure as warrant to take matters into his own hands, first usurping David's particular prerogative by slaughtering Amnon at the sheep-shearing feast in scene 7 and then, in scene 9, after receiving David's pardon for the murder, resolving to usurp David's sovereign prerogative in general. Were he 'honoured / Of tribes and elders and the mightiest ones' (9.147–8), Absalom muses, he would act so that 'everyone that hath a cause to plead / Might come to Absalom and call for right' (151–2). He would assert the sovereign prerogative that David signally fails to assert throughout the play:

> Then in the gates of Zion would I sit
> And publish laws in great Jerusalem,
> And not a man should live in all the land
> But Absalom would do him reason's due.
>
> (153–6)

The rest of the play dramatises the consequences of Absalom's resolution: his rebellion, his defeat and death, and David's proclamation of Solomon as his new heir.

If, however, the play's representation of Tamar's rape and its consequences follows the classical and Old Testament paradigm in its representation of the rape as a crime against legitimate male sovereignty or a call for legitimate male political action against tyranny, other acts of sexual violence in the play problematise this representation. The most prominent of these acts is David's sexual coercion of Bathsheba at the play's beginning, an act that Stephen Guy-Bray contends is a 'proleptic version' (143) of Tamar's rape. The play makes the element of coercion involved in the relationship clear both when Bathsheba protests against Hushai's initial solicitations on David's behalf and, later, when she mourns for her sick newborn whose death the prophet Nathan will pronounce to be punishment for the liaison. Bathsheba, in Whitney-Brown's words, 'is more than a sight or site of David's transgression, more than the silent object of desire. She is a fully speaking subject, exposing and criticizing the contradiction between David's lecherous behavior and the ideology of the godly king' (185). 'What is Bathsheba to please the King', she asks Hushai when he first approaches her, 'Or what is David, that he should desire / For fickle beauty's sake his servant's wife?' (1.76–8), later adding that 'I hate incontinence' (85). 'Oh, what is it to serve the lust of kings?' (5.24), she asks herself as she laments over her sick child, 'How lion-like thy rage when we resist!' (25). Hushai's response to Bathsheba's protests is chilling:

> David, thou knowst, fair dame, is wise and just,
> Elected to the heart of Israel's God;
> Then do not thou expostulate with him
> For any action that contents his soul.
>
> (79–82)

As God's appointed king, David's demands, including the demand for sexual compliance, must be obeyed, and 'do not thou expostulate with him'. Sexual coercion, then, in this instance is not a crime against sovereignty but rather sovereignty's manifestation.

It might be tempting to consider Hushai's lines as merely the cynical rhetoric of a consummate courtier dedicated entirely to satisfying his sovereign's desires. Moreover, the prophet Nathan's parable of the poor man's lamb emphatically presents David's acts as criminal, as David's own judgement upon the parable's villain, the wealthy man who appropriates the poor man's lamb, confirms:

> Now, as the Lord doth live, this wicked man
> Is judged and shall become the child of death.
> Fourfold to the poor man shall he restore
> That without mercy took his lamb away.
>
> (6.29–32)

Significantly, however, it is David who condemns his own assertions of sovereignty, paradoxically but necessarily so: only the divinely appointed sovereign has the right to criminalise his own behaviour, and that is precisely what Nathan shrewdly prompts David to do through the parable. None the less, even if it requires a double movement, David's sexual coercion of Bathsheba ultimately confirms his sovereignty rather than undermining it.

In the play, though, such dialectical thinking is not always required for rape to be considered an assertion of sovereignty. Indeed, immediately after confronting David with the parable and eliciting from him his self-condemnatory judgement, Nathan ventriloquises God and declaims,

> 'I thee anointed King in Israel
> And saved thee from the tyranny of Saul;
> Thy master's house I gave thee to possess;
> His wives into thy bosom did I give,
> And Judah and Jerusalem withal,
> And might, thou knowst, if this had been too small,
> Have given thee more.'

> (6.35–41)

God reminds David that he legitimated David's rule with, among other things, the divinely sanctioned rape of Saul's 'wives'. David's crime, then, is not rape but greed: his sexual coercion of Bathsheba implies that what God gave him was insufficient, 'too small'.

Absalom, or more precisely his adviser Ahithophel, is fully aware of and attempts to appropriate rape's function as a sign of sovereignty. He is, as Whitney-Brown observes, 'a contradictory figure who both acts for female interests in the play yet at other times may seek to identify himself as sovereign by royal subjugation and violation of women' (197). Fulfilling Nathan's prophecy to David that God 'before thy face will take thy wives / And give them to thy neighbour to possess' (6.51–2), Absalom follows Ahithophel's counsel and publicly rapes the ten concubines whom David leaves behind in his palace when he flees Jerusalem during Absalom's revolt. The play does not stage this mass rape, but the biblical narrative relates that 'Ahithophel said unto Absalom, Go in to thy father's concubines, which he hath left to keep the house ... So they spread Absalom a tent upon the top of the house, and Absalom went in to his father's concubines in the sight of all Israel' (2 Samuel, 16:21–2). The play picks up the narrative immediately after the rapes, as Absalom addresses the concubines in an effort rhetorically

to convert the rapes into signs of the transference of sovereignty
from David to himself:

> Now you that were my father's concubines,
> Liquor to his unchaste and lustful fire,
> Have seen his honour shaken in his house,
> Which I possess in sight of all the world.
> I bring ye forth as foils to my renown
> And to eclipse the glory of your king.

(11.1–6)

The concubines bravely resist Absalom's rhetoric: the first
Concubine tells Absalom that the rapes will 'cry for vengeance to the
host of heaven' (11.19), who 'will dart plagues at thy aspiring head /
For doing this disgrace to David's throne' (11.21–2), and the second
Concubine follows this up with a warning that Absalom should
not hope to escape the 'thumping beaks' (11.30) and 'commanding wings' (11.31) of God's angels. Their resistance, however, only
places them in the jeopardy of further violence: Absalom's general
Amasa declares that 'These concubines should buy their taunts
with blood' (11.45). Absalom does not act on Amasa's advice only
because he considers the rapes to have done damage enough: 'let
these foolish women 'scape our hands / To recompense the shame
they have sustained' (11.48–9). Indeed, rape and mass murder inter-
penetrate throughout this play in the rhetoric of divinely appointed
sovereignty. At the beginning of scene 8, for example, David's
fanatical general Joab threatens the Ammonite king Hanun with
the genocidal destruction of the inhabitants of Rabbah, the city
that the Israelite army is besieging. 'Hanun, the God of Israel hath
said, / David the King shall wear that crown of thine' (8.35–6), Joab
trumpets, and

> Israel shall hale thy people hence
> And turn them to the tile-kiln, man and child,
> And put them under harrows made of iron,
> And hew their bones with axes, and their limbs
> With iron swords divide and tear in twain.

(39–43)

This is how Israel will, in Joab's earlier words, 'Subdue the daughters of the gentiles' tribes' (13).

David and Bathsheba leaves us in no doubt about the criminal-
ity of rape, either David's sexual coercion of Bathsheba, Amnon's

rape of Tamar, or Absalom's rape of David's concubines. In each instance, moreover, the play affords the rape victims voices with which to protest against the violence enacted upon their bodies, even though these protests are finally subordinated to the purportedly larger political concerns of the play's male characters. If in these regards the play conforms to the classical and Old Testament rape paradigm reproduced in works like 'The Rape of Lucrece' and *Titus Andronicus*, however, the play interrogatively departs from it by locating rape as foundational to sovereignty in general and David's divine sovereignty in particular. The David who is a rapist and murderer is no less God's favourite, and it is in precisely this paradox that the play locates the essence of David's sovereignty. Bruce Boehrer suggests that the play thus advances a conservative ideological agenda: the play's 'emphasis upon sexual pollution' functions 'to rescue the monarch and his dynasty from the consequences of his own criminal behavior' (62). I would argue in contrast that the play mobilises its critique precisely by foregrounding the sanctified as well as the criminal or polluted aspect of sexual violence. By representing rape in such starkly contradictory terms the play calls into question the distinction upon which the classical paradigm founds legitimate political and patriarchal authority, the distinction between the criminal violation of female bodies and their lawful possession. Through this critique of the foundations of patriarchal authority, *David and Bathsheba* draws attention to the plight of women in a world in which, legitimately or illegitimately, political power is asserted through their bodies in ways that appropriate their trauma and negate their agency.

The play not only draws attention to the process by which male political power asserts itself through the negation of women's trauma and agency, however. Its critique gains force because it places sustained attention on the trauma experienced by Tamar, Bathsheba, and the concubines and does not allow them to be wholly subsumed by the imperatives of male political concerns. One of the important questions Solga asks at the beginning of her study of the ways in which women's trauma and agency have been erased from modern as well as early modern performance and critical discourse is, 'Can we rehearse the (often indeed spectacular) disappearance of violence against women in early modern performance without reproducing it?' (1). Peele's play, I want to suggest, prevents the disappearance of the trauma of sexual violence from both its initial audience's attention and the attention of the modern critic. If elsewhere the play follows the biblical narrative closely, in its representations of the sexual coercion of Bathsheba and the rapes of Tamar and the concubines the play departs from that narrative, and the rape paradigm embedded in it, to give the traumatised women voices with which they express the trauma of their experiences. 'Whither shall I fly, / With folded arms and all-amazèd soul' (4.14–15), cries Tamar as she is ejected from Amnon's residence. She expresses her trauma as a fall from the 'glorious soil' (16) of paradise and exile 'To bare and barren vales with floods made waste, / To desert woods and hills with lightning scorched' (19–21) where she will 'With death, with shame, with hell, with horror sit' (21). Her 'heart is rent / With inward fury of a thousand griefs' (30–1), and in her distress she imagines 'rend[ing] my bloody side' with 'a rusty weapon' (26, 27). She is prevented from suicide by the arrival of Absalom, who vows revenge before urging her to 'Go in, my sister, rest thee in my house, / And God in time shall take this shame from thee' (56–7). Tamar resists Absalom's attempt to incorporate her trauma into the providential narrative in which he sees himself as the central figure, however: 'Nor God nor time will do that good for me' (58), she replies.

Bathsheba similarly resists the erasure of the trauma of her sexual coercion. She may ultimately acquiesce to David's demands, and, as we have seen, the play converts Bathsheba's coerced sexuality into a force working for David's redemption. Moreover, as she works with the prophet Nathan in scene 17 to secure the throne for her son Solomon, she exhibits an agency that goes beyond protest to result in effective and divinely approved political action. None the less, Bathsheba initially voices her objections to David's coercive sexual demands, and she makes it clear that her concerns are not identical with David's and that she is the one who suffers the consequences of David's violence, in however much lyricism he may attempt to disguise that violence. When David greets Bathsheba in the opening scene, he explains to her why he summoned her: 'since thy beauty scorched my conquered soul, / I called thee nearer for my nearer cure' (111–12). Bathsheba does not entirely accept David's strategy of blaming the victim, though: 'One medicine cannot heal our different harms' (124), she later tells him, 'but rather make both rankle at the bone' (125). Bathsheba's harm, her trauma, in this affair is distinct from whatever 'hurt' (122) the smitten David might be feeling, and Bathsheba resists the conflation of the two. In scene 5, as the 'harm' of the affair begins to manifest itself in the illness of David

and Bathsheba's child, Bathsheba's lament elaborates on her sense
of the separateness of her concerns from David's. 'Mourn, Bathsheba',
the lament begins, and 'bewail thy foolishness, / Thy sin, thy shame,
the sorrow of thy soul' (1–2). She finds 'No comfort from the ten-
stringed instrument, / The twinkling cymbal, or the ivory lute' (6–7)
and, tellingly, 'Nor doth the sound of David's kingly harp / Make
glad the broken heart of Bathsheba' (8–9). Indeed, having protested
against 'the lust of kings' (24), she closes the lament by reposing
trust not in David but in 'The grace that God will to His handmaid
send' (27).

In the play's representation of the concubines, the trauma of rape
is much less visible than in the play's representation of the sexual
violence done to Tamar and Bathsheba. As we have seen, the concubines defy their rapist primarily by resisting his appropriation
of their rape as symbols of his sovereignty. None the less, the first
Concubine makes it clear at the beginning of her denunciation of
Absalom that it is not just 'Thy father's honour' (11.17) but also
'ours thus beaten with thy violent arms' (18) that 'Will cry for vengeance to the host of heaven' (19). In a world in which, legitimately
or illegitimately, political power is asserted through women's bodies
in ways that appropriate their trauma and negate their agency,
David and Bathsheba does not allow its audiences or its modern
readers to forget the trauma of women's experiences of sexual
violence.

SOURCES

The Bible is *David and Bathsheba*'s major source. In his introduction
to the Yale edition of the play Blistein remarks that 'while we are
unable to determine which version of the Bible Peele used as his
source, we are sure he used the Bible' (148). Blistein's verdict may
err too far on the side of caution. Exactly which English version
or versions of the Bible Peele employed cannot be determined
with complete certainty, but close analysis indicates that it is most
likely that Peele consulted both the Geneva Bible and the Bishops'
Bible heavily while occasionally turning to other versions such as
the Great Bible. The most extended analysis of the issue remains
Arthur Sampley's 1928 article, 'The Version of the Bible Used
by Peele in the Composition of "David and Bethsabe"'. Sampley
compares the play to the six major sixteenth-century English

translations of the Bible – the Coverdale Bible (1535), Mathew's
Bible (1537), the Great Bible (1539), Taverner's Bible (1539), the
Geneva Bible (1560), and the Bishops' Bible (1568) (79) – along
with a sixteenth-century edition of the Vulgate, and concludes that
'it seems to me in the highest degree probable that Peele made use
of the Bishops' Bible in the composition of *David and Bethsabe*'
(87) and that 'he used some contemporary version of the Latin
Vulgate' (87). According to Sampley, a comparison of the spelling
of the biblical characters' names in the play to their spelling in the
bibles reveals that for the most part Peele took his spellings from the
Bishops' Bible, while the Geneva Bible spellings seem the furthest
removed from Peele's (80–1). Sampley consequently eliminates the
Geneva Bible from further analysis as a possible source, focusing the
remainder of his analysis on a comparison of twelve select passages
from Peele's play to passages from the Bishops' Bible, the Great
Bible, and the Vulgate. The passages from Peele's play were chosen
because they echo one version or another of the Bible particularly
closely.

Sampley's decision to rule out the Geneva Bible from this comparative analysis, however, is logically flawed and has unfortunate
results. From the fact that Peele does not follow the Geneva Bible
in the spelling of his characters' names, it in no way follows that
Peele did not follow it in other matters, and a reinsertion of the
Geneva Bible into Sampley's subsequent analysis strongly suggests
that he did. For nine of Sampley's twelve selected passages, the
Geneva and Bishops' translations are virtually identical. In one
instance, the two versions differ significantly in a way that suggests
that Peele is in this passage echoing the Bishops' rather than the
Geneva rendering: Peele's 'And leave nor name nor issue on the
earth' (9.84) is clearly closer to the Bishops' 'and shall not leave
to my husband neither name nor issue upon the earth' (2 Samuel,
14:7) than to the Geneva's 'and shall not leave to mine husband
neither name nor posterity upon the earth' (2 Samuel, 14:7). In
two instances, however, Peele has clearly conflated the two versions.
2 Samuel, 12:4 reads 'And he spared to take of his own sheep' in
the Bishops' version, 'who refused to take of his own sheep' in the
Geneva version. Peele combines them into 'And he refused and
spared to take his own' (6.24). Similarly, the Bishops' version of 2
Samuel, 17:8 reads 'Thy father is a man also practised in war and
will not lodge with the people', while the Geneva version of the same

verse has 'thy father is a valiant warrior, and will not lodge with the people'. Again, Peele combines the two:

> Besides, the King himself a valiant man,
> Trained up in feats and stratagems of war,
> And will not, for prevention of the worst,
> Lodge with the common soldiers in the field.

(11.106–9)

In nine of Sampley's twelve passages, then, comparison shows that Peele could be echoing either the Bishop's version or the Geneva; in only one passage does a comparison indicate that Peele was echoing the Bishops' version rather than the Geneva; in two passages, comparison strongly suggests that Peele was echoing the Bishops's version *and* the Geneva. In only three instances is Peele closer to the Great Bible than to either the Bishops' version or the Geneva. Following Blistein's analysis, one might also add to this list the Coverdale version, between which and the play Blistein detected four unique parallels, one more than the number of unique parallels he detected between the play and the Geneva version (145).

As the foregoing discussion would indicate, *David and Bathsheba* follows its biblical sources very closely, in both the events it dramatises and in its language. The Old Testament contains two accounts of David's reign, the first found in 2 Samuel and the second in 1 Chronicles. The two accounts, however, emphasise different events – 1 Chronicles does not mention Bathsheba, for example – and for the vast majority of his play Peele draws upon 2 Samuel, specifically chapters 11 through 19, supplemented in the final scene with the first two chapters of 1 Kings, which recount the proclamation of Solomon as David's heir just before David's death. The exact amount of time covered by the play is difficult to determine, in part because the biblical narratives are not always temporally precise and in part because Peele frequently modifies the biblical narrative's chronology for the sake of dramatic compression. 2 Samuel, 5:4–5 informs us that 'David was thirty years old when he began to reign, and he reigned forty years. / In Hebron he reigned over Judah seven years, and six months, and in Jerusalem he reigned thirty and three years over all Israel and Judah.' The events with which the play begins – the siege of Rabbah and David's sexual coercion of Bathsheba – occur at some point early on in David's reign in Jerusalem, while the events with which the play concludes – the defeat of Absalom's rebellion and the declaration of Solomon

as David's heir – are temporally disparate, separated by a lengthy
but indeterminate stretch of time during which David faced two
further rebellions, the first by a man named Sheba (2 Samuel, 20)
and the second by Absalom's younger brother Adonijah (1 Kings,
1). According to the biblical narrative, David declares Solomon to
be his heir after Adonijah's, not Absalom's, rebellion. Perhaps to
avoid the repetition of what are very similar events, however, Peele
has compressed the two rebellions into one.

Peele is not afraid to bend or break the laws of linear time in
his effort to compress time, as in scene 3, when Tamar enters to
visit Amnon immediately after Jonadab has suggested to him that
he request David to send her, or in scene 9, when Joab is able to
make Absalom, supposedly in exile at Geshur, appear in David's
presence within nine lines of being commanded by David to 'Go
fetch my son, that he may live with me' (118). Peele also condenses
time by placing in parallel events that happen serially in the biblical
narrative. Scene 4 provides a good example of this technique, which
Ruth Blackburn has called 'cinematic' (172). The scene reorders
and splices together three distinct episodes in the biblical narrative:
David's frustrated attempt to cover up his adultery by getting Uriah
to sleep with the pregnant Bathsheba (2 Samuel, 11:7–15); Amnon's
rejection of Tamar (2 Samuel, 13:15–22); Absalom's request that
David and his lords and sons attend Absalom's sheep-shearing
feast (2 Samuel, 13:23–27). In the biblical chronology, the cover-up
attempt comes before the final siege of Rabbah, the rape of Tamar
and her rejection after it, and Absalom's request and the feast itself
two years after Tamar's rape. What the biblical narrative chooses
to narrate in serial fashion, Peele has chosen instead to dramatise
as simultaneously occurring and complexly interrelated sequences
of events. Ashley has described *David and Bathsheba* as 'a Biblical
chronicle history' (*Peele*, 144) that 'lacks unity' (148). On the contrary, through dramatic compression of various types Peele is able to
fashion from the episodic biblical narrative the well unified action of
his play. The conclusion of one of the play's earliest students, P.H.
Cheffaud, retains its validity: 'les premiers incidents et les derniers
se trouvent dans la double relation de cause à effet, et de péché à
chatiment [the first incidents and the last are found in the double
relation of cause and effect, and sin and punishment]' (137); consequently, 'l'histoire de David, telle que Peele nous la raconte, est un
veritable theme à la Senèque où l'on voit une maison royale vouée
à la ruine par les crimes de son chef [the history of David, such as

Peele recounts it to us, is a truly Senecan theme in which one sees a royal house dedicated to ruin by the crimes of its head]' (142–3).

David and Bathsheba both amplifies and qualifies its Senecan tragic theme through its use of its second major source, Guilliaume de Saluste du Bartas's Semaines or, as they are better known through Joshua Sylvester's translation, Divine Weeks. The first Semaine, which recounts the Creation, was first published in 1578; the first two days of La Seconde Semaine, beginning with Adam and narrating various aspects of Old Testament history before Abraham, followed in 1584. Five other books of the next two days of La Seconde Semaine were published after Du Bartas's death in 1590 but before Peele's death in 1596: 'The Fathers', 'Jonah', 'Trophies', and 'Magnificence' in 1591, and 'The Law' in 1593 (Prescott, French Poets, 169–72). Du Bartas's work is an encyclopedic religious epic (Auger, 626) stemming from what Lily Campbell has described as 'a movement to substitute divine poetry for the secular poetry which was coming off the presses in the sixteenth century, a movement to substitute Biblical story for secular story, to substitute Christian mythology for a pagan mythology, as well as to substitute prayer and praise of the Christian God for poetry addressed to an unkind mistress' (5). Anne Lake Prescott observes that 'In England Du Bartas was probably the most admired of contemporary European writers, if one excludes Erasmus and the chief figures of the Reformation, and his lengthy descriptions of the creation and history of the world received an adulation seldom given to far better poetry' ('Reception', 144).

English translators of the Semaines include such luminaries as Sir Philip Sidney and James VI (Auger, 625), but, although Sylvester began publishing his translation in 1592 (Sykes, 349), no English translations of the passages on which Peele drew for his play were published before 1594, the date of the play's entry into the Stationers' Register. Moreover, as H. Dugdale Sykes argued in 1924, 'a comparison of his [Peele's] play with the original text of La Seconde Semaine and with Sylvester's translation makes it clear that he borrowed direct from Du Bartas' (349). David and Bathsheba contains very close translations of 115 lines from La Seconde Semaine, taken from three of the books first published in 1584: 'Eden', 'The Ark', and 'The Artifices'. These lines are reproduced either in the commentary notes or, in the case of more extended passages, in the Appendix. All the English translations of these lines are mine. The play's first scene contains translations of 14 lines of Du Bartas's description of Paradise in 'Eden'; another line from the same description is found in scene 4. The one borrowing from 'The Ark', noted by Alexander Dyce in 1861, occurs in Chorus 1. The remaining hundred lines are taken from 'The Artifices', mostly from the conversation between Adam and Seth, and, apart from four lines in scene 12 and three lines in the cancelled fragment after Chorus 2, are all found in the play's concluding scene. Assessing the causes of the English enthusiasm for the *Semaines*, Robert Cummings argues that the books 'were read not for doctrine but for their detachable "beauties" (uncomplicatedly and abundantly represented in Robert Allot's collection of poetical commonplaces, *Englands Parnassus* [1600])' (176). According to Cummings, Allot's anthology contains 112 passages from *La Seconde Semaine*, 110 from Sylvester's translation (190). To this we can add two of the three passages from *David and Bathsheba* reproduced in the anthology: Chorus 1.4–11, and 17.87–9.

Although early modern English readers may have read Du Bartas for isolated poetic passages, Peele's borrowings are deployed to create in *David and Bathsheba* an underlying archetypal pattern that both reinforces and subsumes the play's tragic theme. In the first scene, they emphatically connect David and Bathsheba to Adam and Eve in Eden, implying that their fall repeats the fall of humanity's first parents. Peele draws on lines 40–108 of Du Bartas's *Eden*, a description of Eden itself, in Bathsheba's opening speech and, more extensively, in David's lyrical flight of fancy as he observes Bathsheba bathing. In lines that mark the difference as well as the similarities between the two events, David declaims

> What tunes, what words, what looks, what wonders pierce
> My soul, incensèd with a sudden fire?
> What tree, what shade, what spring, what paradise
> Enjoys the beauty of so fair a dame?
> Fair Eva placed in perfect happiness,
> Lending her praise-notes to the liberal heavens,
> Struck with the accents of archangels' tunes,
> Wrought not more pleasure to her husband's thoughts
> Than this fair woman's words and notes to mine.

> (1.26–34)

Bathsheba may be Eve, the grove in which she is bathing may strike David as Paradise, and David's own sexual desire may incite him to identify with Adam, to want to occupy the position of Adam, but he precisely is not Adam, not 'her husband' (33), a point of which Hushai does not hesitate to remind David in this scene and

elsewhere in the play. David's fall from his paradise is precipitated
by his illicit longing for Paradise. He repeats the Fall by acting on
his forbidden longings to return to what he tropes, with the help of
Du Bartas, as prelapsarian sexual bliss.

The play also presents Tamar's rape as a repetition of the primal
biblical tragedy: 'Whither, alas, ah, whither shall I fly, / With folded
arms and all-amazèd soul' (4.14–15), Tamar cries as she is expelled
from Amnon's palace, 'Cast as was Eva from that glorious soil /
Where all delights sat bating, winged with thoughts, / Ready to
nestle in her naked breasts?' (16–18). The explicit allusions to Eve
and Eden are reinforced by line 17's echo of Du Bartas's description
of Eden's trees, in whose branches 'cent sortes d'oiseaux jour et
nuict s'esbatoient [a hundred kinds of birds day and night frolicked]'
(*Eden*, 83). Peele borrows from Du Bartas to extend the archetypal
pattern throughout the play.

If David and Bathsheba are linked to Adam and Eve, then Amnon,
Absalom, and Solomon are linked to Cain, Abel, and Seth. The can-
celled fragment following Chorus 2 points the way. In this fragment
Absalom seems to be protesting against what he perceives to be the
undeserved favour shown to one of his half-brothers, presumably
Amnon: ' "What boots it, Absalom, unhappy Absalom?" / Sighing, I
say "What boots it, Absalom, / To have disclosed a far more worthy
womb?" ' The lines echo closely Cain's angry musings on Abel in Du
Bartas after God has accepted Abel's sacrifice and rejected Cain's:
'Que te sert-il, Caïn? ô Caïn, que te sert / (Dit-il en souspirant)
d'avoir premier ouvert / Le fecond amarry de la premiere mere
[What use is it, Cain? O Cain, what use is it / (He says sighing)
to have first opened / The fertile womb of the first mother]' (*Les
Artifices*, 267–9). Absalom's murder of Amnon, then, repeats, with a
difference, Cain's murder of Abel: although Absalom is the younger
of the two sons of David – in fact, precisely because Absalom is the
younger of the two – he, like Cain, is envious of the favour shown
his brother, David's eldest son and royal heir, favour most notably
manifested in the play in David's failure to punish Amnon for his
rape of Absalom's sister.

Within this paradigm Peele's borrowings from Du Bartas in scene
17 reveal their function. Taken primarily from Du Bartas's narra-
tion in 'The Artifices' of Adam's lessons to his third son Seth after
Cain has been banished for murdering Abel, the borrowings tightly
identify Solomon with Seth. When Nathan urges David to 'Let
Solomon be made thy staff of age, / Fair Israel's rest, and honour

of thy race' (55–6), he is transferring on to Solomon Du Bartas's description of Seth, 'qui tient de sainct Abel la place, / Baston de sa viellesse, et gloire de sa race [who holds of holy Abel the place, / Staff of his [Adam's] old age, and glory of his race]' (*Les Artifices*, 517–18). The ensuing conversation between David and Solomon substantiates the connection between David's new heir and Adam's only remaining son by translating 53 lines from Adam's conversation with Seth in Du Bartas. Cheffaud may be correct to perceive a Senecan pattern in the tragic consequences that issue from David and Bathsheba's initial adultery, but that pattern is subsumed within the larger biblical paradigm that Peele establishes through his use of Du Bartas, a pattern that goes beyond the utter destruction of the family with which the Senecan pattern concludes and offers in the form of the Seth-like Solomon a collective hope that parallels the personal grace that the penitent David ultimately receives in spite of his sinfulness. *David and Bathsheba* is, in Campbell's words, 'a divine play conscious of its place in divine literature and aware of the traditions and practices of the poets who were writing divine poems' (260), even if Peele's treatment of those traditions and practices does not hesitate to confront their less comfortable elements, such as the political implications of David's status as paradigmatic penitent and sexual violence against women.

DAVID AND BATHSHEBA, BIBLICAL DRAMA, AND PERFORMANCE PROVENANCE

The biblical subject matter of Peele's 'divine drama' makes it unusual for a play written for the Elizabethan professional stage. Although the figure of David was common in early modern European culture in general and Elizabethan literature in particular, and although there are many Continental dramas about David in the period, *David and Bathsheba* is the only extant David play and one of only thirteen or fourteen plays on biblical subjects known to have been written for the early modern English professional stage. Of these plays, *David and Bathsheba* is only one of two to survive the depredations of time and contingency, the other being Thomas Lodge and Robert Greene's Jonah play, *Looking Glass for London and England* (1594). Biblical history was frequently the subject matter of earlier English drama, varying in kind from John Bale's *A Tragedy or Enterlude Manifesting the Chief Promises of God unto Man* (1538) to the great medieval mystery cycles. Murray Roston summarises that 'the most popular themes in the biblical drama of this period were Joseph, Adam, David, Esther, and Susannah' and that 'In each, the good are seen to be vindicated and the guilty to be duly punished' (58). In the middle of the Henrician Reformation, Thomas Watson (consecrated Bishop of Lincoln in 1557) wrote a Latin play entitled *Absalom* (1534–44); the editor of the only surviving manuscript of Watson's play, John Hazel Smith, also notes that in 1562 the Stationers' Register records a play entitled *The Two Sins of David*, now lost (Smith, *Humanist's*, 31).

Scholars have frequently asserted that considerable continuity exists between the earlier drama and the newly developing professional stage of the Elizabethan period. The direct dramatization of biblical history, however, seems to have been one area of discontinuity. According to Blackburn, no Protestant English biblical drama is recorded between 1568 and 1587 (155). Several competing reasons have been suggested for the discontinuity. Suggesting that English writers between 1568 and 1587 might have felt biblical subject matter to be unsafe for dramatic treatment given the Elizabethan government's attempts to suppress the mystery cycles (159), Blackburn attributes the decline of biblical drama by the end of the sixteenth century to increasing Puritan opposition to the theatre (194). In contrast, Roston attributes the end of scriptural drama not to laws or to the Puritan attacks on the theatre but to a rise in the perceived sanctity of the Old Testament. Dramatists, Roston argues, felt increasing scruples about using Old Testament narratives for dramatic purposes and switched instead to exploiting narratives from the Apocrypha and Josephus. 'It was the fear of sacrilege', Roston concludes, that 'brought an end to biblical drama at the close of the sixteenth century' (120).

According to Connolly, however, before biblical drama disappeared from the stage at the end of the sixteenth century, between 1590 and 1602, thirteen biblical dramas are known to have been written for the English professional stage (4). Most of these, Connolly claims, can be assigned to the Admiral's Men: 'After 1594 when the Chamberlain's Men and the Admiral's Men emerged as the two dominant companies, biblical plays become associated almost exclusively with the repertory of the Admiral's Men' (8). Connolly accounts for this concentration through reference to the Admiral's Men's repertorial strategies. Following Knutson's argument that 'one of the strategies employed by the companies which owned Marlowe's plays was to build "a complementary repertory

that duplicated, exploited, or exaggerated certain of their features"
[Knutson 2002, 25]' (9), Connolly states that 'The biblical plays
staged by the Admiral's Men at the Rose and Fortune theatres rep-
licated the themes and motifs of older plays in their collection, particularly the most popular of Marlowe's plays such as *Tamburlaine*
and *The Jew of Malta*. The eponymously titled plays are therefore
characterised by accounts of soldier kings or conquering prophets
whose campaigns are set against an ancient and exotic backdrop'
(20). We have one possible early modern performance record for
David and Bathsheba, an undated entry in Henslowe's diary between
3 and 11 October for payment to workers for the construction of
a gallows by which to hang Absalom by the hair (Foakes, 217).
Although, as Connolly notes, this entry could refer to another play
and does not, therefore, permit us indisputably to assign *David and
Bathsheba* to the Admiral's Men, none the less it concurs generally
with the play's fit with the Admiral's Men's repertorial strategies,
'which makes it possible to suggest that *David and Bethsabe* was
written for the Admiral's Men, and that like the biblical plays of
his contemporaries, Peele's play was destined for performance at
the Rose, with Alleyn in the title role' (8). I am aware of only one
modern stage performance of the play, William Poel's 1932 production, which is briefly described in Robert Speaight's *William Poel and
the Elizabethan Revival* (266–8).

THE TEXT

If we assume that Peele is echoing Marlowe's *1 Tamburlaine* rather
than the other way around in passages such as Absalom's declama-
tion of his desire to 'glut his longing soul / With sole fruition of his
father's crown' (11.139–40), then Peele wrote *David and Bathsheba*
between 1587, when Marlowe's play was first performed, and 14
May 1594, when a 'booke called the booke of David and Bethsaba'
was entered into the Stationers' Register along with *Friar Bacon*,
King Leir, *John of Gaunt*, and *Robin Hood and Little John* (Greg,
261) As Blistein remarks, there is no external or internal evidence
that would allow us to date the play with complete certainty more
precisely than that (142–3). The five plays entered on 14 May were
initially entered to Adam Islip, whose name was then cancelled out
and replaced by Edward White (Greg, 261). Blistein suggests that
'The wardens or clerk who made the entry probably assumed that
Islip was entering them for himself, and so indicated in the Register

until corrected later by Islip or White' but adds that 'no definite reason for the cancellation can be ascertained' (153). W.W. Greg speculates that the play might have been printed in 1594 (261), but no copy of a 1594 edition survives.

When the play was printed in 1599, only Islip's and not White's name appeared on the title page. Three passages from the play were reprinted in *England's Parnassus* (1600), a poetry anthology edited by Robert Allott. There are only three substantive variants between the play and the passages reproduced by Allott. They are recorded in this edition's collation notes. On 29 June 1624 the Stationers' Register records the transfer of 'Salomon and Bersheba' from the widow of Edward White (son of the Edward White to whom the play was initially entered [Blistein, 154–5]) to Edward Alde (Greg, 262). No early edition subsequent to the 1599 quarto is extant, however. Consequently, this edition takes the 1599 quarto as its copy text. Although Greg was aware of only twelve, the ESTC lists fourteen witnesses of the 1599 Q in libraries in North America and the United Kingdom. For this edition I have collated all fourteen, which are housed at the following institutions: the Bodleian Library; the British Library (2); the Folger Shakespeare Library; the Harry Ransom Center, University of Texas at Austin; Harvard University; Haverford College; the Huntington Library; Magdalene College, Cambridge; the National Library of Scotland; National Trust Collections, Petworth House; the University of Illinois, Urbana-Champaign; the Victoria and Albert Museum, Dyce Collection; Worcester College, Oxford (this copy begins at C1).

My collation discovered 23 stop-press variants, all of which are recorded in the collation notes. The play collates A2, B–H, I2. From B1v to G4v, Q's running title alternates regularly between '*Dauid and Bethsabe*' in the inner form and '*Dauid and Bersabe*' in the outer form. In H, the order is reversed, and I1r and I1v both have '*Dauid and Bersabe*' as their running title. There are three discernible spacing variants in the running titles amongst the fourteen quartos. In the Bodleian, University of Illinois, Harvard, and Magdalene College copies of Q, the C1v running title is '*Beth_sabe*'. In all but the Haverford College and Petworth House copies, the D1v running title is '*Bet_hsabe*'. In the Folger, University of Illinois, Harvard, National Library of Scotland, Worcester College, and Magdalene College copies, the H2v running title is '*Bet_hsabe*'. The running title of all copies (excluding the Worcester College copy) at B4v is '*Bersahe*'. The next edition of the play after the 1599 edition is found in volume two of Thomas Hawkins' *The Origin of the English Drama* (1773). Along with Hawkins, the following nineteenth- and twentieth-century editions were consulted in the preparation of this edition and are referred to in the collation notes: Dyce 2 (1829), Dyce 3 (1861), Keltie (1873), Morley (1887), Bullen (1888), Manly (1897), Thorndike (1910), Greg (1912 [1913]), Blistein (1970), and Rabkin (1976).

The 1599 quarto contains some obvious textual problems, which Sampley summarises in five points ('Text', 669). First, in the scene of Tamar's rape (scene 3), Tamar's entrance is temporally perplexing, given that there seems to be insufficient time for her to have been commanded by David to attend her brother Ammon. Moreover, scene 3's opening stage directions list a character, Amnon's page, who 'appears without any business to perform' (669). Second, although in scene 4 Absalom proposes to host the sheep-shearing feast at which he will later kill Amnon, in scene 7 the feast is hosted by Amnon himself. Third, in scene 9 the Widow of Tekoa seems to speak of Absalom as banished, although at no point earlier in the play has David banished him. Fourth and fifth, G4v of the quarto contains a '5. Chorus' that seems to conclude the play, but the chorus (only the second in the play) is followed by a few lines spoken by an already-dead Absalom, the catchword 'Then', and, on H1r, the stage direction '*Trumpets sound ...*', after which follow another two scenes. Sampley explains these textual anomalies as the results of a complex process of abridgement and revision in which the play began as 'a five-act play dealing with the love of David and Bethsabe and the tragedy of Absolon' (669), 'was considerably shortened for reasons connected with the staging of the play' (670), and then was expanded again when 'it was finally thought necessary to execute a revision which would fill out the play to a more desirable length' (670).

Later editors and critics such as Blistein (177–81), Ewbank ('House', 7), and Paul Werstine (246–8) have broadly concurred with Sampley's explanation that the quarto represents some sort of theatrical abridgement and revision of the play. As both Blistein and Ewbank contend, however, there are other ways of explaining the temporal anomalies of Tamar's unexpected entrance and the Widow of Tekoa's reference to banishment than textual corruption, such as Peele's desire to compress events to make a dramatic point. None the less, the difficulties surrounding the '5. Chorus' and the immediately following lines by Absalom remain. While its misnumbering strongly suggests that the text has been abridged, it is not necessarily misplaced, and I retain it in my edition where it is in the quarto. The lines attributed to Absalom following the chorus seem to me to be clearly erroneous, the product perhaps of the compositor's failure to notice a cancelled passage in his manuscript copy or of a stray manuscript leaf from the unabridged version of the play, and in my edition I move them from the main text to the collation notes, accompanied by a full commentary note. Apart from these textual problems, the 1599 quarto is fairly straightforward.

Although it contains a prologue and two choruses, the 1599 quarto is undivided into acts or scenes. This edition follows Greg's 1912 [1913] facsimile edition's division of the play into 17 scenes. To indicate their editorial provenance, the scene divisions, along with additions to stage directions and speech prefixes, have been placed in square brackets in the text. Speech prefixes abbreviated in the quarto have been silently expanded in the text but collated. The quarto's spelling and punctuation have been silently modernised, but instances in which the modernisation required editorial selection among competing alternatives have been collated and explained in the commentary notes. Although, as Sampley demonstrates, the quarto's spellings of character and place names are closer to the spellings found in the Bishop's Bible than the Geneva Bible, the spellings are irregular and do not conform wholly to any version of the Bible to which Sampley compares the play ('Version', 80–1). 'Absalom', for example, is spelled both 'Absalon' and 'Absolon', while 'Bathsheba' is spelled 'Bethsabe' approximately two-thirds of the time and 'Bersabe' about one-third. 'Abishai' has four different variants in the quarto. The play's character and place names have therefore been modernised and regularised in accordance with their spelling in the New King James version of the Bible. The first instances of the modernisations have been recorded in the collation notes. In most cases the modernisation has entailed only minor alteration: 'Uriah' for 'Vrias', for example, or 'Tamar' for 'Thamar'. The most noticeable change is 'Hushai' for the quarto's 'Cusay' or 'Cusai' (The Bishops' Bible alternates between 'Hushai' and 'Chusi', while the Geneva Bible alternates between 'Hushai' and 'Cushi' (Sampley, 'Version', 80)). I have kept substantive emendations to a minimum (a total of 18), preferring to retain the quarto's reading when it made sense, even when the conjectural emendations of previous editors seemed to 'improve' the text.

CONCLUSION

The misplaced fragment and the various textual lacunae discussed in the previous section tantalise us with the glimpse of a fuller version of the play that would represent more clearly than the extant quarto Peele's artistic designs. None the less, even as it stands, *David and Bathsheba* is an aesthetically sophisticated and culturally complex play that challenges its audiences and readers to probe the political, theological, and sexual problems and paradoxes of its biblical subject matter. The play's representation of David as poet, prophet, and, foremost, penitent explores the paradoxical political implications of one of the central problems of the Protestant Reformation, God's grace. Disturbingly, David's strength as God's anointed is not undermined but reinforced by his sinfulness. David is not Tamburlaine, and is better off for that. The play further examines the sinister side of David's divine sovereignty in its representation of sexual violence against women. The play dramatises its chosen slice of David's reign as driven by sexual coercion and violence and their consequences, as a sequence of tragic sexual crimes that are, darkly, the divinely sanctified forms by which patriarchal sovereignty reproduces itself as unlimited. The play may ultimately subsume this 'Senecan' sexual violence in a salvific plan that culminates in Solomon's proclamation as David's heir, but it also gives the victims of sovereign sexual violence the opportunity to voice their traumatic experiences and protest against their victimisation. *David and Bathsheba* is only one of two surviving biblical dramas written for the Elizabethan professional stage and only one of thirteen or fourteen biblical dramas known to have been written for that stage. The play cannot be taken as representative of this lost body of plays, but its intellectual complexity and aesthetic quality demonstrate that Elizabethan playwrights could turn sacred as well as secular history into forceful, engaging contemporary drama.

DAVID AND BATHSHEBA

[List of characters,
in order of appearance

BATHSHEBA, *Uriah the Hittite's wife then David's.*
DAVID, *King of Israel.*
HUSHAI, *David's friend and counsellor.*
JOAB, *son of David's sister Zeruiah and general of David's army.*
ABISHAI, *Joab's brother and leader in David's army.*   5
URIAH, *a Hittite and soldier in David's army.*
HANUN, *King of the Ammonites.*
MAACAH, *mercenary king hired by Hanun.*
AMNON, *David's oldest son.*
JONADAB, *Amnon's friend.*   10
ITHREAM, *David's sixth son.*
TAMAR, *David's daughter.*
ABSALOM, *David's third son.*
NATHAN, *a prophet.*
ADONIJAH, *David's fourth son.*   15
ITTAI, *son of the King of Gath and leader in David's army.*
ZADOK, *high priest.*
AHIMAAZ, *Zadok's son.*
JONATHAN, *Abiathar's son.*
AMASA, *general of Absalom's army during Absalom's revolt.*   20
AHITHOPHEL, *Absalom's chief counsellor.*
ABIATHAR, *high priest.*

Heading List of Characters ... and court attendants] *this edn; not in Q.*
Bathsheba] *this edn; Bersabe Q.*

[*List of Characters*] The characters' names have been modernised in
accordance with their spelling in the New King James Version of the Bible.
Most of the List of Characters' descriptions are explicitly established in
the play itself. The order of David's sons is based on 2 Samuel, 3:2–5. I
Chronicles, 2:16 lists Joab, Abishai, and Asahel as the three sons of David's
sister Zeruiah. For Maacah's status as a mercenary king, see 2 Samuel, 10:6.
For Shimei, see 2 Samuel, 16:5. The list divides the characters into two
groups: those with proper names and those with common names. Within
the groups, the names are listed in order of the characters' appearance on
stage in the play. Chileab, Bathsheba's maid, and Amnon's page are non-
speaking parts.

SHIMEI, *son of Gera, of the house of the former King of Israel, Saul.*
SOLOMON, *David and Bathsheba's son.*
CHILEAB, *David's second son.*   25

The Prologue, *who may also serve as the Chorus*
Bathsheba's maid
Amnon's page
Widow of Tekoa
1 Servant   30
1 Concubine of David
2 Concubine of David
1 Soldier
2 Soldier
Messenger   35

Miscellaneous servants, soldiers, and court attendants]

[Prologue]

[Enter] Prologue.

[Prologue.] Of Israel's sweetest singer now I sing,
His holy style and happy victories,
Whose muse was dipped in that inspiring dew
Archangels stillèd from the breath of Jove,
Decking her temples with the glorious flowers   5

Heading Prologue] *Hawkins (subst); not in Q.* 0.1. SD Enter] *this edn; not in Q.* Prologue] *this edn; Prologus Q.* 1. SH *Prologue*] *this edn; not in Q.*

1.] echoes the formulaic statement of subject with which an epic's opening invocation of a muse or the Muses conventionally begins. 'Sing, goddess, the anger of Peleus' son Achilleus' (1.1), begins Homer's *Iliad*; Milton's *Paradise Lost* commences with 'Of Man's First Disobedience ... / ... / Sing Heav'nly Muse' (1, 6).

Israel's sweetest singer] David, described in the Geneva version of 2 Samuel, 23:1 as the 'sweet singer of Israel'.

2. *style*] stylus or writing implement as well as manner of writing (*OED*, n.). David's 'holy style' or stylus complements the sword with which he has won his 'happy victories' and contrasts with Peele's own 'iron pen'. Contending that 'the holy David's Psalms are a divine poem' (133), Philip Sidney in *The Defence of Poetry* describes an aspect of David's 'holy style', his 'notable *prosopopoeias*, when he maketh you, as it were, see God coming in His majesty, his telling of the beasts' joyfulness and hills leaping', which constitutes 'a heavenly poesy, wherein almost he showeth himself a passionate lover of that unspeakable and everlasting beauty to be seen by the eyes of the mind, only cleared by faith' (140–5).

happy] fortunate, successful.

3. *muse*] source of poetic inspiration. David's muse contrasts with the 'feeble muse' of line 22.

4. *stillèd*] distilled. The imagery of lines 3 to 6 may echo the Geneva version of Deuteronomy, 32:2, the second verse of the song that Moses speaks to the elders of Israel before his death: 'My doctrine shall drop as the rain, and my speech shall still as the dew, as the shower upon the herbs, and as the great rain upon the grass.'

Jove] Jehovah. In scene 2, Joab tells his troops, 'Ye fight the holy battles of Jehovah, / King David's God' (7–8).

52

Heavens rained on tops of Zion and Mount Sinai.
Upon the bosom of his ivory lute
The cherubim and angels laid their breasts,
And when his consecrated fingers struck
The golden wires of his ravishing harp, 10
He gave alarum to the host of heaven,
That, winged with lightning, broke the clouds and cast
Their crystal armour at his conquering feet.
Of this sweet poet, Jove's musician,
And of his beauteous son I press to sing. 15
Then help, divine Adonai, to conduct,
Upon the wings of my well-tempered verse,
The hearers' minds above the towers of heaven,
And guide them so in this thrice-haughty flight

---

6. Zion] Q (Syon). *Modernised silently throughout.* 9. struck] *Hawkins (subst);* strooke Q. 15. his] *Hawkins (subst);* bis Q. press] Q (prease).

6. *Zion*] sacred hill in Jerusalem, in biblical usage often standing for Jerusalem as a whole (Browning, 386).

Mount Sinai] the 'Mountain of God' (Exodus, 3:1) in the Sinai desert, on which Moses encountered the voice of God in the burning bush (Exodus, 3:1–4:17) and received from God the Ten Commandments (Exodus, 19:20–1).

8. *cherubim*] angels. In Exodus, 25:18–21, God instructs Moses to place, facing inward, a golden figure of a cherub with extended wings at each end of the mercy seat that was to sit on the top of the ark of the covenant. Isaiah, 37:16 states that God 'dwellest between the Cherubims'.

9. *struck*] The original spelling, 'strooke', was a form of the past tense of 'stroke' as well as 'strike' but has been modernised as 'struck' in light of the violence of the imagery of the subsequent lines.

11. *alarum*] alarm, call to arms. The original spelling has been retained to preserve the metre.

host army.

12. *That*] who (introducing a non-restrictive relative clause).

13. *crystal armour*] In Marlowe's *1 Tamburlaine*, Zenocrate's tears are figured as 'angels in their crystal armours' (5.1.151).

15. *beauteous son*] Absalom.

press] push forward, strain, advance eagerly (*OED*, v.1, 8a).

16. *Adonai*] God, lit. 'my Lord' (*OED*, n.).

17. *well-tempered*] appropriately measured, balanced, or composed; strong, durable (*OED*, 4b).

19. *thrice-haughty*] lofty, exalted, elevated.

Their mounting feathers scorch not with the fire   20
That none can temper but Thy holy hand.
To Thee for succour flies my feeble muse,
And at Thy feet her iron pen doth use.

21. Thy] *this edn;* thy *Q.*   22. Thee] *this edn;* thee *Q.*   23. Thy] *this edn;*
thy *Q.*

21. *temper*] moderate, restrain. In *The Tale of Troy*, Peele describes
Pyrrhus as 'he whose bloody mind and murdering rage, / Nor awe of Gods,
nor reverence of age, / Could temper' (440–2).

23. *iron*] as a strong metal connotes 'well-tempered' but also, in contrast
to the 'golden wires' (10) of David's harp, suggests that the poetic style of
Peele's 'feeble muse' (22) is less elevated than David's 'holy style' (2).

The Love of David and Fair Bathsheba, with the Tragedy of Absalom

[Sc. 1]

He [*the* Prologue] *draws a curtain and discovers* BATHSHEBA *with her* Maid *bathing over a spring. She sings, and* DAVID *sits above viewing her.*

[*Exit* Prologue.]

Heading Sc. 1] *Bullen (subst); not in Q;* ACT I. SCENE I. *Morley (subst);* Act I. Scene I. *Manly (subst); Sc. i Greg (subst); i Rabkin (subst).* 0.1. SD *the* Prologue] *Dyce 3 (subst); not in Q.* BATHSHEBA] *Q (Bethsabe). Modernised silently throughout.* 0.2. SD *spring.*] *Keltie (subst); spring: QBL 1, 2, P, Hv, Il, Bod, Fol, Tex, NLS, HC, VAM, M; spring, QH.* 0.3. SD *Exit* Prologue.] *this edn; not in Q.*

[*Sc. 1*] The play's opening scene expands 2 Samuel, 11:2–4's terse description of David seeing Bathsheba bathing then commanding her sexual submission. The scene, which takes place at the same time as David's general, Joab, is besieging the Ammonite capital Rabbah, is located at David's palace in Jerusalem. In this scene and the next, Peele replaces anonymous informants and messengers with Hushai, whom the play develops as a powerful civilian counterpart to Joab.

0.1. SD draws a curtain and discovers] Elizabethan amphitheatres possessed two kinds of discovery space, both of which used a curtain: 'One was permanent, a curtained alcove or discovery-space in the tiring-house wall … The other was a special property, a raised platform, or even a curtained "booth" set up on stage, of the kind used in the early years by the travelling players as their tiring house' (Gurr, *Shakespearean Stage*, 149). No special booth is necessary to stage this scene, however, so we might assume that a professional company staging the play in an Elizabethan amphitheatre would use the discovery space in the tiring-house wall.

0.2. SD bathing] suggests that Bathsheba is nude, but her song and subsequent speech indicate that her nudity is shrouded by trees and bushes. Bathsheba's maid might also obstruct the audience's, if not David's, view of Bathsheba's body, which in an Elizabethan performance would presumably be the male body of a boy actor. In Marlowe's *Edward II* Gaveston captures the bisexual erotic potential of this scenario when he imagines 'a lovely boy in Dian's shape' (1.60) who 'Shall bathe him in a spring' (65) holding 'in his sportful hands an olive tree / To hide those parts which men delight to see' (63–4).

0.3. SD above] The tiring-house façade of Elizabethan amphitheatres had two levels: the main stage level, containing doors and the central discovery space, and, above it, an upper gallery of 'lords' rooms', rooms that

55

The Song.

[*Bathsheba.*] Hot sun, cool fire, tempered with sweet air;
    Black shade, fair nurse, shadow my white hair.
    Shine, sun; burn, fire; breathe, air, and ease me;
    Black shade, fair nurse, shroud me and please me.
    Shadow, my sweet nurse, keep me from burning;   5
    Make not my glad cause, cause of mourning.
        Let not my beauty's fire
        Enflame unstaid desire,
        Nor pierce any bright eye
        That wand'reth lightly.   10

Bathsheba. Come, gentle Zephyr, tricked with those perfumes
    That erst in Eden sweetened Adam's love,

0.4. SD *The Song.*] *in left margin of Q.*   1. SH *Bathsheba*] *this edn; not in
Q.*   5. Shadow, my] *Hawkins (subst);* Shadow (my *Q.* nurse, keep]
Hawkins (subst); nurse) keep *Q.*   11. tricked] *Hawkins (subst);* trickt *QP,*
H, Hv, Il, Bod, Fol, Tex, NLS, HC, VAM, M; trick: *QBL 1, 2.*

---

the actors could use as a playing space and in which audience members
could sit during performances for the price of sixpence (Gurr, *Shakespearean
Stage*, 122). An upper playing area may or may not have been available to
touring companies performing in a town hall, church, noble house, or inn
yard (Keenan, *Travelling Players*, 36, 51–2, 83, 97–8).
    2. *fair*] beautiful, gentle; light-coloured (*OED*, adj. and n.1, 1, 8, 17).
Light-coloured skin and beauty were often associated in early modern Western
European culture. Black and white also acquired the polarised moral connotations of good and evil in the Christian tradition (Hall, *Things of Darkness*, 2–11).
    shadow] shade, screen, protect from the sun (*OED*, v., 1a, 3a).
    white] blonde.
    6.] i.e. let me not later regret my sun bathing because of a sun burn.
Beyond its obvious significance, however, the line anticipates the play's
overall dramatic trajectory, in which the 'glad cause' of David's burning
desire for Bathsheba later creates multiple occasions to mourn.
    8. *unstaid*] unrestrained, uncontrolled, unstable (*OED*, adj., 2, 3).
    11. *Zephyr ... perfumes*] Bathsheba's words echo Du Bartas's description
of Eden as a place that 'Zephire emplit d'odeurs [Zephyr fills with odours]'
(*Eden*, 40).
    Zephyr] the west wind, a mild breeze (*OED*, n., 1, 2). In Greek myth,
Zephyrus is one of the four chief Anemoi, sons of the wind god Aeolus and
Eos, goddess of the dawn. The other three are Boreas (the north wind),
Eurus (the east wind), and Notus (the south wind).
    tricked] adorned, decked (*OED*, adj., 1b).
    12. *erst*] first, at first, formerly (*OED*, adv.).

And stroke my bosom with thy silken fan.
This shade, sun-proof, is yet no proof for thee;
Thy body, smoother than this waveless spring   15
And purer than the substance of the same,
Can creep through that his lances cannot pierce.
Thou and thy sister, soft and sacred air,
Goddess of life and governess of health,
Keep every fountain fresh and arbour sweet;   20
No brazen gate her passage can repulse,
Nor bushy thicket bar thy subtle breath.
Then deck thee with thy loose delightsome robes
And on thy wings bring delicate perfumes
To play the wantons with us through the leaves.   25
David. [*Above*] What tunes, what words, what looks, what
     wonders pierce
My soul, incensèd with a sudden fire?
What tree, what shade, what spring, what paradise
Enjoys the beauty of so fair a dame?

---

13. thy] *Dyce 3 (subst);* the *Q.*   14. shade, sun-proof, is] *Hawkins (subst);*
shade (sun proofe) is *Q.*   15. than] *Hawkins (subst);* then *Q.*   16. than]
Hawkins (subst); then *Q.*   20. Keep] *Dyce 3 (subst);* Keepes *Q.*   22. bushy]
Hawkins (subst); bushly *Q.*   26. SH *David*] *Hawkins (subst); Da. Q.*

---

13. *thy*] Q's 'the' awkwardly diminishes the precision of the line's metaphor in so far as it suggests that 'silken fan' might belong to or be something
other than the 'gentle Zephyr' of line 11.
   14. *sun-proof*] Bathsheba's shady bower resembles 'des beaux cabinets à
preuve du soleil [beautiful bowers proof against the sun]' (*Eden*, 44) found
in Du Bartas's Eden.
   proof] barrier, obstacle (see *OED*, n., 9a, b).
   15. *waveless*] The spring or pool in which Bathsheba is bathing is 'waveless' because no breeze has yet entered Bathsheba's shaded grove.
   17. *that*] that which.
   his] the sun's.
   18. *sister*] In Greek myth the Aurai, wind nymphs, are the daughters of
the Anemoi.
   21. *her*] air's.
   22. *thy*] Zephyr's.
   25. *wantons*] playful, carefree, or lustful companions (*OED*, adj. and n.,
3a, 4a).
   us] Bathsheba and her maid, who here is included in Bathsheba's playful
monologue to Zephyr.
   27. *incensèd*] perfumed; set on fire (*OED*).

Fair Eva placed in perfect happiness,   30
Lending her praise-notes to the liberal heavens,
Struck with the accents of archangels' tunes,
Wrought not more pleasure to her husband's thoughts
Than this fair woman's words and notes to mine.
May that sweet plain that bears her pleasant weight   35
Be still enamelled with discoloured flowers,
That precious fount bear sand of purest gold,
And, for the pebble, let the silver streams
That pierce earth's bowels to maintain the source
Play upon rubies, sapphires, chrysolites,   40
The brims let be embraced with golden curls
Of moss that sleeps with sound the waters make
For joy to feed the fount with their recourse;
Let all the grass that beautifies her bower

---

34. Than] *Hawkins (subst);* Then Q.

31–2.] In Du Bartas's Eden, it is the 'cent sortes d'oiseaux [hundred kinds of birds]' (83) who 'marians leurs tons aux doux accents des Anges, / Chantoient et l'heur d'Adam et de Dieu les louanges [marrying their tones with the sweet accents of angels, / Sing the happiness of Adam and the praises of God]' (*Eden*, 85–6).

31. *liberal*] large, generous, bountiful (*OED*, adj., 1a, c).

35.] i.e. May that sweet place where she dwells.

36. *still*] continually.

enamelled … flowers] Du Bartas describes Eden as 'Un temperé climat que la mignarde Flore / Pave du bel esmail des printenieres fleurs [A temperate clime that the pretty Flora / Paves with the beautiful enamel of spring-time flowers]' (*Eden*, 38–9).

discoloured] multicoloured (*OED*, adj., 2a).

37. *That*] may that.

38. *for*] as for.

pebble] 'agate or similar semi-precious stone, found on the beds of streams' (*OED*, n., 2c).

39.] i.e. that flow underground to maintain the fountain's source.

40. *rubies, sapphires, chrysolites*] precious stones red, blue, and green in colour respectively.

41. *The … embraced*] i.e. let the brims be embraced.

42. *sleeps … make*] In Eden, according to Du Bartas, 'Du bruit de cent ruisseaux semond le doux sommeil [The noise of a hundred streams summons sweet sleep]' (*Eden*, 43).

43. *their*] the waters'.

recourse] movement, flow, influx and reflux (*OED*, n.1, 6a, 7a).

44–5.] In Du Bartas's Eden, 'au matin des champs la face verte / Estoit non de rosee, ains de manne couverte [in the morning the green fields / Were not with dew but with manna covered]' (*Eden*, 73–4).

Bear manna every morn instead of dew,   45
Or let the dew be sweeter far than that
That hangs like chains of pearl on Hermon Hill
Or balm which trickled from old Aaron's beard.
Hushai, come up and serve thy lord the King.

Enter HUSHAI [*above*].

Hushai. What service doth my lord the King command?   50
David. See, Hushai, see the flower of Israel,
The fairest daughter that obeys the King
In all the land the Lord subdued to me.
Fairer than Isaac's lover at the well,
Brighter than inside bark of new-hewn cedar,   55
Sweeter than flames of fine perfumèd myrrh,
And comelier than the silver clouds that dance

---

46. than] *Hawkins (subst);* then *Q.*   49. Hushai] *Q (*Cusay*). Modernised
silently throughout.*   49.1. SD] *printed on 49, aligned right, in Q.*   above] *Dyce
3 (subst); not in Q.*   50. SH *Hushai*] *this edn; Cus. Q; Cusay. Hawkins
(subst).*   53. Lord] *Dyce 3 (subst);* lord *Q.*   54. than] *Hawkins (subst);*
then *Q.*   55. than] *Hawkins (subst);* then *Q.*   56. than] *Hawkins (subst);*
then *Q.*   fine perfumèd] *Q (subst);* fire-perfumed *Allott (subst).*   57. than]
Hawkins (subst); then *Q.*

---

45. *manna*] the name that the children of Israel give to the bread God sends
them from heaven each morning during their time in the wilderness after leaving
Egypt (Exodus, 16:16).
   46–8.] The biblical passage to which these lines allude is not explicitly
erotic but political. Psalm 133:1–3 compare the joy of national harmony
('how good and how comely a thing it is, brethen, to dwell even together')
to 'the precious ointment upon the head, that runneth down upon the beard,
even unto Aaron's beard, which went down on the border of his garments:
/ And as the dew of Hermon, which falleth upon the mountains of Zion'.
David's allusion is ironic given that his adultery with Bathsheba causes God
to punish him with civil war (6.46–50).
   47. *Hermon Hill*] is situated in 'the plentiful country about Jerusalem',
according to the Geneva gloss on Psalm 133:3.
   48. *balm*] aromatic oil or ointment (*OED*, n.1).
   54–8.] These lines are reproduced in Robert Allott's verse anthology,
England's Parnassus (1600), under the heading 'Descriptions of Beauty and
Personage'.
   54. *Isaac's lover*] Rebekah, whom the servant of Isaac's father, Abraham,
selects as Isaac's bride because she gives him and his camels water at a well
(Genesis, 24:1–67). She is described as 'very fair to look upon' (Genesis,
24:16).
   56. *myrrh*] aromatic Arabian tree resin (*OED*, n.1, 1a).

On Zephyr's wings before the King of Heaven.
Hushai. Is it not Bathsheba, the Hittite's wife,
    Uriah, now at Rabbah's siege with Joab?   60
David. Go know, and bring her quickly to the King.
    Tell her, her graces hath found grace with him.
Hushai. I will, my lord.   *Exit* HUSHAI *to* BATHSHEBA.
David. Bright Bathsheba shall wash in David's bower,
    In water mixed with purest almond flower,   65
    And bathe her beauty in the milk of kids.
    Bright Bathsheba gives earth to my desires,
    Verdure to earth, and to that verdure flowers,
    To flowers sweet odours, and to odours wings
    That carry pleasures to the hearts of kings.   70

    [*Enter*] HUSHAI [*below*] *to* BATHSHEBA, *she starting*
        as something affright.

Hushai. Fair Bathsheba, the King of Israel
    From forth his princely tower hath seen thee bathe,
    And thy sweet graces have found grace with him.
    Come then and kneel unto him where he stands;

---

58. Zephyr's] *Q; Zephyrus Allott (subst).* King] *Dyce 3 (subst);* king *Q.*
Heaven] *Dyce 3 (subst);* heauen *Q.* 59. SH *Hushai] this edn; Cus. Q;*
Cusay. Hawkins (subst). 60. Uriah] *Q (*Vrias*). Modernised silently through-*
out. Rabbah's] *Dyce 2 (subst);* Rabath *Q.* 61. SH *David] Hawkins*
(subst); Dau. Q. 70.1. SD *Enter] Dyce 3 (subst); not in Q.* below] *Dyce 3*
(subst); not in Q.

    59. *Bathsheba*] Pronounced with stresses on first and final syllable, as also
at lines 64, 71, 76, 105, and 128, 4.158, Chorus 1.21, 5.1, 9, etc.
    60. *Rabbah's siege*] While David is in Jerusalem, the Israelite army com-
manded by Joab is besieging the Ammonite capital city Rabbah. See headnote to scene 2.
    63. SD Exit ... BATHSHEBA] Hushai exits above and descends to the
main stage, presumably by stairs behind the tiring-house façade.
    67–9.] These lines echo Du Bartas's description of 'un doux ventelet
l'halene musquetee, / Coulant dans la forest par l'Eternal plantee [a soft
musk-scented breeze / Flowing in the forest planted by the Eternal]' that
'Donnoit vigueur aux corps, à la terre verdeur, / A la verdure fleurs, aux
fleurs une alme odeur [Gave vigour to bodies, to the earth verdure, / To the
verdure flowers, to the flowers a sweet odour]' (*Eden*, 105–8).
    68. *Verdure*] vegetation, greenery (*OED*, n., 1a).
    70.1. SD starting] reacting in startlement.
    70.2. SD something affright] somewhat affrighted.

The King is gracious and hath liberal hands. 75
Bathsheba. Ah, what is Bathsheba to please the King,
Or what is David, that he should desire
For fickle beauty's sake his servant's wife?
Hushai. David, thou knowst, fair dame, is wise and just,
Elected to the heart of Israel's God; 80
Then do not thou expostulate with him
For any action that contents his soul.
Bathsheba. My lord the King, elect to God's own heart,
Should not His gracious jealousy incense
Whose thoughts are chaste. I hate incontinence. 85
Hushai. Woman, thou wrongst the King and doubtst his
      honour
Whose truth maintains the crown of Israel,
Making him stay that bade me bring thee straight.
Bathsheba. The King's poor handmaid will obey my lord.
Hushai. Then come and do thy duty to His Grace, 90
And do what seemeth favour in his sight.
    Exeunt [HUSHAI, BATHSHEBA, *and* Maid].

76. SH *Bathsheba*] *this edn; Beth. Q; Bethsabe. Hawkins (subst)*. 79. David,
thou] *Hawkins (subst);* Dauid (thou *Q*. dame, is] *Hawkins (subst);* dame)
is *Q*. 83. SH *Bathsheba*] *this edn; Beth. Q; Bethsabe. Hawkins (subst)*
84. His] *this edn;* his *Q*. 85. chaste. I hate] *Manly (subst);* chast, I hate *Q*.
86. and] *Hawkins (subst);* & *Q*. 89. SH *Bathsheba*] *this edn; Beth. Q;
Bethsabe. Hawkins (subst)*. 90. SH *Hushai*] *this edn; Cus. Q; Cusay.
Hawkins (subst)*. 91.1. SD HUSHAI, BATHSHEBA, *and* Maid] *this edn; not
in Q*.

78. *fickle*] false, deceitful, changeable (*OED*, adj.).
servant's] subordinate's, subject's (here referring to Uriah, an officer in
David's army).
80. *Elected ... of*] chosen and beloved by.
81. *expostulate*] question, protest, argue (*OED*, v., 1a, 2a, b).
85. *chaste. I hate*] assumes that 'I' is the first-person singular pronoun,
referring to Bathsheba, who is then the subject of the verb 'hate'. Daniel in
Bullen, however, conjectures 'chaste and hate', and Deighton suggests that
'I' should be taken as 'ay' (110). In both cases, it becomes God, not
Bathsheba, who hates incontinence.
incontinence] unchastity, lack of sexual restraint (*OED*, n., 1a).
88.] i.e. making him wait, he who told me to bring you to him
immediately.
89. *my lord*] David, Bathsheba's king. Women also referred to their hus-
bands as 'my lord', however, and Bathsheba's use of the phrase here ironi-
cally registers her divided loyalty.

David. Now comes my lover tripping like the roe
And brings my longings tangled in her hair.
To joy her love I'll build a kingly bower
Seated in hearing of a hundred streams   95
That, for their homage to her sovereign joys,
Shall, as the serpents fold into their nests,
In oblique turnings wind the nimble waves
About the circles of her curious walks
And with their murmur summon easeful sleep   100
To lay his golden sceptre on her brows.
Open the doors and entertain my love,
Open, I say, and, as you open, sing!
Welcome, fair Bathsheba, King David's darling.

> *Enter* HUSHAI [*above*] *with* BATHSHEBA.

Welcome, fair Bathsheba, King David's darling,   105
Thy bones' fair covering erst discovered fair
And all mine eyes with all thy beauties pierced!

104.1. SD *above*] *Dyce 3 (subst); not in Q.*   105.] *Q begins this line with SH Dauid.*

92. *tripping like the roe*] The speaker in the Song of Solomon anticipates
her beloved's arrival in similar language: 'behold, he cometh leaping by the
mountains, and skipping by the hills. / My well-beloved is like a roe, or a
young hart' (2:8–9).
94. *joy*] enjoy.
96. *for*] by way of.
sovereign] supreme.
97. *as … nests*] i.e. as snakes and serpents nest themselves.
98.] i.e. the nimble waves will wind obliquely.
99. *curious*] intricate, elaborate, artful (*OED*, adj., 7a, 8, 10b).
102. *entertain*] welcome.
104. *darling*] beloved; favourite, minion (*OED*, n.1, 1b).
105–7.] The syntax of these lines has troubled editors. In Q all three lines
end in a comma. Dyce 3 and Bullen change the comma at the end of 105 to
a full stop; Manly changes it to an exclamation mark. Lines 106–7 consequently become a sentence fragment inviting emendation. Dyce 3 comments
that 'To connect this [line 107] with what precedes, a friend would read "Have
all mine eyes"' but concludes that 'the probability is, that a line has dropt out'
(464). Bullen suggests emending 'And all mine eyes' to 'Enthrall'd mine eyes'
(12). Manly emends 'And all' to 'Afar'. Both Dyce and Bullen assume that
the lines fail to make sense because their presumed grammatical subject, 'thy
bones' fair covering', lacks a verb, which their conjectural emendations would
supply. In contrast, I have assumed that lines 106 and 107 are appositional
phrases modifying 'fair Bathsheba' in line 105. This divides lines 105–12 into
two syntactically complete units without positing a need for emendation.
106. *bones' fair covering*] fair skin.

As heaven's bright eye burns most when most he climbs
The crooked zodiac with his fiery sphere
And shineth furthest from this earthly globe,   110
So, since thy beauty scorched my conquered soul,
I called thee nearer for my nearer cure.
Bathsheba. Too near, my lord, was your unarmèd heart
When, furthest off, my hapless beauty pierced,
And would this dreary day had turned to night   115
Or that some pitchy cloud had cloaked the sun
Before their lights had caused my lord to see
His name disparaged, and my chastity!
David. My love, if want of love have left thy soul
A sharper sense of honour than thy king   120
(For love leads princes sometimes from their seats),
As erst my heart was hurt, displeasing thee,
So come and taste thy ease with easing me.

113. SH *Bathsheba*] *this edn; Bethsa. Q; Bethsabe. Hawkins (subst).*
120. than] *Hawkins (subst);* then *Q.*

109. *crooked zodiac*] 'belt of the celestial sphere … within which the apparent motions of the sun, moon, and principal planets take place' (*OED*, n., 1a), crooked in that the undulating path of the sun in its yearly course crosses the equator twice as it moves from the northerly tropic of Cancer to the southerly tropic of Capricorn and back again. The writer of *The Compost of Ptholomeus Prince of Astronomers*, a frequently reprinted digest of Ptolemaic astronomy, explains that the ecliptic and the zodiac 'divideth the one and the other equally, and but not straight, for the zodiac crosseth crookedly, and the places where it crooketh been said equinoctial' (sig. E4v). Blistein notes that Peele uses a similar image in other works: 'Time hath turned his restless wheel about / And made the silver moon and heaven's bright eye / Gallop the zodiac' (*Descensus Astraeae*, 2–4); '[the rising sun] / gallops the zodiac in his fiery [wain]' (*Anglorum Feriae*, 23–4).
112. *for my nearer cure*] for a cure that requires you to be near me.
113. *unarmèd*] unfortified against amorous desire.
114. *hapless*] unlucky, unfortunate.
115. *would*] would that, I wish that.
116. *pitchy*] of the colour and texture of pitch, tar.
117.] i.e. before the clouds had parted sufficiently to allow sunlight through, enabling the King to see Bathsheba's beauty.
119. *want of love*] lack of desire.
120. *than thy king*] than what I, your king, am experiencing.
121. *seats*] thrones; *fig.* royal dignity or responsibility (*OED*, n., 8a, b).
122–3.] i.e. Just as it hurt me to displease you (with my sexual advances), so you can ease yourself by easing me. David seems to be suggesting that Bathsheba's displeasure should be mollified by the knowledge that her sexual compliance will satisfy him, cure his 'hurt'.

Bathsheba. One medicine cannot heal our different harms
    But rather make both rankle at the bone;   125
    Then let the King be cunning in his cure,
    Lest, flattering both, both perish in his hand.
David. Leave it to me, my dearest Bathsheba,
    Whose skill is conversant in deeper cures,
    And, Hushai, haste thou to my servant Joab,   130
    Commanding him to send Uriah home
    With all the speed can possibly be used.
Hushai. Hushai will fly about the King's desire.

                                            Exeunt.

[Sc. 2]

Enter JOAB, ABISHAI, URIAH, *and others,*
with drum and ensign.

---

124. SH *Bathsheba*] *this edn; Beth. Q; Bethsabe. Hawkins (subst).*
133.1. SD] *printed on 133, aligned right, in Q.*

Heading Sc. 2] *Bullen (subst); not in Q;* ACT I. SCENE II. *Morley (subst);*
Act I. Scene II. *Manly (subst); Sc. ii Greg (subst); ii Rabkin (subst).*   o.1. SD
Enter] *QP, BL 1, 2, Hv, Il, Bod, Fol, Tex, NLS, HC, VAM, M; not in QH.*
ABISHAI] *Q (Abisay). Modernised silently throughout.*

---

125. *rankle*] fester.
126. *cunning*] skilful, wise (*OED*, adj., 2a).
127.] i.e. lest, in deceiving us both and making us feel good about our-
selves, you doom us to die a perpetual spiritual death through God's
judgement.

[*Sc. 2*] Located in front of the walls of Rabbah. In the biblical narrative,
David's siege of Rabbah, the capital city of the Ammonites, culminates a
war against the Ammonites that begins when the Ammonite king Nahash
dies and David sends ambassadors to comfort his son and new king, Hanun
(2 Samuel, 10:1–2). Suspecting them to be spies, Hanun mistreats the
ambassadors, and David commences war in revenge (2 Samuel, 10:3–7).
This scene stages the Israelite capture of the city's tower or citadel, which
occurs in the biblical narrative only after the deaths of Uriah and David and
Bathsheba's child (2 Samuel, 12:26–8). By altering the biblical narrative,
conversely, Peele is able to develop Uriah quickly as a wise and heroic martial
figure (he is the one who counsels Joab to assault the tower) whom David
is gravely wronging.
    o.2. SD with drum and ensign] indicates that the entrance is a military
procession.
    ensign] military banner.

Joab. Courage, ye mighty men of Israel,
    And charge your fatal instruments of war
    Upon the bosoms of proud Ammon's sons,
    That have disguised your King's ambassadors,
    Cut half their beards and half their garments off,   5
    In spite of Israel and his daughters' sons!
    Ye fight the holy battles of Jehovah,
    King David's God, and ours and Jacob's God,
    That guides your weapons to their conquering strokes,
    Orders your footsteps, and directs your thoughts   10
    To stratagems that harbour victory.
    He casts His sacred eyesight from on high
    And sees your foes run seeking for their deaths,
    Laughing their labours and their hopes to scorn,
    While twixt your bodies and their blunted swords   15
    He puts on armour of His honour's proof
    And makes their weapons wound the senseless winds.
Abishai. Before this city Rabbah we will lie
    And shoot forth shafts as thick and dangerous

---

12. His] *this edn;* his Q.   16. His] *this edn*; his Q.   18. SH *Abishai*] *this edn; Abis.* Q; *Abisai. Hawkins (subst).*

---

2. *charge*] 'press hard'; 'place (a weapon) in position for action' (*OED*, v., 10, 21a).

3. *proud Ammon's sons*] the Ammonites, a neighbouring people occupying 'land east of the River Jordan' (Browning, 11), with whom the Israelites were frequently at war.

4. *disguised*] disfigured (*OED*, adj., 1a).

5.] 2 Samuel, 10:4 relates that 'Hanun took David's servants, and shaved off the half of their beard, and cut off their garments in the middle, even to their buttocks, and sent them away'.

6. *Israel*] i.e. Abraham's grandson Jacob, whose name was changed to Israel after he had wrestled with God (Genesis, 32:28) and whose descendants constituted the nation of Israel.

his daughters' sons] his descendants, i.e. the Israelites.

11. *harbour*] contain, lodge, shelter (*OED*, v., 1a).

16. *armour … proof*] armour as strong ('proof') as God's promises ('His honour'). See *OED*, proof, n., 9a.

17.] In *1 Tamburlaine*, Tamburlaine brags to his opponent Bajazeth that 'Legions of spirits fleeting in the air / Direct our bullets and our weapons' points / And make your strokes to wound the senseless air' (3.3.156–8).

18. *Rabbah*] the Ammonites' capital city.

lie] deploy our siege.

As was the hail that Moses mixed with fire   20
And threw with fury round about the fields,
Devouring Pharaoh's friends and Egypt's fruits.
Uriah. First, mighty captains Joab and Abishai,
Let us assault and scale this kingly tower,
Where all their conduits and their fountains are;   25
Then we may easily take the city too.
Joab. Well hath Uriah counselled our attempts,
And, as he spoke us, so assault the tower.
Let Hanun now, the King of Ammon's sons,
Repulse our conquering passage if he dare.   30

[*Enter*] HANUN *with King* MAACAH *and others
upon the walls.*

Hanun. What would the shepherd's dogs of Israel
Snatch from the mighty issue of King Ammon,

---

29. Hanun] Q (Hanon). *Modernised silently throughout.* sons] *Dyce 2
(subst);* sonne Q. 30.1. SD *Enter*] *Dyce 3 (subst); not in Q.* MAACAH] Q
(Machaas). *Modernised silently throughout.*

20–1.] Exodus, 9:23 relates that 'Moses stretched out his rod toward
heaven, and the Lord sent thunder and hail, and lightning upon the ground:
and the Lord caused hail to rain upon the land of Egypt'.

24–5.] Both the Bishops' Bible and the Geneva Bible describe the 'tower'
as 'the city of waters' (2 Samuel, 12:27), which the Bishops' version glosses
as 'the chiefest part of the city where the king's palace, and all the conduits
were' and the Geneva version as 'the chief city, and where all the conduits
are'. Among other things, then, the tower or citadel contained the city's
reservoir. The tower could be represented by an onstage booth, such as the
one possibly used in scene 1 as the bower in which Bathsheba is discovered,
but the tiring-house façade with its two levels would serve equally well to
represent Rabbah's tower and walls. In scene 1, Hushai describes David's
position '*above*' (0.2 SD) as David's 'princely tower' (72). Similarly, after
Joab's soldiers have taken Rabbah's tower, Joab appears '*above*' (56.1 SD)
and announces 'Thus have we won the tower' (57), indicating that the tiring-
house façade represents the captured tower at that point.

25. *conduits*] aqueducts.

29. *sons*] Hanun is not the son of the king of Ammon, as Q's 'sonne'
would have it, but rather the king of the sons of Ammon, 'the mighty issue
of King Ammon, / The valiant Ammonites and haughty Syrians' (32–3).

30.2. SD upon the walls] above, on the second level of the tiring-house
façade.

31. *the shepherd's*] David's. David was a shepherd when the prophet
Samuel anointed him as Saul's successor (1 Samuel, 16:11–13).

dogs] the Israelite soldiers.

32. *issue*] offspring.

The valiant Ammonites and haughty Syrians?
'Tis not your late successive victories
Can make us yield or quail our courages,   35
But, if ye dare assay to scale this tower,
Our angry swords shall smite ye to the ground
And venge our losses on your hateful lives.
Joab. Hanun, thy father Nahash gave relief
To holy David in his hapless exile,   40
Lived his fixèd date, and died in peace.
But thou, instead of reaping his reward,
Hast trod it underfoot and scorned our King;
Therefore thy days shall end with violence,
And to our swords thy vital blood shall cleave.   45
Maacah. Hence, thou that bearst poor Israel's shepherd's
      hook,
The proud lieutenant of that baseborn king,
And keep within the compass of his fold,
For, if ye seek to feed on Ammon's fruits
And stray into the Syrians' fruitful meads,   50
The mastiffs of our land shall worry ye
And pull the weezles from your greedy throats.
Abishai. Who can endure these pagans' blasphemies?
Uriah. My soul repines at this disparagement.

---

39. father] *Hawkins (subst);* fathet *Q.*   46. SH *Maacah*] *this edn; Mach. Q;*
Machaas. Hawkins (subst).   53. SH *Abishai*] *this edn; Abis. Q; Abisai.*
Hawkins (subst).

34. *late*] recent.
successive] successful.
35. *Can*] that can.
36. *assay*] attempt.
39. *Nahash gave relief*] Geneva's marginal gloss to 1 Chronicles, 19:2
states that David sent ambassadors to Hanun 'Because Nahash received
David, and his company, when Saul persecuted him'.
41. *fixed date*] allotted life span.
45. *cleave*] stick.
48. *compass*] boundaries, limits.
50. *meads*] meadows (*OED*, n.2).
51. *mastiffs*] large guard or fighting dogs (*OED*, n.).
worry] 'seize by the throat with the teeth and tear or lacerate'; 'kill or
injure by biting and shaking' (*OED*, v., 3a).
52. *weezles*] windpipes (*OED*, n., 1a).
54. *repines*] protests, complains.

Joab. Assault, ye valiant men of David's host,   55
  And beat these railing dastards from their doors!

> *Assault, and they* [JOAB's *soldiers*] *win the tower,*
>   *and* JOAB *speaks above.*

Thus have we won the tower, which we will keep,
Maugre the sons of Ammon and of Syria.

> *Enter* HUSHAI *beneath.*

Hushai. Where is Lord Joab, leader of the host?
Joab. Here is Lord Joab, leader of the host.   60
  Hushai, come up, for we have won the hold.
                              [HUSHAI *exits below, and*]

> *He* [HUSHAI] *comes* [*above*].

Hushai. In happy hour, then, is Hushai come.
Joab. What news, then, brings Lord Hushai from the King?
Hushai. His Majesty commands thee out of hand
  To send him home Uriah from the wars   65
  For matter of some service he should do.

56.1. SD JOAB's soldiers] *this edn; not in* Q.   59. SH *Hushai*] *this edn; Cus.
Q; Cusay. Hawkins (subst).*   61.1. SD HUSHAI *exits below, and*] *this edn; not
in* Q.   61.2. SD] *printed on* 61, *aligned right, in* Q.   HUSHAI] *this edn; not
in* Q.   *above*] *this edn; not in* Q.

---

55. *host*] army.
56. *dastards*] cowards (Florio, *A World of Words* [*LEME*]).
56.1–2. SD] The assault begins on the main stage, as Joab's men 'beat
these railing dastards from their doors' (56), and continues 'above', concluding when the tower has been won and Joab speaks. Joab's soldiers presumably gain access to the space above, representing the tower, by climbing up
scaling ladders in full view of the audience. Compare *1 Henry VI*, 2.1, at the
siege of Orleans.
58. *Maugre*] in spite of.
58.1. SD beneath] on the main stage.
61. *come up*] i.e. come up to the top of the tower (the upper acting area),
whence Joab is speaking.
  hold] fortification.
64. *out of hand*] immediately.

Uriah. 'Tis for no choler hath surprised the King,
   I hope, Lord Hushai, 'gainst his servant's truth.
Hushai. No, rather to prefer Uriah's truth.
Joab. Here, take him with thee, then, and go in peace,   70
   And tell my lord the King that I have fought
   Against the city Rabbah with success
   And scalèd where the royal palace is,
   The conduit heads and all their sweetest springs.
   Then let him come in person to these walls   75
   With all the soldiers he can bring besides
   And take the city as his own exploit,
   Lest I surprise it and the people give
   The glory of the conquest to my name.
Hushai. We will, Lord Joab, and great Israel's God   80
   Bless in thy hands the battles of our King!
Joab. Farewell, Uriah, haste away the King.
Uriah. As sure as Joab breathes a victor here,
   Uriah will haste him and his own return.
             Exeunt [HUSHAI *and* URIAH].
Abishai. Let us descend and ope the palace gate,   85
   Taking our soldiers in to keep the hold.
Joab. Let us, Abishai, and, ye sons of Judah,
   Be valiant and maintain your victory!
                 Exeunt.

---

67. SH *Uriah*] *this edn; Vrias, Q; Urias. Hawkins (subst).*   68. I hope, lord
Hushai,] *Hawkins (subst);* (I hope lord Cusay) *Q.*   80. SH *Hushai*] *this
edn; Cus. Q; Cusay. Hawkins (subst).*   82. Farewell] *Hawkins (subst);*
Earewell *Q.*   84.1. SD] *printed on 84, aligned right, in Q.*   HUSHAI *and*
URIAH] *Dyce 2 (subst); not in Q.*   85. SH *Abishai*] *this edn; Abisa. Q; Abisai.
Hawkins (subst).*   88.1. SD] *printed on 88, aligned right, in Q.*

67–8.] i.e. I hope, Lord Hushai, that King David is not angrily surprised
at something I have done that might have seemed contrary to the obedience
I owe him.
   67. *choler*] anger.
   69.] i.e. No, it is instead an opportunity for you, Uriah, to show your true
devotion and obedience to the King.
   74.] i.e. and we have captured there the aqueduct reservoir.
   78. *surprise*] attack suddenly and stealthily.
   80. *great*] may great.
   82. *haste away the King*] i.e. bring the King back here hastily ('haste' is
transitive here).
   84. *him*] David.

[Sc. 3]

[*Enter*] AMNON, JONADAB, ITHREAM,
and Amnon's Page.

Jonadab. [*To Amnon*] What means my lord, the King's
beloved son,
That wears upon his right triumphant arm
The power of Israel for a royal favour,
That holds upon the tables of his hands
Banquets of honour and all thoughts' content,   5
To suffer pale and grisly abstinence
To sit and feed upon his fainting cheeks
And suck away the blood that cheers his looks?
Amnon. Ah, Jonadab, it is my sister's looks,
On whose sweet beauty I bestow my blood,   10
That make me look so amorously lean.

Heading Sc. 3] *Bullen (subst); not in Q;* ACT I. SCENE III. *Morley (subst);*
Act I. Scene III. *Manly (subst); Sc. iii Greg (subst);* iii *Rabkin (subst).*   0.1. SD
Enter] *Dyce 3 (subst); not in Q.*   AMNON] *Q (Ammon). Modernised silently
throughout.*   ITHREAM] *Q (Iethray). Modernised silently throughout.*   1. SH
Jonadab] *Hawkins (subst); Ionad. Q.*   *to Amnon*] *this edn; not in Q.*   9. SH
Amnon] *this edn; Ammo. Q; Ammon. Hawkins (subst).*   11. make] *Dyce 3
(subst); makes Q.*

[*Sc. 3*] Located in Amnon's residence in Jerusalem. The scene's events are
narrated in 2 Samuel, 13:1–14. Peele relocates the events temporally, moving
them from after to before David's final conquest of Rabbah, and compresses
them by omitting the business of David visiting the supposedly sick Amnon
then sending for Tamar. Immediately after Jonadab has outlined his plan
to Amnon, Tamar enters, leaving no interval for David to have visited or
commanded Tamar to attend Amnon, even though she claims that 'the King
commanded' (34) her. Sampley takes this compression to be an indication
that the play in its current state is an abridgement of a fuller version in
which David's visit and subsequent command to Tamar were dramatised,
additionally noting that the scene introduces a character, the page, who has
no lines in the play in its current condition ('Text', 661).
    1. *King's beloved son*] Amnon, King David's oldest son.
    3. *favour*] token of special affection.
    4–5.] Jonadab's metaphor compares Amnon's hands to banqueting tables,
at which his favourites feast on the honour and content that Amnon's royal
bounty provides.
    9. *my sister's*] Tamar's.
    10.] i.e. whose beauty steals the colour from my cheeks.

Her beauty, having seized upon my heart,
So merrily consecrate to her content,
Sets now such guard about his vital blood
And views the passage with such piercing eyes   15
That none can 'scape to cheer my pining cheeks,
But all is thought too little for her love.
Jonadab. Then from her heart thy looks shall be relieved,
And thou shalt joy her as thy soul desires.
Amnon. How can it be, my sweet friend Jonadab,   20
Since Tamar is a virgin and my sister?
Jonadab. Thus it shall be: lie down upon thy bed,
Feigning thee fever-sick and ill at ease,
And, when the King shall come to visit thee,
Desire thy sister Tamar may be sent   25
To dress some dainties for thy malady;
Then, when thou hast her solely with thyself,
Enforce some favour to thy manly love.
See where she comes. Entreat her in with thee.

Enter TAMAR.

Tamar. What aileth Amnon with such sickly looks   30
To daunt the favour of his lovely face?

---

18. SH *Jonadab*] *Hawkins (subst); Iona. Q.*   21. Tamar] *Q (*Thamar*).
Modernised silently throughout.   22. SH *Jonadab*] *Hawkins (subst); Iona. Q.*

---

13. *merrily*] happily, agreeably. Dyce 3, Morley, Bullen, Manly, Thorndike,
and Rabkin emend to 'merely', i.e. completely or absolutely, thus eliminating
the contrast between a tranquil past in which Amnon's heart was 'consecrate
to her [Tamar's] content' and the 'now' (14) in which Tamar's beauty has
so 'seized' (12) it that none of its 'vital blood' (14) 'can 'scape to cheer my
[Amnon's] pining cheeks' (16).
    consecrate] consecrated.
    14. *his*] i.e. my, or my heart's.
    15. *the passage*] i.e. the passage of blood from Amnon's heart to his face.
    16. *none*] none of Amnon's heart's blood.
    19. *joy*] enjoy.
    26. *dress some dainties*] prepare some delicacies.
    28.] persuade Tamar to reciprocate your manly desire (by force if
necessary).
    29. *Entreat ... thee*] i.e. Beg her to come in with you.
    31. *daunt*] overcome, subdue, cast down (*OED*, v., 1, 3b).

Amnon. Sweet Tamar, sick and wish some wholesome cates
Dressed with the cunning of thy dainty hands.
Tamar. That hath the King commanded at my hands.
Then come and rest thee while I make thee ready   35
Some dainties easeful to thy crazèd soul.
Amnon. I go, sweet sister, easèd with thy sight.

                                                        Exeunt.

                    JONADAB [*remains*].

Jonadab. Why should a prince, whose power may command,
Obey the rebel passions of his love,
When they contend but 'gainst his conscience   40
And may be governed or suppressed by will?
Now, Amnon, loose those loving knots of blood
That sucked the courage from thy kingly heart,
And give it passage to thy withered cheeks.–

32. SH *Amnon*] *this edn; Am. Q; Ammon. Hawkins (subst).* 32. and]
Hawkins (subst); & *Q.* 34. SH *Tamar*] *this edn; Tham. Q; Thamar. Hawkins
(subst).* 36. dainties easeful] *this edn;* daintie seasefull *QHC;* dainties, ease-
full *QP, BL 1, 2, Bod, Tex, Hv, Il, Fol, H, NLS, VAM, WC, M.* 37. SH
Amnon] *this edn; Am. Q; Ammon. Hawkins (subst).* 37.2. SD] *Bullen
(subst); on same line as 37.1, aligned right, in Q.* JONADAB [*remains*].] *this
edn; Restet Jonadab. Q.* 38. SH *Jonadab*] *Hawkins (subst); Ion. Q.*
42. loose] *Q (*lose). 43. sucked] *Q (*sokte*).*

32. *sick*] I am sick.
cates] food, delicacies.
33. *Dressed ... cunning*] prepared with the skill.
36. *crazèd*] broken, cracked, diseased (*OED*, adj., 1, 4).
40.] when those passions urge that which conscience alone forbids.
(Jonadab addresses these remarks as if to the absent Amnon.)
42. *loose*] loosen. 'Loose' modernises Q's 'lose' following Hawkins, Dyce,
Morley, Bullen, Thorndike, and Rabkin. Manly and Blistein retain the
original spelling, but the immediate context – Amnon is being urged to 'lose'
'knots' – strongly suggests that the verb is a variant form of 'loose'. 'Lose'
is clearly a variant form of 'loose' in the SD opening scene 10 and in lines
12 and 14 of scene 15.
43. *sucked*] modernises Q's 'sokte' following Dyce, Morley, Bullen,
Thorndike, and Rabkin. Hawkins modernises as 'soaked'. *OED*, soak, v. 8b
offers 'suck out' as one of soak's meanings.

Now, Tamar, ripened are the holy fruits   45
That grew on plants of thy virginity,
And rotten is thy name in Israel.
Poor Tamar, little did thy lovely hands
Foretell an action of such violence
As to contend with Amnon's lusty arms,   50
Sinewed with vigour of his kindless love.
Fair Tamar, now dishonour hunts thy foot
And follows thee through every covert shade,
Discovering thy shame and nakedness
Even from the valleys of Jehoshaphat   55
Up to the lofty mounts of Lebanon,
Where cedars, stirred with anger of the winds
Sounding in storms the tale of thy disgrace,
Tremble with fury and with murmur shake
Earth with their feet and with their heads the heavens, 60
Beating the clouds into their swiftest rack
To bear this wonder round about the world.   *Exit.*

---

60. Earth] *Hawkins (subst);* Eearth Q.

---

47. *rotten*] continues the metaphor beginning with 'ripened' in line 45.
The rapid transition from 'ripened' to 'rotten' anticipates the suddenness
and violence with which Amnon plucks Tamar's 'holy fruits' – violating her
sexually and destroying her reputation as a marriageable female in a patriarchal society – and then discards her.
50. *lusty*] strong; lustful.
51. *kindless*] unkind; unnatural (*OED*, adj., 1); incestuous.
52. *hunts thy foot*] dogs your footsteps.
54. *Discovering*] uncovering, revealing.
58. *disgrace*] By raping and, in scene 4, abandoning Tamar, Amnon will
have ruined Tamar's honour as a woman in a patriarchal society.
61. *rack*] 'mass of cloud moving quickly' (*OED*, n.2, 2a).

[Sc. 4]

[*Enter*] AMNON *thrusting out* TAMAR[*, and* ITHREAM].

Amnon. Hence from my bed, whose sight offends my soul
    As doth the parbreak of disgorgèd bears!
Tamar. Unkind, unprincely, and unmanly Amnon,
    To force and then refuse thy sister's love,
    Adding unto the fright of thy offence   5
    The baneful torment of my published shame!
    Oh, do not this dishonour to thy love,
    Nor clog thy soul with such increasing sin!
    This second evil far exceeds the first.

Heading Sc. 4] *Greg (subst); not in Q.*   0.1. SD *Enter*] *Dyce 3 (subst); not*
in Q.   *and* ITHREAM] *this edn; not in Q; and* JETHRAY *Dyce 3 (subst).*   1. SH
Amnon] *this edn; Am. Q; Ammon. Hawkins (subst).*   3. SH *Tamar*] *this edn;*
Thama. Q; Thamar. Hawkins (subst).

[*Sc. 4*] The scene begins immediately outside Amnon's residence, from
which Tamar is thrust at the beginning, and concludes at David's palace,
'This ground before the King my master's doors' (175), in Uriah's words.
The scene reorders and splices together three distinct episodes in the biblical narrative: David's frustrated attempt to cover up his adultery by getting
Uriah to sleep with the pregnant Bathsheba (2 Samuel, 11:7–15); Amnon's
rejection of Tamar (2 Samuel, 13:15–22); Absalom's request that David and
his lords and sons should attend Absalom's sheep-shearing feast (2 Samuel,
13:23–7). In the biblical chronology, the cover-up attempt comes before
the final siege of Rabbah, the rape of Tamar and her rejection after it, and
Absalom's request and the feast itself two years after Tamar's rape. What
the biblical narrative chooses to narrate in serial fashion, Peele has chosen
instead to dramatise as simultaneously occurring and complexly interrelated
sequences of events.
    2. *parbreak*] vomit (*OED*, n.).
    disgorgèd bears] bears that have just vomited. According to Pliny the Elder,
the breath of a bear is 'pestilential and deadly, insomuch as no beast will
touch where a bear hath breathed' (*Natural History*, 10.53).
    4. *refuse ... love*] reject and humiliate the sister whom you should love.
    6. *baneful*] harmful, destructive.
    9.] closely follows Tamar's protest in the biblical account that 'this evil
(to put me away) is greater than the other that thou diddest unto me' (2
Samuel, 13:16). By rejecting Tamar, Amnon refuses to make the appropriate
restitution for raping her, which Deuteronomy, 22:29 specifies as giving 'the
maid's father fifty shekels of silver, and she shall be his wife'. Earlier in the
biblical narrative, Tamar attempts to prevent Amnon from raping her by
suggesting that he seek David's permission to marry her (2 Samuel, 13:13).

Amnon. Ithream, come thrust this woman from my sight,   10
    And bolt the door upon her if she strive.   [*Exit.*]
Ithream. Go, madam, go, away, you must be gone.
    My lord hath done with you. I pray depart.
                              He shuts her out [then exits].
Tamar. Whither, alas, ah, whither shall I fly,
    With folded arms and all-amazèd soul,   15
    Cast as was Eva from that glorious soil
    Where all delights sat bating, winged with thoughts,
    Ready to nestle in her naked breasts?
    To bare and barren vales with floods made waste,
    To desert woods and hills with lightning scorched;   20
    With death, with shame, with hell, with horror sit.
    There will I wander from my father's face;
    There Absalom, my brother Absalom,
    Sweet Absalom, shall hear his sister mourn;
    There will I live with my windy sighs,   25
    Night ravens and owls to rend my bloody side,
    Which with a rusty weapon I will wound

10. SH *Amnon*] *this edn; Am. Q; Ammon. Hawkins (subst).*   11. SD] *Exit.*]
Dyce 3 (subst); not in Q.   13. SD *then exits*] *Dyce 3 (subst); not in Q.*   14. SH
Tamar] *this edn; Tham. Q; Thamar. Hawkins (subst).*   17. Where] *Manly
(subst);* (Where *Q.*   thoughts] *QP, HC, Fol, VAM, WC (subst);* though
ts *QBod, Hv, Ill, BL1, H, M;* thoug hts *QBL 2, Tex, NLS.*   18. breasts?]
Manly (subst); breasts) *Q.*   23. Absalom] *Q* (Absolon*). Modernised silently
throughout.*

13. SD] Perhaps Ithream closes a stage door as he leaves, signifying that
he is following Amnon's orders (10–11) and bolting the door to prevent
Tamar's re-entry into Amnon's palace. Tamar must remain on stage, but in
such a way that we understand that she is barred from Amnon's presence.
    15. *folded arms*] a conventional sign of melancholy or emotional distress.
    16. *glorious soil*] Eden.
    17.] The line may draw its imagery from Du Bartas's description of Eden's
trees, in whose branches 'cent sortes d'oiseaux jour et nuict s'esbatoient [a
hundred kinds of birds day and night frolicked]' (*Eden*, 83).
    bating] fluttering impatiently (*OED*, v.1, 2a).
    21. *sit*] I will sit.
    25. *live*] Following a conjecture in Dyce 2, Dyce 3, Keltie, Morley, Bullen,
Manly, Thorndike, Blistein, and Rabkin emend to 'lure'. Although the
emendation may improve the sense of lines 25–6 slightly, 'live' is intelligible.
    26. *rend*] rip, tear.

And make them passage to my panting heart.
Why talkst thou, wretch, and leav'st the deed undone?

Enter ABSALOM.

Rend hair and garments, as thy heart is rent   30
With inward fury of a thousand griefs,
And scatter them by these unhallowed doors
To figure Amnon's resting cruelty
And tragic spoil of Tamar's chastity!
Absalom. What causeth Tamar to exclaim so much?   35
Tamar. The cause that Tamar shameth to disclose.
Absalom. Say; I, thy brother, will revenge that cause.
Tamar. Amnon, our father's son, hath forcèd me
And thrusts me from him as the scorn of Israel.
Absalom. Hath Amnon forcèd thee? By David's hand   40
And by the covenant God hath made with him,
Amnon shall bear his violence to hell,
Traitor to heaven, traitor to David's throne,
Traitor to Absalom and Israel.
This fact hath Jacob's Ruler seen from heaven   45
And, through a cloud of smoke and tower of fire,

28. make] *Hawkins (subst);* makee *Q.* 35. SH *Absalom*] *this edn; Abs.
Q; Absalon. Hawkins (subst).* 36. SH *Tamar*] *this edn; Tham. Q; Thamar.
Hawkins (subst).* 37. SH *Absalom*] *this edn; Absa. Q; Absalon. Hawkins
(subst).* 38. SH *Tamar*] *this edn; Tham. Q; Thamar. Hawkins (subst).*
40. SH *Absalom*] *this edn;Abs. Q;Absalon. Hawkins (subst).* 45. Ruler] *this
edn;* ruler *Q.* 46-7. fire, / As] *Dyce 3 (subst);* fire / (As *Q.*

28. *them*] the ravens and owls.
29. *the deed*] i.e. suicide.
32. *these unhallowed doors*] the doors of Amnon's residence, from which
Tamar has just been ejected, signified by a stage door.
33. *figure*] portray, represent symbolically (*OED*, v., 4, 6), emblazon.
resting] remaining, abiding (*OED*, v.1, 3a).
34. *spoil*] ruin, pillage, rape (*OED*, n., 2a, 8a).
39. *scorn*] shame.
45. *fact*] deed.
46. *cloud ... fire*] God appeared to the Israelites during their exodus from
Egypt as a 'pillar of a cloud' by day and 'by night in a pillar of fire' (Exodus,
13:21).

As he rides vaunting him upon the greens,
Shall tear his chariot wheels with violent winds
And throw his body in the bloody sea;
At him the thunder shall discharge his bolt,   50
And his fair spouse, with bright and fiery wings,
Sit ever burning on his hateful bones;
Myself, as swift as thunder or his spouse,
Will hunt occasion with a secret hate
To work false Amnon an ungracious end.   55
Go in, my sister, rest thee in my house,
And God in time shall take this shame from thee.
Tamar. Nor God nor time will do that good for me.

                                             Exit TAMAR.

ABSALOM [*remains*].

Enter DAVID *with his train.*

David. My Absalom, what mak'st thou here alone
And bears such discontentment in thy brows?   60
Absalom. Great cause hath Absalom to be displeased
And in his heart to shroud the wounds of wrath.
David. 'Gainst whom should Absalom be thus displeased?

---

47. greens,] *Dyce 3 (subst);* greenes) *Q.*   58. SH *Tamar*] *this edn; Tham. Q; Thamar. Hawkins (subst).*   58. SD] *this edn; printed at the beginning of 58.1 in Q.*   TAMAR] *this edn; Tham Q; Thamar Hawkins (subst).*   58.1. SD ABSALOM [*remains*].] *this edn; restat Absolon. Q.*   61. SH *Absalom*] *this edn; Abs. Q; Absalon. Hawkins (subst).*

---

47. *he*] Amnon.
vaunting him] boasting, bragging, displaying himself proudly (*OED*, v., 1a, 3c).
upon the greens] as he rides his chariot over the grassy earth.
50. *the thunder*] the thunderer, Jove.
51. *his fair spouse*] Jove's consort, Juno.
52. *Sit*] shall sit in judgement.
53. *thunder … spouse*] i.e. Jove's thunderbolt or the vengeful anger of his queen, Juno.
54. *hunt occasion*] seek an opportunity.
55. *ungracious*] damnable.
58. *Nor*] Neither.
58.3. SD *train*] retinue of attendants.
59. *mak'st thou*] are you doing.
62. *shroud*] harbour, conceal (*OED*, v.1, 2a, 5).

Absalom. 'Gainst wicked Amnon, thy ungracious son,
  My brother and fair Tamar's by the King,   65
  My stepbrother by mother and by kind.
  He hath dishonoured David's holiness
  And fixed a blot of lightness on his throne,
  Forcing my sister Tamar when he feigned
  A sickness, sprung from root of heinous lust.   70
David. Hath Amnon brought this evil on my house
  And suffered sin to smite his father's bones?
  Smite, David, deadlier than the voice of heaven,
  And let hate's fire be kindled in thy heart!
  Frame in the arches of thy angry brows,   75
  Making thy forehead like a comet shine,
  To force false Amnon tremble at thy looks!
  Sin with his sevenfold crown and purple robe
  Begins his triumphs in my guilty throne;
  There sits he watching with his hundred eyes   80
  Our idle minutes and our wanton thoughts,
  And with his baits made of our frail desires

64. SH *Absalom*] this edn; *Abs. Q; Absalon. Hawkins (subst).*   73. than] *Hawkins (subst);* then *Q.*

65–6.] David had each of his six sons by a different woman. Amnon's mother was Ahinoam, an 'Israelite'; Absalom's mother was Maacah, 'daughter of Talmai the King of Geshur' (2 Samuel, 3:2–3). The Geneva gloss to 2 Samuel, 13:1 states that 'Tamar was Absalom's sister both by father and mother, and Amnon only by father'. Only implicit in these lines, Absalom's sense of the superiority of his and his sister Tamar's birth over that of their stepbrother Amnon's is possibly the subject of Absalom's lament in the misplaced fragment following the second chorus in Q: 'What boots it, Absalom, unhappy Absalom, / ... / To have disclosed a far more worthy womb', Absalom declaims.

68. *lightness*] profligacy.

70. *heinous*] hateful, atrocious (*OED*, adj., 1a).

72. *to smite ... bones*] i.e. to dishonour his father.

75. *Frame*] 'shape, compose, give (specified) expression to (the countenance, face)' (*OED*, v., 5d).

angry] 'But when King David heard all these things, he was very wroth' (2 Samuel, 13:21).

78. *sevenfold*] The Deadly Sins were conventionally seven in number.

80. *hundred eyes*] alludes to Argus, the hundred-eyed Titan in Greek myth whom Hera appoints to guard Io, a nymph-turned-heifer with whom Zeus has been having an affair. Hermes frees Io by charming Argus asleep then killing him (Grimal, 58–9). Sin's 'hundred eyes' synechdochically represent its all-seeing nature.

Gives us the hook that hales our souls to hell.
But with the spirit of my kingdom's God
I'll thrust the flattering tyrant from his throne   85
And scourge his bondslaves from my hallowed court
With rods of iron and thorns of sharpened steel.
Then, Absalom, revenge not thou this sin;
Leave it to me, and I will chasten him.
Absalom. I am content. Then grant my lord the King   90
Himself with all his other lords would come
Up to my sheep feast on the plain of Hazor.
David. Nay, my fair son, myself with all my lords
Will bring thee too much charge, yet some shall go.
Absalom. But let my lord the King himself take pains.   95
The time of year is pleasant for Your Grace,
And gladsome summer in her shady robes,
Crownèd with roses and with planted flowers,
With all her nymphs shall entertain my lord,
That from the thicket of my verdant groves   100
Will sprinkle honey dews about his breast
And cast sweet balm upon his kingly head.
Then grant thy servant's boon, and go, my lord.

90. SH *Absalom*] *this edn; Abs. Q; Absalon. Hawkins (subst).*   93. SH
David] *Hawkins (subst); Da. Q.*   95. SH *Absalom*] *this edn; Abs. Q; Absalon.
Hawkins (subst).*   98. flowers] *QP, BL 1, 2, H, Fol, Hv, Il, Tex, Il, Bod,
VAM, WC, M (subst);* flower *QHC.*

85.] David's statement is confusing. Nowhere in the biblical narrative
and nowhere else in the play is it suggested that Amnon is a king in his own
right. He is David's oldest son and heir to the throne of Israel, however, so
David may be threatening to disinherit him.

    tyrant] Renaissance political theorists distinguished legitimate kings from
tyrants on legal and psychological grounds. A tyrant was one who acquired
sovereign power illegitimately or used it to abrogate the law in pursuit of his
own personal pleasures and interests; governed by passion rather than reason,
the tyrant was cruel, sexually excessive, and effeminate (Bushnell, 36).

89.] In the biblical narrative (2 Samuel, 13) as in the play, not David but
Absalom 'chasten[s]' Amnon, by killing him at the sheep-shearing feast.

90–2. *Then ... Hazor*] In the biblical narrative Absalom arranges the
sheep-shearing feast two years after Tamar's rape. The Geneva glosses to 2
Samuel, 13:20 and 23, however, make clear the feast's nature as a calculated
trap: Absalom initially 'dissembled it [his desire for revenge] till occasion
served'; he arranges the feast 'thinking thereby to fulfill his wicked purpose'.

94. *charge*] burden, expense.

95. *take pains*] make a special effort.

103. *boon*] request.

David. Let it content my sweet son Absalom
  That I may stay, and take my other lords.   105
Absalom. But shall thy best belovèd Amnon go?
David. What needeth it that Amnon go with thee?
Absalom. Yet do thy son and servant so much grace.
David. Amnon shall go, and all my other lords,
  Because I will give grace to Absalom.   110

Enter HUSHAI *and* URIAH, *with others.*

Hushai. Pleaseth my lord the King, his servant Joab
  Hath sent Uriah from the Syrian wars.
David. Welcome, Uriah, from the Syrian wars.
  Welcome to David as his dearest lord.
Uriah. Thanks be to Israel's God and David's grace   115
  Uriah finds such greeting with the King!
David. No other greeting shall Uriah find
  As long as David sways the elected seat
  And consecrated throne of Israel.
  Tell me, Uriah, of my servant Joab.   120
  Fights he with truth the battles of our God
  And for the honour of the Lord's anointed?
Uriah. Thy servant Joab fights the chosen wars
  With truth, with honour, and with high success

---

104. SH *David*] *Hawkins (subst); Dau. Q.*   106. SH *Absalom*] *this edn;
Abs. Q; Absalon. Hawkins (subst).*   107. SH *David*] *Hawkins (subst); Dau.
Q.*   108. SH *Absalom*] *this edn; Abs. Q; Absalon. Hawkins (subst).*   109. SH
David] *Hawkins (subst); Dau. Q.*   113. SH *David*] *Hawkins (subst); Dau.
Q.*   117. SH *David*] *Hawkins (subst); Dau. Q.*   118. David] *Hawkins
(subst);* Dauids *Q.*   122. Lord's] *Q (subst).*

108.] i.e. Yet do me, your son and obedient subject, this favour.
110. *give grace to*] bestow favour on.
111. *Pleaseth*] May it please.
114. *dearest lord*] favourite noble.
116. *Uriah*] that Uriah.
with] from.
117.] i.e. I will always greet Uriah with special welcome.
118. *David*] Q's 'Dauids' is not coherent as either plural or genitive.
121. *truth*] loyalty.
122. *the Lord's anointed*] David.
123. *the chosen wars*] the wars he has been chosen to wage.

And 'gainst the wicked King of Ammon's sons   125
Hath by the finger of our sovereign's God
Besieged the city Rabbah and achieved
The court of waters, where the conduits run,
And all the Ammonites' delightsome springs.
Therefore he wisheth David's mightiness   130
Should number out the host of Israel
And come in person to the city Rabbah,
That so her conquest may be made the King's
And Joab fight as his inferior.
David. This hath not God and Joab's prowess done   135
Without Uriah's valours, I am sure,
Who, since his true conversion from a Hittite
To an adopted son of Israel,
Hath fought like one whose arms were lift by heaven
And whose bright sword was edged with Israel's wrath.   140
Go therefore home, Uriah, take thy rest;
Visit thy wife and household with the joys
A victor and a favourite of the King's
Should exercise with honour after arms.
Uriah. Thy servant's bones are yet not half so crazed   145
Nor constitute on such a sickly mould
That for so little service he should faint

---

134. And] *Hawkins (subst);* Aud *Q.*

125. *King of Ammon's sons*] Hanun, King of the Ammonites, and his brethren.
126. *by the finger*] by the guiding hand.
127. *achieved*] taken, conquered.
128. *court of waters*] ie. the city's reservoir (hence its strategic military importance), located in the 'kingly tower' (2.24) taken by Joab and his men in scene 2. See note to 2.24–5.
130. *David's mightiness*] David in his mightiness.
131. *number out ... Israel*] fill out the roster of Israel's army.
133. *That ... her conquest*] so that the conquest of Rabbah.
134. *as his inferior*] as his subject.
137–8.] Uriah's conversion from a Hittite to an Israelite was akin to a modern change in citizenship and required that he be circumcised.
139. *lift*] lifted.
140. *edged*] sharpened.
144. *after arms*] after engagement in military activity.
146. *constitute*] constituted, assembled.

82   DAVID AND BATHSHEBA

And seek, as cowards, refuge of his home,
Nor are his thoughts so sensually stirred
To stay the arms with which the Lord would smite   150
And fill their circle with His conquered foes
For wanton bosom of a flattering wife.
David. Uriah hath a beauteous, sober wife,
Yet young and framed of tempting flesh and blood.
Then, when the King hath summoned thee from arms,   155
If thou unkindly shouldst refrain her bed,
Sin might be laid upon Uriah's soul
If Bathsheba by frailty hurt her fame.
Then go, Uriah, solace in her love;
Whom God hath knit to thee, tremble to loose.   160
Uriah. The King is much too tender of my ease.
The ark, and Israel, and Judah dwell
In palaces and rich pavilions,

---

148. seek, as cowards,] *Hawkins (subst);* seeke (as cowards) *Q.*   150. Lord]
Dyce 3 (subst); lord *Q.*   151. His] *this edn;* his *Q.*   153. SH *David*] *Hawkins
(subst); Da. Q.*   160. loose] *Q (*lose*).*

---

150. *stay*] stop, restrain.
151. *their circle*] the circle of Uriah's arms. The implicit contrast is
between the motion of Uriah's arms when engaging God's enemies and the
circle his arms would form when embracing his wife Bathsheba.
153. *sober*] modest.
156. *refrain*] refrain from.
158.] If Bathsheba should wantonly injure her reputation. (David advises
Uriah to perform his role as sexual partner to his wife, lest she look elsewhere
for pleasure. See note 180 below for 2 Samuel's explanation of David's secret
motive in prompting Uriah to do this.)
160.] Compare the marriage service in the Anglican Book of Common
Prayer: 'Those whom God hath joined together, let no man put asunder.'
160. *loose*] modernises Q's 'lose' following Dyce 3, Keltie, Morley, Bullen,
and Thorndike. Hawkins, Dyce 2, Manly, Greg, Blistein, and Rabkin retain
the original spelling, and 'lose' is intelligible, but the verb with which 'lose'
is in opposition, 'hath knit', suggests that the meaning is loose, i.e. untie or
set free. See 3.42, in which Amnon is urged to 'loose' 'knots'.
161–70.] closely echo the Bishops' Bible version of Uriah's reply: 'Urias
answered David, The ark, and Israel, and Judah dwell in pavilions, and my
lord Joab, and the servants of my lord abide in the open fields, and shall I
then go into mine house, to eat and drink, and lie with my wife? By thy life,
and by the life of thy soul, I will not do this thing' (2 Samuel, 11:11).
161. *tender of*] considerate of, thoughtful for (*OED*, adj., 9a).
162. *ark*] ark of the covenant, for which a permanent temple had yet to
be built and was therefore still housed in a tent-like structure or pavilion.

But Joab and his brother in the fields,
Suffering the wrath of winter and the sun.   165
And shall Uriah, of more shame than they,
Banquet and loiter in the work of heaven?
As sure as thy soul doth live, my lord,
Mine ears shall never lean to such delight
When holy labour calls me forth to fight.   170
David. Then be it with Uriah's manly heart
As best his fame may shine in Israel.
Uriah. Thus shall Uriah's heart be best content.
Till thou dismiss me back to Joab's bands,
This ground before the King my master's doors   175

He lies down.

Shall be my couch, and this unwearied arm
The proper pillow of a soldier's head,
For never will I lodge within my house
Till Joab triumph in my secret vows.
David. Then fetch some flagons of our purest wine,   180
That we may welcome home our hardy friend
With full carouses to his fortunes past
And to the honours of his future arms.
Then will I send him back to Rabbah siege
And follow with the strength of Israel.   185

---

166. Uriah, of] *Manly (subst);* Vrias (of *Q.*   than] *Hawkins (subst);* then *Q.*
they] *Manly (subst);* they) *Q.*   175.1. SD] *printed on 175, aligned right, in Q.*

---

166. *more shame*] less noble status. Line 174 makes it clear that Uriah is
one of Joab's subordinate officers.

167. *in*] in doing.

174. *bands*] troops.

178–9.] The meaning of these lines is not entirely clear. Were a comma
to be inserted between 'triumph' and 'in', they could conjecturally mean, 'I
have vowed the deepest vow that I will never lodge within my house until
Joab triumph at Rabbah'.

180.] The Geneva glosses to 2 Samuel, 11:8 and 13 state David's motiva-
tions explicitly: thinking 'that if Uriah lay with his wife, his [David's] fault
might be cloaked,' David 'made him drink more liberally than he was wont
to do, thinking hereby he would have lain by his wife'.

flagons] large drinking cups.

183. *his future arms*] his future military career.

185. *strength*] army.

Enter one [a servant] with the flagons of wine.

Arise, Uriah, come and pledge the King.

He [URIAH] riseth.

[The servant gives full glasses of wine to DAVID,
URIAH, ABSALOM, and HUSHAI.]

Uriah. If David think me worthy such a grace,
    I will be bold and pledge my lord the King.
David. Absalom and Hushai both shall drink
    To good Uriah and his happiness.   190
Absalom. We will, my lord, to please Uriah's soul.
David. I will begin, Uriah, to thyself
    And all the treasure of the Ammonites,
    Which here I promise to impart to thee
    And bind that promise with a full carouse.   195

[He drinks.]

Uriah. What seemeth pleasant in my sovereign's eyes,
    That shall Uriah do till he be dead.

[He drinks.]

David. Fill him the cup;
[The servant refills URIAH's glass.]
                     follow, ye lords that love
Your sovereign's health, and do as he hath done.

[The other lords drink.]

185.1. SD *a servant*] *this edn;* not in Q.   186.1. SD] *printed on 186, aligned*
right, in Q. URIAH] *this edn; not in* Q.   186.2. SD] *this edn; not in* Q.
189. SH *David*] *Hawkins (subst); Dau.* Q.   191. SH *Absalom*] *this edn; Abs.*
Q; *Absalon. Hawkins (subst).*   192. SH *David*] *Hawkins (subst); Dau.*
Q.   195.1. SD *He drinks.*] *Dyce 3 (subst); not in* Q.   197.1. SD *He drinks.*]
this edn; not in Q.   198. SH *David*] *Hawkins (subst); Dau.* Q.   198. SD
The servant … glass.] *this edn; not in* Q.   199.1. SD *The other lords drink.*] *this*
edn; not in Q.

186. *pledge*] offer a toast to.
188.] It is possible that Uriah begins to drink at this point, but protocol
might dictate that he, and the others, wait for David to begin.
195. *carouse*] large draft of wine.
196. *What*] Whatever.

Absalom. Ill may he thrive or live in Israel   200
     That loves not David or denies his charge!
     Uriah, here is to Abishai's health,
     Lord Joab's brother and thy loving friend.

                    [*He drinks.*]

Uriah. I pledge Lord Absalom and Abishai's health.

                    He drinks.

Hushai. Here now, Uriah, to the health of Joab   205
     And to the pleasant journey we shall have
     When we return to mighty Rabbah's siege.

                    [*He drinks.*]

Uriah. Hushai, I pledge thee all, with all my heart.
     Give me some drink, ye servants of the King,
     Give me my drink.   210

          [*The servant refills* URIAH's *glass, and*] [*h*]*e drinks.*

David. Well done, my good Uriah, drink thy fill,
     That in thy fullness David may rejoice.
Uriah. I will, my lord.

                    [*He drinks.*]

Absalom. Now, Lord Uriah, one carouse to me.
Uriah. No, sir, I'll drink to the King;   215
     Your father is a better man than you.

___

200. SH *Absalom*] *this edn;Abs. Q;Absalon. Hawkins (subst).*   202. Abishai]
Q (Abisai). Modernised silently throughout.   203.] *Hawkins (subst); printed
as one line with previous line in Q.* and] *Hawkins (subst);* & *Q.* 203.1. SD
He drinks.] *Dyce 3 (subst); not in Q.* 204.1. SD] *printed on 204, aligned
right, in Q.* 205. SH *Hushai*] *this edn; Cus. Q; Cusay. Hawkins
(subst).*   207. Rabbah's] *this edn;* Rabath *Q.* 207.1. SD *He drinks.*] *Dyce
3 (subst); not in Q.* 210.1. SD] *printed on 210, aligned right, in Q.* The
servant ... and] *this edn; not in Q.* 211. SH *David*] *Hawkins (subst);* Da.
Q. 213.1. SD *He drinks.*] *this edn; not in Q.* 214. SH *Absalom*] *this edn;*
Abs. Q;Absalon. Hawkins (subst).   216. than] *Hawkins (subst);* then *Q.*

201. *charge*] order, command.
202-3.] These lines are clearly iambic pentameter lines printed without a
line break in Q.

David. Do so, Uriah; I will pledge thee straight.
Uriah. I will indeed, my lord and sovereign,
    Ay, once in my days be so bold.
David. Fill him his glass.   220
Uriah. Fill me my glass.

        He [URIAH] *gives him* [*a servant*] *the glass.*

David. Quickly, I say.
Uriah. Quickly, I say.

    [*The servant fills the glass and hands it back to* URIAH.]

Here, my lord, by your favour now I drink to you.

           [*He drinks.*]

David. I pledge thee, good Uriah, presently.   225

        He drinks.

Absalom. Here then, Uriah, once again for me
    And to the health of David's children.
Uriah. David's children?

---

217. SH *David*] *Hawkins (subst); Dau. Q.*   219. Ay] *Rabkin (subst);* I *Q.*
221.1. SD] *printed on 221, aligned right, in Q.*   URIAH] *this edn; not in Q.*
a servant] *this edn; not in Q; conj Dyce 3.*   222. SH *David*] *Hawkins (subst);*
Dau. Q.   223.] *Dyce 3 (subst), conj Dyce 2; printed as one line with previous*
line in Q.   223.1. SD *The servant … URIAH.*] *this edn; not in Q; His glass is*
filled. Manly (subst).   224.] *this edn; Q begins line with* SH*Vrias..*   224.1. SD
He drinks.] *Dyce 3 (subst); not in Q.*   225. SH *David*] *Hawkins (subst); Dau.*
Q.   225.1. SD] *printed on 225, aligned right, in Q.*   226. SH *Absalom*] *this*
edn; Abs. Q; Absalon. Hawkins (subst).

   217. *straight*] immediately.
   219. *in my days*] in my life.
   222–3.] are printed as one line in Q, but 'Vrias' is italicised. Proper nouns
in the play are not italicised, but speech headings are, suggesting that Vrias
is a speech heading rather than part of David's speech. The immediately
preceding two lines and lines 227–30 provide other examples of the drunken
Uriah parroting the dialogue addressed to him.
   224. *by your favour*] with your permission. (Uriah is thoroughly drunk by
this time. Compare *Antony and Cleopatra*, 2.7, where Antony and others get
Lepidus stupefactorily drunk by toasting him repeatedly and thereby obliging
him to reciprocate by downing his drink.)

Absalom. Ay, David's children. Wilt thou pledge me, man?
Uriah. Pledge me, man?   230
Absalom. Pledge me, I say, or else thou lov'st us not.
Uriah. What, do you talk, do you talk?
    I'll no more; I'll lie down here.
David. Rather, Uriah, go thou home and sleep.
Uriah. Oho, sir, would you make me break my sentence?   235

                He lies down.

    Home, sir? No indeed, sir! I'll sleep upon mine arm
    Like a soldier, sleep like a man as long as I live in Israel.
David. [*Aside*] If naught will serve to save his wife's renown,
    I'll send him with a letter unto Joab
    To put him in the forefront of the wars,   240
    That so my purposes may take effect.
    [*To* HUSHAI *and servants*] Help him in, sirs.
            Exit DAVID *and* ABSALOM.
Hushai. Come, rise, Uriah; get thee in and sleep.
Uriah. I will not go home, sir, that's flat.
Hushai. Then come and rest thee upon David's bed.   245

        [URIAH *rises.*]

Uriah. On afore, my lords, on afore.

                Exeunt.

---

229. SH *Absalom*] *this edn; Abs. Q; Absalon. Hawkins (subst).*   229. Ay]
Hawkins (subst); I *Q.*   230. man?] *Keltie (subst);* man. *Q.*   231. SH
Absalom] *this edn; Abs. Q; Absalon. Hawkins (subst).*   235.1. SD] *aligned
right in Q.*   238. SD *Aside*] *Dyce 3; not in Q.*   242. SD] *To* HUSHAI *and
servants*] *this edn; not in Q.*   242.1. SD] *printed on 242, aligned right, in Q.*
245.1. SD URIAH *rises.*] *this edn; not in Q.*   246.1. SD] *printed on 246,
aligned right, in Q.*

---

232. *do you talk*] Uriah's expression dismisses as childish prattle Absalom's
attempt in the previous lines to get Uriah to drink to him (and David's other
children) as well as to David.
    235. *my sentence*] the vow Uriah made in lines 174–9 not to go home until
Joab has conquered Rabbah.
    238. *renown*] reputation, fame. David reckons that, if Uriah is killed in
battle, Bathsheba will no longer be an adulterous wife. See 2 Samuel, 11:15.
    246. *afore*] before (*OED*).

[Chorus 1]

[Enter] Chorus.

[Chorus.] Oh, proud revolt of a presumptuous man,
Laying his bridle in the neck of sin,
Ready to bear him past his grave to hell!
Like as the fatal raven that in his voice
Carries the dreadful summons of our deaths   5
Flies by the fair Arabian spiceries,
Her pleasant gardens and delightsome parks,
Seeming to curse them with his hoarse exclaims,
And yet doth stoop with hungry violence
Upon a piece of hateful carrion,   10
So wretched man, displeased with those delights
Would yield a quickening savour to his soul,
Pursues with eager and unstanchèd thirst
The greedy longings of his loathsome flesh.
If holy David so shook hands with sin,   15
What shall our baser spirits glory in?

Heading Chorus 1] *Greg (subst); not in Q;* [SECOND] CHORUS. *Bullen
(subst);* I Chorus *Rabkin (subst).* 0.1. SD *Enter] Dyce 3 (subst); not in
Q.* 1. SH *Chorus] Dyce 3 (subst); not in Q.* 7. parks] *Q (subst);* parts
Allott (subst).

2.] i.e. abandoning control or restraint to sin (see *OED*, bridle, n., 1a).
4–14.] These lines are reproduced in Robert Allott's verse anthology,
England's Parnassus (1600), under the heading 'Man'. Dyce 3 (469) observes
that Peele borrows the simile from Du Bartas: 'Ainsi que les corbeaux, d'une
penne venteuse, / Passent les bois pleurans de L'Arabie heureuse, / Meprisent
les jardins et parcs delicieux / Qui de fleurs esmaillez vont parfumant les
cieux, / Et s'arrestent, gloutons, sur la salle carcasse, / D'un criminel rompu
n'a guere à coups de masse [Just as the swift-winged ravens / Pass the rainy
woods of happy Arabia, / Scorn the delightful gardens and parks / That
perfume the heavens with enamelled flowers, / And come to a halt, gluttons,
on the dirty carcass / Of a criminal bludgeoned to death]' (*L'Arche*, 521–6).
4–5.] In Marlowe's *The Jew of Malta*, Barabas compares himself to 'the
sad presaging raven that tolls / The sick man's passport in her hollow beak'
(2.1.1–2).
8. *exclaims*] exclamations, cries.
12. *Would*] that would.
quickening savour] enlivening smell.
13. *unstanchèd*] unquenched.

This King, by giving Lust her rein,
Pursues the sequel with a greater ill:
Uriah in the forefront of the wars
Is murdered by the hateful heathen's sword,   20
And David joys his too dear Bathsheba.
Suppose this past and that the child is born
Whose death the prophet solemnly doth mourn.
[Exit Chorus.]

[Sc. 5]

Enter BATHSHEBA with her Handmaid.

Bathsheba. Mourn, Bathsheba; bewail thy foolishness,
Thy sin, thy shame, the sorrow of thy soul.
Sin, shame, and sorrow swarm about thy soul,
And in the gates and entrance of my heart
Sadness with wreathèd arms hangs her complaint.   5

17. king, by] *Manly (subst), Dyce 2 conj;* kingly *Q.* rein] *Q (*raigne*).*
23. SD] *Dyce 3 (subst); not in Q.*

Heading Sc. 5] *Greg (subst); not in Q;* SCENE IV. *Bullen (subst);* ACT II.
SCENE I. *Morley (subst);* Act II. Scene I. *Manly (subst);* iv *Rabkin (subst).*
1. SH Bathsheba] *this edn; Beth. Q; Bethsabe. Hawkins (subst).*

---

17. *King, by*] Q's 'kingly' renders nonsense of lines 17 and 18. Dyce conjectures 'king by'; Bullen emends to 'kingly [ruler] giving'; Morley emends
to 'kingly spirit'; Manly revises the line to 'This king, by giuing vnto lust
her raigne'. Hawkins, Keltie, Thorndike, Greg, Blistein, and Rabkin retain
'kingly'.

rein] Manly, Greg, and Blistein retain Q's spelling, 'raigne', but all other
editions modernise 'raigne' as 'rein', consonant with line 2's equestrian
metaphor. Q uses 'raigne' once more in the play, when Nathan tells David
in scene 17 to 'let Solomon reign [Q raigne]' (48).

21. *joys*] enjoys.

22. *the child*] David and Bathsheba's firstborn son, unnamed. See 2
Samuel, 11:27.

23. *the prophet*] David, who was commonly considered to be a prophet as
well as poet and king in the Renaissance.

[*Sc. 5*] Conjecturally, in this scene Bathsheba is located in the part of
David's palace, perhaps her own private chambers, whence she is summoned
to David in scene 6. Her lament corresponds to no specific part of the biblical
narrative.

5. *wreathèd*] folded (*OED*, adj., 2). Tamar flees Amnon's palace with
'folded arms' at 4.15. Folded arms conventionally signified melancholy.

No comfort from the ten-stringed instrument,
The twinkling cymbal, or the ivory lute,
Nor doth the sound of David's kingly harp
Make glad the broken heart of Bathsheba.
Jerusalem is filled with thy complaint,   10
And in the streets of Zion sits thy grief.
The babe is sick, sick to the death, I fear,
The fruit that sprung from thee to David's house,
Nor may the pot of honey and of oil
Glad David or his handmaid's countenance.   15
Uriah, woe is me to think hereon,
For who is it among the sons of men
That saith not to my soul, 'The King hath sinned,
David hath done amiss, and Bathsheba
Laid snares of death unto Uriah's life'?   20
My sweet Uriah, fallen into the pit
Art thou and gone even to the gates of hell
For Bathsheba, that wouldst not shroud her shame.
Oh, what is it to serve the lust of kings?
How lion-like thy rage when we resist!   25
But, Bathsheba, in humbleness attend
The grace that God will to His handmaid send.

            Exit BATHSHEBA [*and her* Handmaid].

9. Bathsheba] *Q* (Bersabe). *Modernised silently throughout.*   27. His] *this edn;* his *Q.*   27. SD BATHSHEBA] *this edn;* Beth *Q;* Beth[sabe *Manly (subst).*   *and her* Handmaid] *this edn; not in Q; with* MAID *Manly (subst).*

7. *twinkling*] All previous editions except Greg emend to 'tinkling', but fast-moving, metallic cymbals might twinkle, and none of the three other musical instruments listed in lines 6 to 8 is immediately preceded by an adjective describing its sound. *OED* records the sixteenth-century use of 'twinkling' as a noun denoting 'a tinkling sound' or 'the production of such a sound' (n.2), and in *A Knight's Conjuring* (1607) Thomas Dekker mentions the 'twinkling' of Orpheus's harp (D2r).

14. *pot ... oil*] Deuteronomy, 8:8 describes the land God has promised the Israelites as a 'land of oil olive, and honey'.

15. *Glad*] gladden.

23. *that ... shame*] you who refused to conceal from public view her shame.

25.] The lion is traditionally a royal beast.

27. *His handmaid*] i.e. Bathsheba herself, not the Handmaid accompanying her in this scene.

[Sc. 6]

> [*Enter*] DAVID *in his gown walking sadly*[, *with servants*].

[*David.*] The babe is sick, and sad is David's heart,
To see the guiltless bear the guilty's pain.
David, hang up thy harp, hang down thy head,
And dash thy ivory lute against the stones!
The dew that on the Hill of Hermon falls　　　　　　5
Rains not on Zion's tops and lofty towers,
And David's thoughts are spent in pensiveness.
The plains of Gath and Ashkelon rejoice.
The babe is sick, sweet babe, that Bathsheba
With woman's pain brought forth to Israel.　　　　　10

> *Enter* NATHAN.

But what saith Nathan to his lord the King?
Nathan. Thus Nathan saith unto his lord the King:
There were two men, both dwellers in one town;

Heading Sc. 6] *Greg (subst); not in Q;* SCENE V. *Bullen (subst);* Act II.
Scene II. *Manly (subst);* v *Rabkin (subst).*　0.1. SD] *this edn; Dauid in his
gowne walking sadly. To him Nathan. Q; Enter* DAVID *in his gown, walking
sadly:* Servants *attending. Dyce 3 (subst).　Enter*] *Dyce 3 (subst); not in Q.*
1. SH *David*] *Hawkins (subst); not in Q.*　10.1. SD] *printed on 10, aligned
right, in Q.*　11.] *Q follows this line with the SD Nathan to Dauid.*

[*Sc. 6*] Located in David's palace. The scene dramatises 2 Samuel,
12:1–24.

5–6.] Psalm 133:3 compares collective peace and harmony to 'the dew of
Hermon, which falleth upon the mountains of Zion'. In these lines, David
asserts that the 'dew' of Hermon Hill does not fall 'on Zion's tops', thus
expressing his sense of collective as well as personal distress. See note to
1.46–8.

7–8.] Following Dyce 3, Keltie, Morley, Bullen, Manly, Thorndike,
Blistein, and Rabkin invert the order of these lines. Dyce merely asserts that
the lines 'are transposed', without offering any reason, and subsequent
editors have adopted this emendation with no attempt at explanation. The
presence of the co-ordinating conjunction 'And' at the beginning of line 7
and the absence of a co-ordinating conjunction at the beginning of line 8
might suggest that the order of the two lines has been inverted if we consider
them as independent clause components of a compound sentence. They do,
however, make sense in the order Q gives them, as they are printed here.

8. *Gath and Ashkelon*] Philistine cities.

12–68.] Nathan's parable and David's penitent response are related in 2
Samuel, 12:1–15. Peele follows the language of the biblical account closely.

The one was mighty and exceeding rich
In oxen, sheep, and cattle of the field,   15
The other poor, having nor ox, nor calf,
Nor other cattle, save one little lamb,
Which he had bought and nourished by the hand,
And it grew up, and fed with him and his,
And ate and drank as he and his were wont,   20
And in his bosom slept, and was to live
As was his daughter or his dearest child.
There came a stranger to this wealthy man,
And he refused and spared to take his own
Or of his store to dress or make him meat,   25
But took the poor man's sheep, partly poor man's store,
And dressed it for this stranger in his house.
What, tell me, shall be done to him for this?
David. Now, as the Lord doth live, this wicked man
Is judged and shall become the child of death.   30
Fourfold to the poor man shall he restore
That without mercy took his lamb away.
Nathan. Thou art the man, and thou hast judged thyself.
David, thus saith the Lord thy God by me:
'I thee anointed King in Israel   35

---

20. ate] *Morley (subst);* eat Q.   28. What, tell me,] *Hawkins (subst);* What
(tell me) Q.   29. SH *David*] *Hawkins (subst); Dau.* Q.   29. Lord] *Dyce 3
(subst);* lord Q.   33. SH *Nathan*] *Hawkins (subst); Nath.* Q.   34. Lord] *Q
(subst).*

---

15. *cattle of the field*] livestock generally, not just cattle.
16. *nor ox*] neither ox.
20. *ate*] Q's 'eat' functions as the past tense here.
21–2.] Compare 2 Samuel, 12:3: 'and slept in his bosom, and was unto
him as his daughter'.
25. *store*] stock, supplies; plenty, abundance (*OED*, n., 1a, 4b).
dress] prepare.
26. *partly … store*] i.e. a significant portion of all the poor man owned.
30. *child of death*] In its gloss on 2 Samuel, 12:5, the Geneva Bible supplies
this phrase as the literal Hebrew of 'shall surely die' in David's pronounce-
ment that 'the man that hath done this thing, shall surely die'.
35.] Samuel anoints David king in 1 Samuel, 16:13.

And saved thee from the tyranny of Saul;
Thy master's house I gave thee to possess;
His wives into thy bosom did I give,
And Judah and Jerusalem withal,
And might, thou knowst, if this had been too small,   40
Have given thee more.
Wherefore, then, hast thou gone so far astray
And hast done evil and sinned in My sight?
Uriah thou hast killèd with the sword;
Yea, with the sword of the uncircumcised   45
Thou hast him slain, wherefore from this day forth
The sword shall never go from thee and thine.
For thou hast ta'en this Hittite's wife to thee,
Wherefore, behold, I will', saith Jacob's God,
'In thine own house stir evil up to thee;   50
Yea, I before thy face will take thy wives
And give them to thy neighbour to possess.
This shall be done to David in the day,
That Israel openly may see thy shame.'

---

40. might, thou knowest,] *Hawkins (subst);* might (thou knowest) *Q.*
43. My] *this edn;* my *Q.*   48. ta'en] *Hawkins (subst);* tane *Q.*   49. will,
sayth Jacob's God,] *Hawkins (subst);* wil (saith Iacobs God) *Q.*

36.] Saul, the King of Israel at the time of David's anointing, began to persecute David after David slew the Philistine champion Goliath and thus permitted the previously stymied Israelite army to rout the Philistines in an important battle. See 1 Samuel, 18:6–8.

39. *Judah*] one of the twelve tribes of Israel, located in southern Palestine. David reigned over Judah for seven years before becoming king of the remaining eleven tribes and uniting Israel after the assassination of Ishbosheth (2 Samuel, 5:1–5).

45. *uncircumcised*] The Israelites used circumcision as a sign of difference between them and neighbouring peoples. God tells Moses and Aaron that 'if a stranger dwell with thee, and will observe the Passover of the Lord, let him circumcise all the males, that belong unto him, and then let him come and observe it, and he shall be as one that is born in the land: for none uncircumcised person shall eat thereof' (Deuteronomy, 12:48).

47.] i.e. You and your kingdom will experience unceasing wars.

49. *Jacob's God*] Jacob was son of Isaac and Rebekah and father of the twelve sons from whom the tribes of Israel took their names. He is renamed Israel after wrestling with the Angel of God and refusing to let go of him until blessed (Genesis, 32:28).

53. *in the day*] openly, publicly.

David. Nathan, I have against the Lord, I have   55
    Sinned, oh, sinned grievously, and, lo,
    From heaven's throne doth David throw himself
    And groan and grovel to the gates of hell!

                        He falls down.

Nathan. David, stand up. [DAVID *stands.*] Thus saith the
    Lord by me,
    'David the King shall live', for He hath seen   60
    The true repentant sorrow of thy heart,
    But, for thou hast in this misdeed of thine
    Stirred up the enemies of Israel
    To triumph and blaspheme the God of hosts
    And say, 'He set a wicked man to reign   65
    Over His lovèd people and His tribes',
    The child shall surely die that erst was born,
    His mother's sin, his kingly father's scorn.

                        Exit NATHAN.

55. Nathan,] *QBL 1, 2, Bod, Fol, H, HC, Il, Tex, NLS, VAM (subst);*
Nathan; *QHv* Lord] *Q (subst).* 58.1. SD] *printed on 58, aligned right, in*
Q. 59. SH *Nathan*] *Hawkins (subst); Nath. Q.* 59. SD DAVID *stands.*] *this*
edn; not in Q. 59. Lord] *Q (subst).* 60. He] *this edn;* he *Q.* 66. Over
His] *this edn;* Ouer his *Q.* and His] *this edn;* and his *Q.* 68. SD] *printed*
on 68.1, aligned right, in Q.

──

55–6. I have against ... grievously] recalls David's declaration to God in
Psalm 51:4 that 'Against thee, against thee only have I sinned'. According
to the headnote in the Geneva Bible, David composed the psalm, the first
of seven Penitential Psalms, after he 'was rebuked by the prophet Nathan
for his great offence'.
    57.] This line might suggest that at some point, perhaps when Nathan
enters at 10.1 SD and presents David with a case for his judgement, David
ceases to pace sadly and sits on his throne, from which he now throws
himself. This would require David's throne to be brought on stage at the
beginning of the scene.
    62. *for*] because.
    67.] On the fatal sickness of the child as divine vengeance, see 2 Samuel,
12:14.
    erst] just now. (Also in line 84.)
    68.] i.e. the child that bears witness to his mother's sin and his kingly
father's shameful conduct. (Also in line 78.)

David. How just is Jacob's God in all His works!
  But must it die that David loveth so?   70
  Oh, that the mighty One of Israel
  Nill change His doom and says the babe must die,
  Mourn, Israel, and weep in Zion gates.
  Wither, ye cedar trees of Lebanon!
  Ye sprouting almonds with your flowering tops,   75
  Droop, drown, and drench in Hebron's fearful streams!
  The babe must die that was to David born,
  His mother's sin, his kingly father's scorn.

DAVID sits sadly.

Enter HUSHAI to DAVID and his train.

1 Servant. What tidings bringeth Hushai to the King?
Hushai. To thee, the servant of King David's court,   80
  This bringeth Hushai: as the prophet spoke,
  The Lord hath surely stricken to the death
  The child new-born by that Uriah's wife
  That by the sons of Ammon erst was slain.

---

69. SH *David*] *Hawkins (subst); Da. Q.* 69. His] *this edn;* his *Q.*
71. One] *Dyce 3 (subst);* one *Q.* 72. His] *this edn;* his *Q.* 76. streams]
Hawkins (subst); streames *QP, BL 1, 2, Bod, Tex, Il, H, Hv, Fol, NLS, VAM,
WC, M;* streame *QHC.* 78.1. SD] *aligned right in Q.* 79. SH *1 Servant*]
Dyce 3 (subst); Seruus. Q. 82. Lord] *Q (subst).*

72–3.] i.e. will not change his judgement, saying that the babe must die
and that Israel and iron-gated Zion must weep.
  72. *Nill*] Will not.
  doom] judgement.
  74. *Lebanon*] 'a mountain range in Syria which runs for about 280 km.
(180 miles) parallel to the eastern Mediterranean coast' (Browning, 233),
upon which grew the cedars and firs out of which Solomon constructed his
temple and palace (1 Kings, 5:5–10).
  76. *Hebron's*] Hebron was the city where David reigned as King of Judah
for seven years before becoming King of Israel and relocating to Jerusalem
(2 Samuel, 5:5).
  78.1. SD sits] David could sit on the ground or on his throne.

1 Servant. Hushai, be still. The King is vexèd sore.   85
  How shall he speed that brings this tidings first,
  When, while the child was yet alive, we spoke
  And David's heart would not be comforted?
David. Yea, David's heart will not be comforted.
  What murmur ye, the servants of the King?   90
  What tidings telleth Hushai to the King?
  Say, Hushai, lives the child, or is he dead?
Hushai. The child is dead that of Uriah's wife
  David begat.
David.   Uriah's wife, sayst thou?
  The child is dead; then ceaseth David's shame.   95
  Fetch me to eat, and give me wine to drink,
  Water to wash, and oil to clear my looks;
  Bring down your shawms, your cymbals, and your pipes.

---

85. SH *1 Servant*] *Dyce 3 (subst); Seruus. Q.*   89. SH *David*] *Hawkins
(subst); Da. Q.*   93–4. wife / David] *Hawkins (subst); no line break in
Q.*   94. SH *David*] *Hawkins (subst); Da. Q.*

85–8.] These lines closely follow 2 Samuel, 12:18, but whereas in the biblical narrative the anonymous servants, having heard the news of the child's
death, speak these words among themselves before David perceives their
whispering and guesses its meaning, Peele converts these words into dialogue
and makes Hushai specifically the bearer of bad news, thus adding to the
development of his character as a tough-minded but loyal servant of David.

86. *speed*] fare.

87. *while*] even while.

we spoke] 2 Samuel, 12:18 reports that 'the servants of David feared to tell
him that the child was dead: for they said, Behold, while the child was yet
alive, we spake to him'.

93–4.] The emended lineation converts the lines into two regular iambic
pentameter lines, the second begun by Hushai and sharply completed by
David.

98–100.] These verses echo Psalm 98:5–6, 'Sing praise to the Lord upon
the harp, even upon the harp with a singing voice. / With shawms and sound
of trumpets sing loud before the Lord the King.' In *Anglorum Feriae*, in which
he celebrates Elizabeth's Accession Day, Peele reworks the imagery of these
lines into praise of Elizabeth: 'London's Shepherd ... / praiseth the Mighty
One of Israel' (108–9) with 'the sound of cymbals, trumps, and shawms'
(105) and 'with the strings of his unfeigned heart / Tunes his true joy for all
those days of peace, / Those quiet days that Englishmen enjoy / Under our
Queen' (110–13).

98. *shawms*] 'mediaeval musical instrument[s] of the oboe class, having
a double reed enclosed in a globular mouthpiece' (*OED*, n., 1a). 2 Samuel,

Let David's harp and lute, his hand and voice,
Give laud to Him that loveth Israel   100
And sing His praise that shendeth David's fame,
That put away his sin from out his sight
And sent his shame into the streets of Gath.
Bring ye to me the mother of the babe,
        [*Exit a servant to summon* BATHSHEBA.]
That I may wipe the tears from off her face,   105
And give her comfort with this hand of mine,
And deck fair Bathsheba with ornaments,
That she may bear to me another son,
That may be lovèd of the Lord of Hosts.
For where he is, of force must David go,   110
But never may he come where David is.

*They [servants] bring in water, wine, and oil, music,
and a banquet.*

[*Enter* BATHSHEBA.]

Fair Bathsheba, sit thou and sigh no more,
And sing and play, you servants of the King.

100. Him] *this edn;* him *Q.*   101. His] *this edn;* his *Q.*   104.1. SD *Exit …*
BATHSHEBA.] *this edn; not in Q.*   109. Lord] *Q (subst).*   111.1. SD *servants*] *this edn; not in Q.*   111.2. SD *Enter* BATHSHEBA.] *Dyce 2 (subst); not
in Q.*

12 does not mention shawms, but they can be found in conjunction with
other musical instruments in Psalm 98:5–6.
    100. *laud*] praise.
    101. *shendeth*] shields, defends (*OED*, v.2).
    108. *another son*] Solomon. 2 Samuel, 12:24 relates that 'David comforted
Bathsheba his wife, and went in unto her, and lay with her, and she bore a
son, and he called his name Salomon: also the Lord loved him'.
    110. *he*] David and Bathsheba's dead child. In the biblical narrative, after
receiving news of the child's death David comments, 'While the child was
yet alive, I fasted and wept: for I said, Who can tell whether God will have
mercy on me, that the child may live. / But now being dead, wherefore
should I now fast? Can I bring him again any more? I shall go to him, but
he shall not return to me' (2 Samuel, 12:22–3). The grave, where David too
must go, is 'Where he is'.
    of force] of necessity.

Now sleepeth David's sorrow with the dead,
And Bathsheba liveth to Israel.   115

They use all solemnities together and sing, etc.

Now arms and warlike engines for assault
Prepare at once, ye men of Israel,
Ye men of Judah and Jerusalem,
That Rabbah may be taken by the King,
Lest it be callèd after Joab's name,   120
Nor David's glory shine in Zion streets!
To Rabbah marcheth David with his men
To chastise Ammon and the wicked ones.

Exeunt omnes.

[Sc. 7]

Enter ABSALOM *with two or three.*

Absalom. Set up your mules, and give them well to eat,
And let us meet our brothers at the feast.
Accursèd is the master of this feast,
Dishonour of the house of Israel,

115.1. SD etc.] *Q (& c.).*   116.] *Q begins line with SH Dauid.*   123.1. SD]
printed on 123, aligned right, in Q.

Heading Sc. 7] *Greg (subst); not in Q;* SCENE VI. *Bullen (subst);* ACT II.
SCENE II. *Morley (subst);* Act II. Scene III. *Manly (subst);* vi *Rabkin (subst).*
1. SH *Absalom] this edn; Abs. Q; Absalon. Hawkins (subst).*

115.1. SD solemnities] 'observance of ceremony or special formality on
important occasions' (*OED*, n., 1).
116. *engines*] devices, machines.

[*Sc. 7*] Located on the plains of Hazor, 'an important city north of the
Sea of Galilee' (Browning, 142). Contradicting both the biblical account and
4.90–110, Amnon rather than Absalom is the sheep-shearing feast's host.
The event is briefly related in 2 Samuel, 13:28–9.
3. *the master ... feast*] Amnon. See previous note.

His sister's slander, and his mother's shame.   5
Shame be his share that could such ill contrive,
To ravish Tamar and, without a pause,
To drive her shamefully from out his house.
But may his wickedness find just reward!
Therefore doth Absalom conspire with you   10
That Amnon die what time he sits to eat,
For in the holy temple have I sworn
Wreak of his villainy in Tamar's rape.
And here he comes. Bespeak him gently, all,
Whose death is deeply gravèd in my heart.   15

Enter AMNON *with* ADONIJAH *and* JONADAB
to ABSALOM *and his company.*

Amnon. Our shearers are not far from hence, I wot,
And Amnon to you all his brethren
Giveth such welcome as our fathers erst
Were wont in Judah and Jerusalem,
But specially, Lord Absalom, to thee,   20
The honour of thy house and progeny.
Sit down and dine with me, King David's son,

15.1. SD ADONIJAH] *Q (Adonia). Modernised silently throughout.*   16. SH
Amnon] *this edn; Am. Q; Ammon. Hawkins (subst).*

---

5. *His sister's*] Tamar's. See 4.64–8 and note to 4.65–6.

his mother's shame] This phrase echoes the description of David and
Bathsheba's dead son as 'His mother's sin, his kingly father's scorn' (6.68),
perhaps calling into question the legitimacy of Amnon's birth. The phrase
could, however, be simply alluding to the shamefulness of Amnon's rape of
Tamar. See note to 4.65–6.

10. *you*] the '*two or three*' (0.1 SD) with whom Absalom enters the scene.

11. *what time*] when.

12. *holy temple*] Absalom's reference is anachronistic, as God did not
permit David to build Him a temple, but rather gave that work to Solomon
(2 Samuel, 7:1–16; 1 Chron. 17:4–14).

13. *Wreak*] revenge.

14. *Bespeak him*] Speak to him.

15. *gravèd*] engraved.

16. *wot*] know.

18. *erst*] formerly.

21. *progeny*] descendants; family (*OED*, n., 1a).

Thou fair young man, whose hairs shine in mine eye
Like golden wires of David's ivory lute.
Absalom. Amnon, where be thy shearers and thy men,   25
That we may pour in plenty of thy vines,
And eat thy goats' milk, and rejoice with thee?
Amnon. Here cometh Amnon's shearers and his men.
Absalom, sit and rejoice with me.

Here enter a company of shepherds, and dance and sing.

Drink, Absalom, in praise of Israel.   30
Welcome to Amnon's fields from David's court.
Absalom. [*Stabbing* AMNON] Die with thy draught, perish and
die accursed,
Dishonour to the honour of us all!
Die for the villainy to Tamar done,
Unworthy thou to be King David's son.   35

Exit ABSALOM.

Jonadab. Oh, what hath Absalom for Tamar done?
Murdered his brother, great King David's son.
Adonijah. Run, Jonadab, away, and make it known
What cruelty this Absalom hath shown.

[*Exit* JONADAB.]

Amnon, thy brother Adonijah shall   40
Bury thy body among the dead men's bones,
And we will make complaint to Israel
Of Amnon's death and pride of Absalom.

Exeunt omnes.

---

23. eye] *QP, BL 1, 2, Bod, Tex, Il, H, Hv, Fol, NLS, VAM, WC, M (subst);*
ey *QHC.*   25. SH *Absalom*] *this edn; Abs. Q; Absalon. Hawkins (subst).*
28. SH *Amnon*] *this edn; Am. Q; Ammon. Hawkins (subst).*   30.] *Q begins
this line with SH Am.*   32. SH *Absalom*] *this edn; Abs. Q; Absalon. Hawkins
(subst).*   32. SD *Stabbing* AMNON] *Dyce 3 (subst); not in Q.*   35. King]
Hawkins (subst); Kings Q.   35. SD* ABSALOM] *this edn; Absa Q; Absalon.
Hawkins (subst).*   36. SH *Jonadab*] *Hawkins (subst); Ionad. Q.*   38. SH
Adonijah] *this edn; Adon. Q; Adonia. Hawkins (subst).*   39.1. SD *Exit*
JONADAB.] *this edn; not in Q.*   43.1. SD] *printed on 43, aligned right, in Q.*

---

26. *pour ... vines*] plentifully drink your wine.
35. *King*] Q's 'Kings' is not coherent as either plural or genitive.

[Sc. 8]

Enter DAVID *with* JOAB, ABISHAI, HUSHAI,
  with drum and ensign against Rabbah.

[*David.*] This is the town of the uncircumcised,
  The city of the kingdom; this is it,
  Rabbah, where wicked Hanun sitteth king.
  Dispoil this King, this Hanun, of his crown,
  Unpeople Rabbah and the streets thereof,   5
  For in their blood and slaughter of the slain
  Lieth the honour of King David's line.
  Joab, Abishai, and the rest of you,
  Fight ye this day for great Jerusalem!

      [*Enter* HANUN *and others on the walls.*]

Joab. And see where Hanun shows him on the walls.   10
  Why then do we forbear to give assault,
  That Israel may, as it is promisèd,
  Subdue the daughters of the gentiles' tribes?
  All this must be performed by David's hand.
David. Hark to me, Hanun, and remember well,   15

Heading Sc. 8] *Greg (subst); not in Q;* SCENE VII. *Bullen (subst);* ACT II.
SCENE III. *Morley (subst);* Act II. Scene IV. *Manly (subst);* vii *Rabkin
(subst).*   O.I. SD ABISHAI] *Q (Abyssus). Modernised silently throughout.*
1. SH *David] Hawkins (subst); not in Q.*   3. Hanun] *Q (*Hannon*).
Modernised silently throughout.*   8. Abishai] *Q (Abyshai). Modernised silently
throughout.*   9.1. SD *Enter* HANUN *and others on the walls.] Dyce 3; not in Q.*
15. SH *David] Hawkins (subst); Da. Q.*

  [*Sc. 8*] Fulfilling David's declaration at the conclusion of scene 6 that 'To
Rabbah marcheth David with his men / To chastise Ammon and the wicked
ones' (122–3), this scene is located before the walls of the city of Rabbah,
whose tower Joab and his soldiers captured in scene 2. The biblical account
narrates the capture of the tower and the siege and capture of the whole city
as one continuous sequence of events (2 Samuel, 12:26–31), occurring after
the death of David and Bathsheba's child and before the rape of Tamar.
Peele has arranged these three narrative strands in parallel fashion.
  2. *The city of the kingdom*] Both the Bishops' Bible and the Geneva Bible
use this phrase to describe Rabbah (2 Samuel, 12:26).
  10. *him*] himself.
  12. *as it is promisèd*] 2 Samuel, 3:18 states that 'the Lord hath spoken of
David, saying, By the hand of my servant David I will save my people Israel
out of the hands of the Philistims, and out of the hands of all their enemies'.

As sure as He doth live that kept my host
What time our young men by the pool of Gibeon
Went forth against the strength of Ishbosheth
And twelve to twelve did with their weapons play,
So sure art thou and thy men of war   20
To feel the sword of Israel this day
Because thou hast defièd Jacob's God
And suffered Rabbah with the Philistine
To rail upon the tribe of Benjamin.

Hanun. Hark, man, as sure as Saul thy master fell   25
And gored his sides upon the mountain tops
And Jonathan, Abinadab, and Malchishua
Watered the dales and deeps of Ashkelon
With bloody streams that from Gilboa ran
In channels through the wilderness of Ziph   30
What time the sword of the uncircumcised
Was drunken with the blood of Israel,
So sure shall David perish with his men
Under the walls of Rabbah, Hanun's town.

---

16. He] *Dyce 3 (subst);* he *Q.*   23. Philistine] *Hawkins (subst);* Philistime *Q.*
27. Malchishua] *Q* (Melchisua).   31. uncircumcised] *Hawkins (subst);*
vncircumsed *Q.*

17–19.] The incident to which David alludes in these lines is recounted
in 2 Samuel, 2:12–16.

17. *What time*] when.

18. *Ishbosheth*] son of Saul and, after Saul's death in battle, King of Israel
for two years until assassinated in his bed (2 Samuel, 2:10, 4:6–7). During
Ishbosheth's short reign David was King of Judah (2 Samuel, 2:4). After
Ishbosheth's assassination David became King of Israel as well as Judah (2
Samuel, 5:3–5).

19.] In the biblical account, the forces of Ishbosheth and David encounter
each other on opposite sides of the pool of Gibeon. Their respective generals,
Abner and Joab, send twelve of their men out to fight each other, '[a]nd
every one caught his fellow by the head and thrust his sword in his fellow's
side, so they fell down together' (2 Samuel, 2:16).

23. *Philistine*] Q's 'Philistime' may not be a typographical error, as the
Geneva Bible uses 'Philistim' or 'Philistims' for Philistines, which is the
spelling in the Bishops' Bible. See note to line 12.

24. *Benjamin*] the youngest of Jacob's twelve sons; the tribe of Benjamin
was closely associated with the tribe of Judah (Browning, 35).

25–32.] 1 Samuel, 31:1–6 recounts the Philistines' defeat of the Israelites
on Mount Gilboa, during which Saul and three of his sons, Jonathan,
Abinadab, and Malchishua, die.

32. *Was drunken with*] was awash with.

Joab. Hanun, the God of Israel hath said,   35
     David the King shall wear that crown of thine
     That weighs a talent of the finest gold
     And triumph in the spoil of Hanun's town
     When Israel shall hale thy people hence
     And turn them to the tile-kiln, man and child,   40
     And put them under harrows made of iron,
     And hew their bones with axes, and their limbs
     With iron swords divide and tear in twain.
     Hanun, this shall be done to thee and thine
     Because thou hast defièd Israel.   45
     To arms, to arms, that Rabbah feel revenge
     And Hanun's town become King David's spoil!

                     Alarm, excursions, assault.

                                        Exeunt omnes.

40. tile-kiln] *Q* (tile-kill*).*   47.2. SD] *this edn; follows 47.1 SD without a line break in Q.*

---

37. *talent*] an ancient unit of weight ranging from 50 to 90 lb (*OED*, n., 1a). Hanun's crown is described as weighing a talent of gold in 2 Samuel, 12:30. The Geneva marginal gloss to 1 Chronicles, 20:2 defines a talent of gold as 'the value of seven thousand and seventy crowns, which is about threescore pound weight'.

38. *spoil*] despoiling, ravaging; spoils of war.

39. *hale*] drag, forcibly remove.

40–3.] The Bishops' version of 2 Samuel, 12:31 describes David's slaughter of the inhabitants of Rabbah as follows: 'And he carried away the people that was therein, and put them under saws, and under iron harrows, and under axes of iron, and thrust them into the tile-kiln.' Peele turns this description into a threat, uttered by the hard-nosed Joab rather than by David himself, perhaps in order to maintain the play's characterisation of David as a king reluctant to involve himself directly in the shedding of blood. The killing methods described in these lines – incineration, ploughing bodies into the earth, and dismemberment – suggest a genocidal desire not only to inflict pain upon but also utterly to annihilate the Ammonites.

40. *tile-kiln*] brick oven, oven used to cremate the conquered enemy.

41. *harrows*] 'heavy frame of timber (or iron) set with iron teeth or tines, which is dragged over ploughed land to break clods, pulverize and stir the soil, root up weeds, or cover in the seed' (*OED*, n., 1a).

47.1–2. SD] The sequence of actions indicated by this stage direction begins with the sound of drum or trumpet ('*Alarm*') to signal the onset of attack by Joab's soldiers on the tiring-house façade representing the tower, followed by the entrance of Hanun's soldiers from the façade on to the stage to repulse the attack ('*excursions*'), and culminating in Joab's soldiers' final attack on the façade ('*assault*') and exit offstage into the tower through the façade's doors ('*Exeunt omnes*').

[Sc. 9]

> [*Trumpets*] *and* [*enter*] DAVID *with* HANUN'*s crown*[,
> *with* JOAB, ABISHAI, *and soldiers*].

David. Now clattering arms and wrathful storms of war
    Have thundered over Rabbah's racèd towers,
    The wreakful ire of great Jehovah's arm
    That for His people made the gates to rend
    And clothed the cherubim in fiery coats   5
    To fight against the wicked Hanun's town.
    Pay thanks, ye men of Judah, to the King,
    The God of Zion and Jerusalem,
    That hath exalted Israel to this
    And crownèd David with this diadem!   10
Joab. Beauteous and bright is he among the tribes.
    As when the sun attired in glist'ring robe

Heading Sc. 9] *Greg (subst); not in Q.*   o.1. SD] *Hawkins (subst); follows*
8.47.1 SD without a line break in Q.   Trumpets] *this edn; Then the trumpets,*
Q.   enter] *Dyce 3 (subst); not in Q.*   , *with* JOAB, ABISHAI, and *soldiers*] *this*
edn; not in Q.   1. SH David] *Hawkins (subst); Dau. Q.*   4. His] *this edn;*
his *Q.*   7. King] *Q (subst).*

[*Sc. 9*] This scene can be plausibly located in David's palace in Jerusalem
after Rabbah has been taken by the Israelites. The opening trumpets herald
David's triumphant return to his city and to the throne that, wearing Hanun's
crown, he ascends shortly after his entrance. David's concluding command
to 'you men of Israel' (140) to 'Depart with me' (140) and 'ransack Ammon's
richest treasuries' (142) indicates that David will be leaving Jerusalem again
to spoil the rest of the Ammonites' territories (as 2 Samuel, 12:31 states that
he does *before* returning to Jerusalem), leaving Jerusalem free from the royal
presence that might check the plans that Absalom declares in lines 145–58
to usurp David's authority.

    2. *racèd*] levelled to the ground, demolished, razed (*OED*, race, v.2, 4).

    3. *wreakful*] revengeful.

    4. *made ... rend*] tore apart the gates.

    5. *cherubim*] angels. See note to Prologue 8. The biblical narrative does
not record the presence of any angels at the siege of Rabbah. See 2 Samuel,
12:29–21.

    10. *diadem*] crown.

    11–15.] Dyce observes that these lines echo *The Faerie Queene*, 1.5.2.1–5:
'At last the golden Orientall gate / Of greatest heauen gan to open faire, /
And *Phoebus* fresh, as bridegrome to his mate, came dauncing forth, shaking
his deawie haire: / And hurld his glistring beames through gloomy aire.'

Comes dancing from his oriental gate
And bridegroom-like hurls through the gloomy air
His radiant beams, such doth King David show,   15
Crowned with the honour of his enemy's town.
Shining in riches like the firmament,
The starry vault that overhangs the earth,
So looketh David King of Israel.
Abishai. Joab, why doth not David mount his throne,   20
Whom heaven hath beautified with Hanun's crown?

[DAVID *ascends his throne wearing* HANUN's *crown.*]

Sound trumpets, shawms, and instruments of praise
To Jacob's God for David's victory!

Enter JONADAB.

Jonadab. Why doth the King of Israel rejoice,
Why sitteth David crowned with Rabbah's rule?   25
Behold, there hath great heaviness befall'n
In Amnon's fields by Absalom's misdeed,

21.1. SD] *this edn; not in* Q.

13. *oriental*] eastern.
17. *firmament*] heavens.
21.1. SD throne] a moveable stage property on a dais, perhaps canopied
(Gurr, *Shakespearean Stage*, 149).
22–3.] See note to 6.98–100.
23.1. SD *JONADAB*] Daniel in Bullen suggests that Jonadab's entrance
should be delayed and that 'the first speech given to him here should be
delivered by a messenger', presumably because when he fled the bloody
sheep-shearing feast in scene 7 he knew that at least one of David's sons,
Adonijah, was still alive, and it therefore does not seem to make sense either
that he should announce the slaughter of all of David's sons in lines 24 to 31
or that seven lines later he should blatantly contradict this announcement.
Moreover, in the biblical narrative the source of the initial bad news is
unspecified (2 Samuel, 13:30), while Jonadab is the one to announce that
only Amnon has been killed (2 Samuel, 13:32–3). If, however, Jonadab flees
the feast immediately after Adonijah commands him to 'Run, Jonadab, away,
and make it known / What cruelty this Absalom hath shown' (7.38–9), his
first speech might reflect his ignorance concerning the outcome of the slaughter that was still ongoing when he exited scene 7. His subsequent declaration
that 'In Israel is left of David's seed!' (38) would then logically express his
joy and relief as he observes the entrance of Adonijah and David's other sons.
27. *Absalom's misdeed*] i.e. his slaying of his brother in scene 7.

And Amnon's shearers and their feast of mirth
Absalom hath overturnèd with his sword,
Nor liveth any of King David's sons   30
To bring this bitter tidings to the King.
David. Ay me, how soon are David's triumphs dashed,
How suddenly declineth David's pride!
As doth the daylight settle in the west,
So dim is David's glory and his gite.   35
Die, David, for to thee is left no seed
That may revive thy name in Israel.
Jonadab. In Israel is left of David's seed!

Enter ADONIJAH *with other sons.*

Comfort your lord, you servants of the King.—
Behold, thy sons return in mourning weeds,   40
And only Amnon Absalom hath slain.
David. Welcome, my sons; dearer to me you are
Than is this golden crown or Hanun's spoil.
Oh, tell me, then, tell me, my sons, I say,
How cometh it to pass that Absalom   45
Hath slain his brother Amnon with the sword?
Adonijah. Thy sons, O King, went up to Amnon's fields
To feast with him and eat his bread and oil,
And Absalom upon his mule doth come,
And to his men he saith, 'When Amnon's heart   50
Is merry and secure, then strike him dead,
Because he forcèd Tamar shamefully,

---

29. Absalom] *Q (Absalon). Modernised silently throughout.* 38. SH *Jonadab*]
Hawkins (subst); Iona. Q. 42. SH *David*] *Hawkins (subst); Da. Q.*
43. Than] *Hawkins (subst); Then Q.* 47. SH *Adonijah*] *this edn; Ado. Q;
Adonia. Hawkins (subst).*

35. *gite*] dress or gown; *fig.* splendour, magnificence. *OED,* gite / gide,
n. provides the literal definition, then specifies Peele's figurative use of the
word using as examples this line and line 456 of Peele's *The Tale of Troy,*
'Done is thy pride, dim is thy glorious gite'.
36–7.] Although Absalom is still alive, David here may be anticipating his
banishment.
38.] As Amnon's dear friend, Jonadab reacts incredulously to what David
has just said.

And hated her, and threw her forth his doors'.
And this did he, and they with him conspire
And kill thy son in wreak of Tamar's wrong.   55
David. How long shall Judah and Jerusalem
Complain and water Zion with their tears?
How long shall Israel lament in vain,
And not a man among the mighty ones
Will hear the sorrows of King David's heart?   60
Amnon, thy life was pleasing to thy lord
As to mine ears the music of my lute
Or songs that David tuneth to his harp,
And Absalom hath ta'en from me away
The gladness of my sad distressèd soul.   65

                                        Exeunt omnes.

DAVID [*remains*]. *Enter* Widow of Tekoa.

---

61. lord] *this edn;* Lord *Q.* 64. ta'en] *Hawkins (subst);* tane *Q.* 65.1. SD] *printed on 65, aligned right, in Q.* 65.2. SD DAVID remains] *this edn; Manet Dauid Q.* Tekoa] *Q (Thecoa). Modernised silently throughout.*

---

55. *wreak*] revenge.
56–8.] These lines recall Psalm 80:4, 'O Lord God of hosts, how long wilt thou be angry against the prayer of thy people?'
61. *to thy Lord*] i.e. to me, David.
65.2. SD] Daniel in Bullen suggests that 'One or more scenes are wanting here; the loss deprives the scene with the "Widow" of all motive: David has not banished Absalon nor taken any course to revenge the death of Amnon' (44). Peele's dramatic compression of events here does strain temporal logic in so far as it provides Joab with implausibly little time to locate and instruct the widow. Yet the play need not show us David banishing Absalom: Absalom has fled, in effect banishing himself, and it might be to this self-banishment that the widow refers in line 97. The biblical narrative, in fact, does not explicitly state that David banishes Absalom. The lack of motivation that Daniel takes as evidence of the loss or abridgement of scenes in the play, then, is already there in the play's source and is merely accentuated by the undeniably extreme or, in Blistein's words, 'injudicious' (181) dramatic compression of time. In the biblical narrative, three years elapse between David being informed of Absalom's revenge and flight and the incident with the Widow of Tekoa (2 Samuel, 13:38, 14).
Tekoa] 'town in the tribe of Judah (2 Chr. xi. 6), on the range of hills which rise near Hebron, and stretch eastward towards the Dead Sea' (Smith, 680).

Widow. [*Kneels*] God save King David, King of Israel,
    And bless the gates of Zion for his sake!
David. Woman, why mournest thou? Rise from the earth;
    Tell me what sorrow hath befall'n thy soul.
Widow. [*Rises*] Thy servant's soul, O King, is troubled sore,   70
    And grievous is the anguish of her heart,
    And from Tekoa doth thy handmaid come.
David. Tell me and say, thou woman of Tekoa,
    What aileth thee or what is come to pass.
Widow. Thy servant is a widow in Tekoa.   75
    Two sons thy handmaid had, and they, my lord,
    Fought in the field, where no man went betwixt,
    And so the one did smite and slay the other.
    And lo, behold, the kindred doth arise
    And cry on him that smote his brother,   80
    That he therefore may be the child of death,
    'For we will follow and destroy the heir'.
    So will they quench that sparkle that is left
    And leave nor name nor issue on the earth
    To me or to thy handmaid's husband dead.   85
David. Woman, return, go home unto thy house.
    I will take order that thy son be safe;
    If any man say otherwise than well,

66. SD *Kneels*] *Dyce 3 (subst); not in Q.* 68. SH *David*] *Hawkins (subst);*
Dau. Q. 70. SD *Rises*] *Dyce 3 (subst); not in Q.* 71. grievous] *Hawkins*
(subst); greenous *Q.* 76. they, my lord,] *Hawkins (subst);* they (my lord)
Q. 88. than] *Hawkins (subst);* then *Q.*

66–144.] These lines closely follow the narrative and language of 2
Samuel, 14. In the biblical account, however, Joab must go to Geshur to
fetch Absalom (23), and Absalom remains in Jerusalm for two years before
he is allowed to see David (28). Peele omits mention of Absalom's burning
of Joab's fields in order to get his attention and prompt him to intercede with
David on Absalom's behalf (29–32) and compresses the remaining incidents
into one continuous event.
    77.] i.e. fought in a field, where no one separated them; or, fought on the
battlefield, where there was no safe ground between the two armies.
    78. *the one ... the other*] i.e. one of the brothers slew the other. See 2
Samuel, 14:6, 'the one smote the other and slew him'.
    81. *may be ... death*] i.e. may be put to death.
    83. *that sparkle*] the spark of life.
    84. *nor name*] neither name.
    85. *husband dead*] dead husband.
    87. *take order*] give orders.
    88.] i.e. If any man disagree.

Bring him to me and I shall chastise him,
For, as the Lord doth live, shall not a hair   90
Shed from thy son or fall upon the earth.
Woman, to God alone belongs revenge.
Shall then the kindred slay him for his sin?
Widow. Well hath King David to his handmaid spoke,
But wherefore then hast thou determinèd   95
So hard a part against the righteous tribes
To follow and pursue the banishèd,
Whenas to God alone belongs revenge?
Assuredly thou sayst against thyself.
Therefore call home again the banishèd,   100
Call home the banishèd, that he may live
And raise to thee some fruit in Israel.
David. Thou woman of Tekoa, answer me,
Answer me one thing I shall ask of thee:
Is not the hand of Joab in this work?   105
Tell me, is not his finger in this fact?
Widow. It is, my lord, his hand is in this work.
Assure thee, Joab, captain of thy host,
Hath put these words into thy handmaid's mouth,
And thou art as an angel from on high   110
To understand the meaning of my heart.
Lo where he cometh to his lord the King.

Enter JOAB.

David. Say, Joab, didst thou send this woman in
To put this parable for Absalom?

---

90. Lord] *Q (subst)*.   103. SH *David*] *Hawkins (subst); Da. Q.*   107. SH
Widow] *Hawkins (subst);Wid. Q.*

92. *to God ... revenge*] 'Vengeance and recompense are mine', God
declares in Deuteronomy, 32:35.
97. *the banishèd*] Absalom. Neither the biblical narrative nor the play
represents David banishing Absalom, but Peele here follows his biblical
source, in which the Widow of Tekoa refers to Absalom as 'banishèd' (2
Samuel, 14:13).
106. *fact*] deed.
108–9.] See 2 Samuel, 14:19, 'thy servant Joab bade me, and he put all
these words in the mouth of thine handmaid'.
114.] i.e. To offer this implied comparison on behalf of Absalom, in order
to urge David to forgive him for murdering his brother Amnon.

Joab. Joab, my lord, did bid this woman speak,   115
　　　And she hath said, and thou hast understood.
David. I have, and am content to do the thing.
　　　Go fetch my son, that he may live with me.

　　　　　　　　JOAB *kneels.*

Joab. Now God be blessèd for King David's life!
　　　Thy servant Joab hath found grace with thee   120
　　　In that thou sparest Absalom thy child.
　　　A beautiful and fair young man is he;
　　　In all his body is no blemish seen.
　　　His hair is like the wire of David's harp
　　　That twines about his bright and ivory neck.   125
　　　In Israel is not such a goodly man,
　　　And here I bring him to entreat for grace.
　　　　　　　　　　　　[JOAB *rises and exits.*]

　　　　　　Enter ABSALOM *with* JOAB.

David. Hast thou slain in the fields of Hazor—
　　　Ah, Absalom my son! Ah, my son Absalom!
　　　But wherefore do I vex thy spirit so?   130
　　　Live, and return from Geshur to thy house,
　　　Return from Geshur to Jerusalem.
　　　What boots it to be bitter to thy soul?

118.1. SD] *aligned right in Q.*   127. SD JOAB *rises and exits.*] *this edn; not in Q.*

122–3.] According to 2 Samuel, 14:25, 'Now in all Israel there was none to be so much praised for beauty as Absalom: from the sole of his foot even to the top of his head there was no blemish in him'.
　129.] The line anticipates David's lament over Absalom in 2 Samuel, 18:33, 'O my son Absalom, my son, my son Absalom: would God I had died for thee, O Absalom, my son, my son.' The text was set by Thomas Tomkins (1572–1656) in his 'When David heard that Absalom was slain', one of the most exquisitely moving *a capella* choral compositions of the English Renaissance.
　130. *wherefore*] why.
　131. *Geshur*] 'principality in the north-eastern corner of Bashan, adjoining the province of Argob (Deut. iii. 14) and the kingdom of Aram' (Smith, 208). Absalom was the grandson of the king of Geshur (2 Samuel, 3.3).
　133. *boots it*] use is it.

Amnon is dead, and Absalom survives.
Absalom. Father, I have offended Israel,   135
    I have offended David and his house.
    For Tamar's wrong hath Absalom misdone,
    But David's heart is free from sharp revenge,
    And Joab hath got grace for Absalom.
David. Depart with me, you men of Israel,   140
    You that have followed Rabbah with the sword,
    And ransack Ammon's richest treasuries.
    Live, Absalom my son, live once in peace;
    Peace with thee and with Jerusalem!
                             Exeunt omnes.

ABSALOM [*remains*].

Absalom. David is gone, and Absalom remains,   145
    Flowering in pleasant springtime of his youth.
    Why liveth Absalom and is not honoured
    Of tribes and elders and the mightiest ones,
    That round about his temples he may wear
    Garlands and wreaths set on with reverence,   150
    That everyone that hath a cause to plead
    Might come to Absalom and call for right?
    Then in the gates of Zion would I sit
    And publish laws in great Jerusalem,
    And not a man should live in all the land   155
    But Absalom would do him reason's due.
    Therefore I shall address me as I may
    To love the men and tribes of Israel.   *Exit.*

---

135. SH *Absalom*] *this edn; Abs. Q; Absalon. Hawkins (subst).* 144.2. SD
ABSALOM [*remains*].] *this edn; Manet Absolon. Q.* 145. SH *Absalom*] *this
edn; Abs. Q; Absalon. Hawkins (subst).* 158. SD] *printed on 158.1, aligned
right, in Q.*

137.] Absalom has avenged the wrong done to Tamar.
144. *Peace with thee*] May peace be with you.
154. *publish*] proclaim.
156. *do ... due*] deal justly and reasonably with him.
157. *address me*] undertake.

[Sc. 10]

Enter DAVID, ITTAI, ZADOK, AHIMAAZ, JONATHAN,
with others, DAVID *barefoot with some loose covering*
over his head, and all mourning.

David. Proud Lust, the bloodiest traitor to our souls,
    Whose greedy throat nor earth, air, sea, or heaven
    Can glut or satisfy with any store,
    Thou art the cause these torments suck my blood,
    Piercing with venom of thy poisoned eyes   5
    The strength and marrow of my tainted bones.
    To punish Pharaoh and his cursèd host
    The waters shrank at great Adonai's voice,
    And sandy bottom of the sea appeared,
    Offering his service at His servant's feet;   10

Heading Sc. 10] *Greg (subst); not in Q;* SCENE VIII. *Bullen (subst);*
ACT III. SCENE I. *Morley (subst);* Act II. Scene V. *Manly (subst);* viii
Rabkin (subst). 0.1. SD ITTAI] *Q (Ithay). Modernised silently throughout.*
ZADOK] *Q (Sadoc). Modernised silently throughout.* AHIMAAZ] *Q (Ahimaas).*
Modernised silently throughout. *loose*] *Q (lose).* 1. SH *David*] *Hawkins*
(subst); Dau. Q. 8. shrank] *this edn;* shrinke *Q;* shrunk *Hawkins (subst).*
10. His] *this edn;* his *Q.*

[*Sc. 10*] Located on the Mount of Olives, 'a hill about 1.6 km. (1 mile)
long to the east of Jerusalem, separated from it by the Kidron valley'
(Browning, 272). David has fled to the Mount of Olives from Jerusalem
because of Absalom's rebellion. The scene is based on 2 Samuel, 15:14–37,
but Peele shapes the biblical account into a moment of intense dejection
for David. David and his companions prostrate themselves at line 19 of the
scene; although his companions gradually stand up as the scene progresses,
David remains lying down and does not arise, despite exhortations from his
companions, until the end of the scene 115 lines later.
    0.1–3. SD] This stage direction derives from 2 Samuel, 15:30, 'And
David went up the Mount of Olives and wept as he went up, and had his
head covered, and went barefooted: and all the people that was with him,
had every man his head covered, and as they went up, they wept'.
    2. *nor earth*] neither earth.
    3. *glut*] fill completely, satisfy greedily, indulge to excess (*OED*, v.1).
    7–10.] Exodus, 14:21–2 relates Moses' parting of the Red Sea in order to
allow the children of Israel to escape Pharaoh and the Egyptians.
    8. *shrank*] Q's 'shrinke' functions as the past tense here.
    Adonai's] God's.
    10.] i.e. obligingly presenting a dry crossing for the feet of Moses, the
Lord's servant.

And, to inflict a plague on David's sin,
He makes his bowels traitors to his breast,
Winding about his heart with mortal gripes.
Ah, Absalom, the wrath of heaven inflames
Thy scorchèd bosom with ambitious heat,   15
And Satan sets thee on a lusty tower,
Showing thy thoughts the pride of Israel
Of choice to cast thee on her ruthless stones.
Weep with me, then, ye sons of Israel!

He lies down, and all the rest after him.

Lie down with David, and with David mourn   20
Before the Holy One that sees our hearts;
Season this heavy soil with showers of tears,
And fill the face of every flower with dew.
Weep, Israel, for David's soul dissolves,
Lading the fountains of his drownèd eyes,   25
And pours her substance on the senseless earth.
Zadok. Weep, Israel, oh, weep for David's soul,
Strewing the ground with hair and garments torn
For tragic witness of your hearty woes!

---

21. One] *Dyce 3 (subst)*; one Q.

---

12. *bowels*] children. '[T]hine own bowels which do call thee sire' (3.1.29), the Duke tells Claudio in *Measure for Measure*, 'Do curse the gout, serpigo, and the rheum / For ending thee no sooner' (31–2).

13. *gripes*] grasps, clutches (*OED*, n.1).

16–18.] These lines recall Satan's temptation of Christ in Matthew, 4:5–11, in which Satan first sets Jesus on a 'pinnacle of the temple' (5) in Jerusalem and bids him 'cast thyself down: for it is written, that he will give his angels charge over thee, and with their hands they shall lift thee up, lest at any time thou shouldest dash thy foot against a stone' (6). Satan then 'took him [Jesus] up into an exceeding high mountain, and showed him all the kingdoms of the world, and the glory of them, / And said to him, All these will I give thee, if thou wilt fall down, and worship me' (8–9).

16. *lusty*] mighty. Peele elsewhere uses 'lusty' as a simple (and positive) adjective to describe inanimate objects: 'Her lusty mantle waving in the wind' (*The Arraignment of Paris*, 1.3.122), for example. Marlowe's Doctor Faustus uses the adjective to describe a place in his declaration that he wants to 'conjure in some lusty grove' (*Doctor Faustus, A-Text*, 1.1.153).

25. *Lading*] drawing or scooping liquid from, emptying (*OED*, lade, v., 5a, 6).

27, 30.] Zadok is a high priest; Ahimaaz is his son.

Ahimaaz. Oh, would our eyes were conduits to our hearts   30
  And that our hearts were seas of liquid blood
  To pour in streams upon this holy mount
  For witness we would die for David's woes!
Jonadab. Then should this Mount of Olives seem a plain
  Drowned with a sea that with our sighs should roar   35
  And in the murmur of his mounting waves
  Report our bleeding sorrows to the heavens
  For witness we would die for David's woes.
Ittai. Earth cannot weep enough for David's woes.
  Then weep, you heavens, and, all you clouds, dissolve,   40
  That piteous stars may see our miseries
  And drop their golden tears upon the ground
  For witness how they weep for David's woes!
Zadok. Now let my sovereign raise his prostrate bones
  And mourn not as a faithless man would do,   45
  But be assured that Jacob's righteous God,
  That promised never to forsake your throne,
  Will still be just and pure in His vows.

[*All but* DAVID *rise.*]

David. Zadok, high priest, preserver of the ark,
  Whose sacred virtue keeps the chosen crown,   50
  I know my God is spotless in His vows
  And that these hairs shall greet my grave in peace,

---

34. SH *Jonadab*] *Hawkins (subst); Iona. Q.*   39. SH *Ittai*] *this edn; Ith. Q;
Ithay. Hawkins (subst).*   48. His] *this edn;* his *Q.*   48.1. SD *All but* DAVID
rise.] *this edn; not in Q.*   49. SH *David*] *Hawkins (subst); Da. Q.*   51. His]
this edn; his *Q.*

34. *Mount of Olives*] See headnote to this scene.
47.] At the beginning of David's reign over Israel, God promises David
that 'thine house shall be stablished and thy kingdom forever before thee,
even thy throne shall be stablished forever' (2 Samuel, 7:16).
49. *the ark*] the ark of the covenant, a sacred chest in which were contained the stone tables God gave to Moses on Mount Sinai, on which were
written the Ten Commandments. See notes to Prologue 8 and 4.162.
50. *keeps*] guards.
51.] I know that God honours all vows made in purity of heart.
52. *these hairs*] i.e. my body.
shall ... peace] In 2 Samuel, 7.10–11 God promises David that 'I will give
thee rest from all thine enemies' and 'when thy days be fulfilled, thou shalt
sleep with thy fathers'.

But that my son should wrong his tendered soul
And fight against his father's happiness
Turns all my hopes into despair of him,   55
And that despair feeds all my veins with grief.
Ittai. Think of it, David, as a fatal plague,
    Which grief preserveth but preventeth not,
    And turn thy drooping eyes upon the troops
    That, of affection to thy worthiness,   60
    Do swarm about the person of the King.
    Cherish their valours and their zealous loves
    With pleasant looks and sweet encouragements.
David. Methinks the voice of Ittai fills mine ears.
Ittai. Let not the voice of Ittai loathe thine ears,   65
    Whose heart would balm thy bosom with his tears.
David. But wherefore go'st thou to the wars with us?
    Thou art a stranger here in Israel
    And son to Achish mighty King of Gath;
    Therefore return, and with thy father stay.   70
    Thou cam'st but yesterday, and should I now
    Let thee partake these troubles here with us?
    Keep both thyself and all thy soldiers safe;
    Let me abide the hazards of these arms,
    And God requite the friendship thou hast showed.   75
Ittai. As sure as Israel's God gives David life,
    What place or peril shall contain the King,
    The same will Ittai share in life and death.

---

64. SH *David*] *Hawkins (subst); Da. Q.*   65. SH *Ittai*] *this edn; Ith. Q;*
Ithay. Hawkins (subst).   69. Achish] *Q (Achis).*   76. SH *Ittai*] *this edn;*
Ith. Q; Ithay. Hawkins (subst).

---

53. *tendered*] cherished, loved (*OED*, tender, v.2).
57–8.] i.e. grief does not remedy or cure despair but rather maintains or
lengthens it.
60. *of*] out of.
65. *loathe*] be loathsome to.
66. *Whose*] he (Ittai) whose.
balm] soothe, heal.
69. *King of Gath*] David found refuge with Achish King of Gath while
being pursued by Saul (1 Samuel, 27:1).
72. *partake*] partake of.
74. *abide*] undergo, suffer.

David. Then, gentle Ittai, be thou still with us,
   A joy to David and a grace to Israel.   80
   Go, Zadok, now, and bear the ark of God
   Into the great Jerusalem again.
   If I find favour in His gracious eyes,
   Then will He lay His hand upon my heart
   Yet once again before I visit death,   85
   Giving it strength and virtue to mine eyes
   To taste the comforts and behold the form
   Of His fair ark and holy tabernacle.
   But if He say, 'My wonted love is worn,
   And I have no delight in David now,'   90
   Here lie I armèd with an humble heart
   T'embrace the pains that anger shall impose,
   And kiss the sword my Lord shall kill me with.
   Then, Zadok, take Ahimaaz thy son
   With Jonathan, son to Abiathar,   95
   And in these fields will I repose myself
   Till they return from you some certain news.
Zadok. Thy servants will with joy obey the King
   And hope to cheer his heart with happy news.
           Exit ZADOK, AHIMAAZ, *and* JONATHAN.
Ittai. Now that it be no grief unto the King,   100
   Let me for good inform His Majesty
   That with unkind and graceless Absalom
   Ahithophel, your ancient counsellor,
   Directs the state of this rebellion.

---

79. SH *David*] *Hawkins (subst); Da. Q.* 83. His] *this edn;* his *Q.*
84. He] *this edn;* he *Q.* His] *this edn;* his *Q.* 88. His] *this edn;* his *Q.*
89. He] *this edn;* he *Q.* 93. Lord] *this edn;* lord *Q.* 100. SH *Ittai*] *this
edn; Ith. Q; Ithay. Hawkins (subst).* 103. Ahithophel] *Q (*Achitophel*).*
Modernised silently throughout.

   79. *still*] continually.
   89. *wonted*] accustomed, usual.
   94. *Ahimaaz*] pronounced as four syllables.
   95. *Abiathar*] high priest with Zadok (2 Samuel, 20:25).
   97.] until Ahimaaz and Jonathan bring back certain news from you.
   101. *for good*] with virtuous intent.
   102. *unkind*] unnatural, lawless (*OED*, kind, adj., 1a, 2a), and also unfeel-
ing, lacking in kindness (*OED*, unkind, adj., 6a).

David. Then doth it aim with danger at my crown.   105
    O Thou that holdst his raging bloody bound
    Within the circle of the silver moon,
    That girds earth's centre with his watery scarf,
    Limit the counsel of Ahithophel,
    No bounds extending to my soul's distress,   110
    But turn his wisdom into foolishness!

       Enter HUSHAI *with his coat turned and head covered.*

Hushai. Happiness and honour to my lord the King!
David. What happiness or honour may betide
    His state that toils in my extremities?
Hushai. Oh, let my gracious sovereign cease these griefs,   115
    Unless he wish his servant Hushai's death,
    Whose life depends upon my lord's relief.
    Then let my presence with my sighs perfume
    The pleasant closet of my sovereign's soul.

---

115. SH *Hushai*] *this edn; Cus. Q; Cusay. Hawkins (subst).*

106–7.] i.e. O Thou who places limits on natural disorder, preventing inferior natural elements such as the raging sea from overwhelming the heavenly elements beyond 'the circle' or orbit 'of the silver moon'. (Psalm 89:9 declares that God 'rulest the raging of the sea: when the waves thereof arise, thou stillest them'; see Manly, 458).

107. *circle*] orbit. In early modern astronomy all things within the circle or orbit of the moon, i.e. all things earthly, were subject to change and death, while the heavenly realms above the moon's circle were immutable.

108. *watery scarf*] the seas.

109–11.] David asks God to limit Ahithophel's counsel just as He restrains within their bounds the potentially destructive elements of the natural world, such as the sea, thus turning the natural imagery of 106–8 into political allegory.

110.] i.e. do not aggravate and extend my suffering.

111.1. SD turned] In the biblical account Hushai's coat is torn (2 Samuel, 15:32) not turned, but, as Blistein observes, Hushai's turned coat could be an anticipatory visual sign of the duplicitous mission to Absalom's court that David is about to command him to undertake (271).

head covered] In 2 Samuel, 15:32 Hushai enters 'having earth upon his head'.

113–14. *may … extremities*] i.e. can come to anyone who, like me, has to deal with the straitened circumstances we are encountering in my kingdom.

117. *relief*] happiness.

119. *closet*] private chamber.

David. No, Hushai, no. Thy presence unto me   120
  Will be a burden since I tender thee,
  And cannot break thy sighs for David's sake.
  But if thou turn to fair Jerusalem
  And say to Absalom, as thou hast been
  A trusty friend unto his father's seat,   125
  So thou wilt be to him and call him King,
  Ahithophel's counsel may be brought to naught.
  Then, having Zadok and Abiathar,
  All three may learn the secrets of my son,
  Sending the message by Ahimaaz   130
  And friendly Jonathan, who both are there.
[*Hushai.*] Then rise, referring the success to heaven.
David. [*Rises*] Hushai, I rise, though with unwieldy bones
  I carry arms against my Absalom.

                                                    Exeunt.

---

120. SH *David*] *Hawkins (subst); Da. Q.*   132. SH *Hushai*] *Hawkins (subst);*
last line of David's speech beginning at 120 in Q.   133. SH *David*] *Hawkins*
(subst); Da. Q.   133. SD *Rises*] *Bullen (subst); not in Q.*   134.1. SD] *printed*
on 134, aligned right, in Q.

121. *tender*] regard, cherish, love (*OED*, v.2, 3a, d).
122. *break*] interrupt, cause to cease. Hawkins, Dyce, Keltie, Morley,
Bullen, Thorndike, Manly, and Rabkin emend to 'brook', but Greg and
Blistein retain Q's 'breake', Blistein because 'David may be saying that he
cannot make Cusay [Hushai] "breake" (i.e. stop) sighing' (271).
123. *turn*] return.
124. *as*] just as.
125. *seat*] throne; *fig.* royal authority (*OED*, n., 8a, b).
128–9.] Then, since you have Zadok and Abiathar there with you, the
three of you may be able to learn what Absalom and Ahithophel are up to.
132. *referring … heaven*] i.e. appealing to heaven to assure success.

[Sc. II]

[*Enter*] ABSALOM, AMASA, AHITHOPHEL,
with the Concubines of David *and others, in great state.*
ABSALOM *crowned.*

Absalom. [*To the Concubines*] Now you that were my father's
    concubines,
Liquor to his unchaste and lustful fire,
Have seen his honour shaken in his house,
Which I possess in sight of all the world.
I bring ye forth for foils to my renown   5
And to eclipse the glory of your king,
Whose life is, with his honour, fast enclosed
Within the entrails of a jetty cloud,
Whose dissolution shall pour down in showers
The substance of his life and swelling pride.   10
Then shall the stars light earth with rich aspects,

Heading Sc. II] *Greg (subst); not in* Q; SCENE IX. *Bullen (subst);* ACT III.
SCENE II. *Morley (subst);* Act II. Scene VI. *Manly (subst);* ix *Rabkin (subst).*
0.1. SD *Enter*] *this edn; not in* Q.   1. SH *Absalom*] *this edn; Abs.* Q; *Absalon.*
Hawkins (subst).   1. *To the Concubines*] *this edn; not in* Q.

[*Sc. II*] Located in David's palace in Jerusalem, which Absalom has now
occupied. The scene dramatises events recounted in 2 Samuel, 16:15–17:16.
    0.1. SD *Concubines of David*] According to 2 Samuel, 15:16, when he fled
Jerusalem David 'left ten concubines to keep the house'.
    4. *in sight of all the world*] Absalom thus fulfills God's declaration, made
through the prophet Nathan, that 'I before thy face will take thy wives / And
give them to thy neighbour to possess. / This shall be done to David in the
day / That Israel openly may see thy shame' (6.51–4).
    5. *foils*] background material used to enhance the radiance of gems (*OED*,
n.1, 5a, b).
    9. *pour down*] dissolve.
    11–16.] Absalom's boasting is Tamburlainian in its hyperbole and cosmic
vocabulary. Tamburlaine vaunts to the conquered Bajazeth, for example,
that 'The chiefest god, first mover of that sphere / Enchased with thousands
ever-shining lamps, / Will sooner burn the glorious frame of heaven / Than
it should so conspire my overthrow' (*1 Tamburlaine*, 4.2.8–11).
    11. *light*] beam their light upon.
    aspects] looks, glances; in astrological terminology, the combined regards
of planets and other heavenly bodies upon human observers, upon whom
these regards exercise a good or bad influence depending upon the particular
combination (*OED*, n., 1b, 4). In Peele's *Edward I*, Lluellen declares, 'The
angry heavens frown on Britain's face / To eclipse the glory of fair Cambria,
/ With sore aspectes the dreadful planets lour' (16.1–3).

And heaven shall burn in love with Absalom,
Whose beauty will suffice to chase all mists
And clothe the sun's sphere with a triple fire
Sooner than his clear eyes should suffer stain   15
Or be offended with a louring day.
[*1 Concubine.*] Thy father's honour, graceless Absalom,
And ours thus beaten with thy violent arms,
Will cry for vengeance to the host of heaven,
Whose power is ever armed against the proud,   20
And will dart plagues at thy aspiring head
For doing this disgrace to David's throne.
[*2 Concubine.*] To David's throne, to David's holy throne,
Whose sceptre angels guard with swords of fire
And sit as eagles on his conquering fist,   25
Ready to prey upon his enemies.
Then think not thou, the captain of his foes,
Were thou much swifter than Asahel was,
That could outpace the nimble-footed roe,
To 'scape the fury of their thumping beaks   30
Or dreadful scope of their commanding wings.
Ahithophel. Let not my lord the King of Israel
Be angry with a silly woman's threats,
But, with the pleasure he hath erst enjoyed,

---

13. chase] *Hawkins (subst);* chast *Q.*   15. than] *Hawkins (subst);* then *Q.*
17. SH *1 Concubine*] *Hawkins (subst); Concub. Q.*   23. SH *2 Concubine*]
Hawkins (subst); 2. *Q.*   28. than] *Hawkins (subst);* then *Q.* Asahel] *Q*
(Azahell).   32. SH *Ahithophel*] *this edn; Achip. Q; Achitophel. Hawkins (subst).*

---

12. *burn in love with*] i.e. ardently love and approve of.
19. *host*] (a) large company of angels and (b) army.
23–6.] These lines continue the dependent clause with which the first
Concubine's speech concludes at line 22.
28. *Were thou*] even if you were.
Asahel] brother of Joab and Abishai.
29.] According to 2 Samuel, 2:18, 'Asahel was as light on foot as a wild
roe'.
30–1. *their ... their*] (referring to the eagle-like angels in lines 24–5).
33. *Be angry with*] be angered by.
34.] 2 Samuel, 16:21–2 relates that 'Ahithophel said unto Absalom, Go in
to thy father's concubines, which he hath left to keep the house ... So they
spread Absalom a tent upon the top of the house, and Absalom went in to his
father's concubines in the sight of all Israel.'
erst] heretofore.

Turn them into their cabinets again   35
Till David's conquest be their overthrow.
Absalom. Into your bowers, ye daughters of disdain,
  Gotten by fury of unbridled lust,
  And wash your couches with your mourning tears
  For grief that David's kingdom is decayed.   40
[*1 Concubine.*] No, Absalom, his kingdom is enchained
  Fast to the finger of great Jacob's God,
  Which will not loose it for a rebel's love.
                                              Exeunt [Concubines].
Amasa. If I might give advice unto the King,
  These concubines should buy their taunts with blood.   45
Absalom. Amasa, no, but let thy martial sword
  Empty the veins of David's armèd men,
  And let these foolish women 'scape our hands
  To recompense the shame they have sustained.

---

37. SH *Absalom*] *this edn; Abs. Q; Absalon. Hawkins (subst).*   41. SH *1
Concubine*] *Hawkins (subst); 1. Q.*   43. loose] *Q (*lose*).*   43.1. SD] *printed
on 43, aligned right, in Q.* Concubines] *Dyce 2 (subst); not in Q.*   46. SH
Absalom] *this edn; Abs. Q; Absalon. Hawkins (subst).*   47. veins] *Hawkins
(subst);* paines *Q.*

35. *cabinets*] private chambers; here, the seraglio, embodying the 'pleasure'
that David has heretofore 'enjoyed' (34) and that now is to be banished along
with the concubines.
36.] i.e. until the defeat of King David will also mean the end for the
concubines.
37. *daughters of disdain*] i.e. women deserving nothing but disdain.
38.] i.e. you whose presence here is the wild product of unrestrained lust
(with a suggestion too that they themselves were conceived in unbridled lust).
39. *wash your couches*] i.e. wet with your tears the soft beds on which you
practised your lust.
43. *loose*] modernises Q's 'lose' following Dyce, Keltie, Morley, Bullen,
Thorndike, and Rabkin. Hawkins, Manly, Greg, and Blistein retain the original
spelling, but the immediate context, in which 'lose' is set in opposition to 'enchained'
(41), suggests that the verb's primary meaning is to loose, set free, or untie.
47. *veins*] Hawkins, Dyce, Keltie, Morley, Bullen, Manly, and Thorndike
make this emendation of Q's 'pains'. As alternatives, Dyce 2 conjectures
'plains' (Rabkin adopts this conjecture) and Blistein 'panes', but the immediate context strongly favours 'veins': Absalom bids Amasa to 'let thy martial
sword / Empty the veins of David's armèd men' (46–7) as a substitute for the
'blood' (45) of the concubines.
48–9.] Absalom urges his general, Amasa, to let the concubines remain
unpunished as a way of showing that the sin of their transgressions was really
David's; they are only his kept women.

First, Absalom was by the trumpet's sound   50
Proclaimed through Hebron King of Israel,
And now is set in fair Jerusalem
With complete state and glory of a crown.
Fifty fair footmen by my chariot run,
And to the air, whose rupture rings my fame,   55
Where'er I ride they offer reverence.
Why should not Absalom, that in his face
Carries the final purpose of his God,
That is, to work him grace in Israel,
Endeavour to achieve with all his strength   60
The state that most may satisfy his joy,
Keeping His statutes and His covenants pure?
His thunder is entangled in my hair,
And with my beauty is His lightning quenched;
I am the man He made to glory in   65
When, by the errors of my father's sin,
He lost the path that led into the land
Wherewith our chosen ancestors were blessed.

Enter HUSHAI.

Hushai. Long may the beauteous King of Israel live,
To whom the people do by thousands swarm!   70
Absalom. What meaneth Hushai so to greet his foe?
Is this the love thou showedst to David's soul,

---

62. His statutes] *this edn;* his statutes *Q.* His covenants] *this edn;* his
couenants *Q.* 64. His] *this edn;* his *Q.* 65. He] *this edn;* he *Q.* 69. SH
Hushai] *this edn; Cus. Q; Cusay. Hawkins (subst).* 71. SH *Absalom*] *this
edn; Abs. Q; Absalon. Hawkins (subst).*

50–6.] These lines summarise the onset of Absalom's rebellion, recounted
in 2 Samuel, 15:1–12.

53. *complete*] Stressed on the first syllable.
state] regal splendour (*OED*, n., 16).

55. *whose ... fame*] i.e. the clamorous rupturing sound of which (shouting,
trumpets, etc.) sings aloud my fame.

57–8. *in his face ... God*] i.e. in his handsome countenance, the beauty of
which signifies his being chosen the instrument of God's will.

59. *to ... Israel*] i.e. to fulfill God's purpose and glorify Israel.

64.] i.e. heaven's lightning is virtually extinguished by my dazzling beauty.
quenched] controlled.

67. *He*] David.

To whose assistance thou hast vowed thy life?
Why leav'st thou him in this extremity?
Hushai. Because the Lord and Israel chooseth thee,   75
And, as before I served thy father's turn
With counsel acceptable in his sight,
So likewise will I now obey his son.
Absalom. Then welcome, Hushai, to King Absalom!
And now, my lords and loving counsellors,   80
I think it time to exercise our arms
Against forsaken David and his host.
Give counsel first, my good Ahithophel,
What times and orders we may best observe
For prosperous manage of these high exploits.   85
Ahithophel. Let me choose out twelve thousand valiant men,
And, while the night hides with her sable mists
The close endeavours cunning soldiers use,
I will assault thy discontented sire,
And, while with weakness of their weary arms,   90
Surcharged with toil to shun thy sudden power,
The people fly in huge disordered troops
To save their lives and leave the King alone,
Then will I smite him with his latest wound
And bring the people to thy feet in peace.   95
Absalom. Well hath Ahithophel given his advice.

75. SH *Hushai*] *this edn; Cus. Q; Cusay. Hawkins (subst).*   79. SH *Absalom*]
this edn; Abs. Q; Absalon. Hawkins (subst).   86. SH *Ahithophel*] *this edn;
Achi. Q; Achitophel. Hawkins (subst).*   87. and, while] *Hawkins (subst);* and
(while *Q.*   88. use,] *Hawkins (subst);* vse) *Q.*   96. SH *Absalom*] *this edn;
Abs. Q; Absalon. Hawkins (subst).*

78. *his son*] Absalom. Hushai argues: if I ever owed obedience to King
David, does it not follow that I owe obedience to his son Absalom? Thus
dealing sophistically with the fact that Absalom is now in rebellion against
his father David.
82. *forsaken*] i.e. forsaken by God and by Hushai and Absalom.
85. *manage*] management.
87. *sable*] black.
90. *weary*] wearying.
91. *Surcharged*] overcharged, overburdened.
94. *latest*] final, fatal.

        Yet let us hear what Hushai counsels us,
        Whose great experience is well worth the ear.
Hushai. Though wise Ahithophel be much more meet
        To purchase hearing with my lord the King   100
        For all his former counsels than myself,
        Yet, not offending Absalom or him,
        This time it is not good nor worth pursuit,
        For well thou knowst thy father's men are strong,
        Chafing as she-bears robbèd of their whelps.   105
        Besides, the King himself a valiant man,
        Trained up in feats and stratagems of war,
        And will not, for prevention of the worst,
        Lodge with the common soldiers in the field.
        But now, I know, his wonted policies   110
        Have taught him lurk within some secret cave,
        Guarded with all his stoutest soldiers,
        Which, if the forefront of his battle faint,
        Will yet give out that Absalom doth fly,

99. SH *Hushai*] *this edn; Cus. Q; Cusay. Hawkins (subst).*   101. than]
Hawkins (subst); then *Q.*

    99. *meet*] fitting, suitable.
    101. *For*] because of.
    105. *Chafing*] fretting, becoming enraged (*OED*, v., 10a).
    whelps] cubs, young.
    106-9.] These lines combine the Geneva and Bishops' versions of the
    latter half of 2 Samuel, 17:8: 'thy father is a valiant warrior, and will not
    lodge with the people' (Geneva); 'thy father is a man also practised in war,
    and will not lodge with the people' (Bishops'). The next verse (9) of 2
    Samuel, 17, makes the point clear: King David has chosen not to lodge with
    his soldiers in order to protect his personal safety. Instead, 'he is hid now in
    some pit, or in some other place'. See lines 110-15 below, for Peele's elabora-
    tion upon this information.
    106. *himself*] himself is.
    108. *will not … worst*] i.e. will not hesitate, in order to prevent the worst.
    110. *wonted*] customary, habitual.
    111. *him*] him to.
    112. *stoutest*] hardiest and strongest.
    113. *battle*] battalion, division, army (*OED*, n., 8a).
    faint] weaken, retreat.
    114.] David's soldiers will nevertheless report it as a fact that Absalom
    has fled – even though they presumably know this to be untrue.

And so thy soldiers be discouragèd.   115
David himself withal, whose angry heart
Is as a lion's letted of his walk,
Will fight himself and all his men to one
Before a few shall vanquish him by fear.
My counsel, therefore, is with trumpet's sound   120
To gather men from Dan to Beersheba,
That they may march in number like sea sands
That nestle close in one another's neck.
So shall we come upon him in our strength
Like to the dew that falls in showers from heaven,   125
And leave him not a man to march withal.
Besides, if any city succour him,
The numbers of our men shall fetch us ropes,
And we will pull it down the river's stream,
That not a stone be left to keep us out.   130
Absalom. What says my lord to Hushai's counsel now?
Amasa. I fancy Hushai's counsel better far
        Than that is given us from Ahithophel,
        And so I think doth every soldier here.
All. Hushai's counsel is better than Ahithophel's.   135

---

121. Beersheba] *Q* *(*Bersabe*). Modernised silently throughout.* 123. one]
Hawkins (subst); not in Q. 128. numbers] *Hawkins (subst);* nnmbers *Q.*
131. SH *Absalom*] *this edn; Abs. Q; Absalon. Hawkins (subst).* 132. SH
Amasa] *Hawkins (subst); Ama. Q.* 133. Than] *Hawkins (subst);* Then *Q.*
135. than] *Hawkins (subst);* then *Q.*

115.] i.e. and in that way Absalom's soldiers will be disheartened by the
(false) rumour that he has fled the battle.

116. *withal*] also, moreover, likewise (*OED*, adv., 1a).

117. *letted*] hindered, impeded (*OED*, adj.).

118. *to one*] i.e to the last man.

121. *from Dan to Beersheba*] from one end of Israel to another (see 2
Samuel, 17:11).

123. *in one another's neck*] Hawkins, Dyce, Bullen, Keltie, Morley, Manly,
and Thorndike emend Q's 'in another's neck' to 'in one another's neck',
thus plausibly regularising the line's metre. The phrase means 'marching in
close ranks'.

127. *succour*] help, aid.

128. *The numbers*] a number.

129.] i.e. and we will pull that city into the river.

133. *that*] that which.

from] by.

Absalom. Then march we after Hushai's counsel all.
Sound trumpets through the bounds of Israel!
And muster all the men will serve the King,
That Absalom may glut his longing soul
With sole fruition of his father's crown.   140

            Exeunt.

     [AHITHOPHEL *and* HUSHAI *remain.*]

Ahithophel. Ill shall they fare that follow thy attempts,
That scorns the counsel of Ahithophel.   *Exit.*

       [HUSHAI *remains*].

Hushai. Thus hath the power of Jacob's jealous God
Fulfilled His servant David's drifts by me
And brought Ahithophel's advice to scorn.   145

   Enter ZADOK, ABIATHAR, AHIMAAZ, *and* JONATHAN.

---

136. SH *Absalom*] *this edn; Abs. Q; Absalon. Hawkins (subst).* 140.1. SD]
printed on 140, aligned right, in Q. 140.2. SD AHITHOPHEL *and* HUSHAI
remain.] *this edn; not in Q; Exeunt all except* ACHITOPHEL *and* CUSAY. *Bullen
(subst).* 141. SH *Ahithophel*] *this edn; Ach. Q; Achitophel. Hawkins (subst).*
142. SD *Exit.*] *Bullen (subst); not in Q.* 142.1. SD HUSHAI *remains*] *this
edn; Restat Cusay. Q.* 144. His] *this edn; his Q.*

---

136. *after*] in accordance with.

138. *will*] who are willing to. (Absalom here speaks of himself as the king.)

139–40.] Richard of Gloucester, the future Richard III, speaks of how he
will 'Torment myself to catch the English crown', *3 Henry VI*, 3.2.179.

139. *glut his longing soul*] In the anonymous *Locrine*, occasionally attributed to Peele, the ghost of Almanact announces that 'now revenge shall glut
my longing soul' (sig. F1v). As he dies, Tamburlaine exhorts his eyes to
'Pierce through' Zenocrate's 'coffin ... / And glut your longings with a
heaven of joy' (*2 Tamburlaine*, 5.4.226–7). Faustus requests Helen from
Mephistopheles 'To glut the longing of my heart's desire' (*Doctor Faustus*,
B-Text, 5.1.86).

140.] i.e. with the defeat of King David, thereby fulfilling my one overwhelming desire. The line echoes Marlowe's Tamburlaine, who in *1
Tamburlaine*, 2.7.12–29 justifies his rebellion against the King of Persia as
the result of his divinely sanctioned and natural desire for 'the ripest fruit of
all' (27), which is 'The sweet fruition of an earthly crown' (29).

143. *jealous*] i.e. vigilant in protecting Israel's rights. (Hushai sees a divine
purpose in frustrating Ahithophel's sway over Absalom, and confesses here
that this was his intent, not a wish to aid Absalom.)

Zadok. God save Lord Hushai and direct his zeal
    To purchase David's conquest 'gainst his son!
Abiathar. What secrets hast thou gleaned from Absalom?
Hushai. These, sacred priests that bear the ark of God:
    Ahithophel advised him in the night   150
    To let him choose twelve thousand fighting men
    And he would come on David at unwares
    While he was weary with his violent toil,
    But I advised to get a greater host
    And gather men from Dan to Beersheba   155
    To come upon him strongly in the fields.
    Then send Ahimaaz and Jonathan
    To signify these secrets to the King,
    And will him not to stay this night abroad
    But get him over Jordan presently,   160
    Lest he and all his people kiss the sword.
Zadok. Then go, Ahimaaz and Jonathan,
    And straight convey this message to the King.
Ahimaaz. Father, we will, if Absalom's chief spies
    Prevent not this device and stay us here.   165

                                                    Exeunt.

---

148. SH *Abiathar*] *Hawkins (subst); Abia. Q.*   149. These,] *Hawkins*
(subst); These *Q.*   God:] *Hawkins (subst);* God, *Q.*   164. SH *Ahimaaz*] *this*
edn; Ahim. Q; Ahimaas. Hawkins (subst).   165.1. SD] *printed on 165, aligned*
right, in Q.

---

148. *from Absalom*] i.e. about Absalom's plans and military strength.
149. *priests*] Zadok and Abiathar, who are on stage with their sons,
Ahimaaz and Jonathan.
150. *him*] Absalom.
152. *at unwares*] by surprise, unexpectedly.
159. *will*] urge.
160. *presently*] at once.
161. *kiss the sword*] die by the sword.
163. *straight*] at once.
164–5.] 2 Samuel, 17:17–21 recounts that Ahimaaz and Jonathan are
forced to hide in a well in order to escape Absalom's spies and reach David
with their information.
165. *Prevent*] anticipate.
device] plan, strategy.

[Sc. 12]

[*Enter*] SHIMEI [*alone*].

Shimei. The man of Israel that hath ruled as King,
   Or rather as the tyrant of the land,
   Bolstering his hateful head upon the throne
   That God unworthily hath blessed him with,
   Shall now, I hope, lay it as low as hell   5
   And be deposed from his detested chair.
   Oh, that my bosom could by nature bear
   A sea of poison to be poured upon
   His cursèd head that sacred balm hath graced
   And consecrated King of Israel!   10
   Or would my breath were made the smoke of hell,
   Infected with the sighs of damnèd souls
   Or with the reeking of that serpent's gorge
   That feeds on adders, toads, and venomous roots,
   That, as I opened my revenging lips   15
   To curse the shepherd for his tyranny,

Heading Sc. 12] *Greg (subst); not in Q;* SCENE X. *Bullen (subst);* ACT III.
SCENE III. *Morley (subst);* Act II. Scene VII. *Manly (subst);* x *Rabkin
(subst).* 0.1. SD *Enter*] *Dyce 3 (subst); not in Q.* SHIMEI] *Q (Semei).
Modernised silently throughout.* alone] *this edn; solus Q.*

[*Sc. 12*] In the biblical narrative, this scene takes place in the environs
of Bahurim, which the Geneva gloss to 2 Samuel, 16:5 states 'was a city in
the tribe of Benjamin'. The scene dramatises 2 Samuel, 16:5–13, 17:21–2,
and 18:1–5. In the biblical narrative, the events dramatised in scene 11 take
place between the Shimei's cursing and the arrival of Ahimaaz and Jonathan.
   0.1. SD *SHIMEI*] 'a man of the family of the of the house of Saul' and
'the son of Gera' (2 Samuel, 16:5).
   1.] King David.
   3. *Bolstering*] propping up.
   7. *could ... bear*] could, by its own natural properties, produce.
   10. *consecrated*] ordained.
   11. *would*] would that.
   13–15.] Shimei's cursing resembles Bajazeth's declaration in *1 Tamburlaine*
that his 'life' is 'more loathsome to my vexèd thought / Than noisome par-
break of the Stygian snakes / Which fills the nooks of hell with standing air,
/ Infecting all the ghosts with cureless griefs!' (5.2.255–8).
   13. *gorge*] throat.
   16. *the shepherd*] David, whom Shimei angrily demotes from king back to
his lowly origins.

My words might cast rank poison to his pores
And make his swoll'n and rankling sinews crack
Like to the combat blows that break the clouds
When Jove's stout champions fight with fire!   20
See where he cometh that my soul abhors.
I have prepared my pocket full of stones
To cast at him, mingled with earth and dust,
Which, bursting with disdain, I greet him with.

[*Enter*] DAVID, JOAB, ABISHAI, ITTAI, *with others.*

Come forth, thou murderer and wicked man!   25
The Lord hath brought upon thy cursèd head
The guiltless blood of Saul and all his sons,
Whose royal throne thy baseness hath usurped,
And to revenge it deeply on thy soul
The Lord hath given the kingdom to thy son,   30
And he shall wreak the trait'rous wrongs of Saul.

24.1. SD *Enter*] *Dyce 3 (subst); not in Q.*   25.] *Q begins line with SH Semei.*
26. Lord] *Q (subst).*   30. Lord] *Q (subst).*

---

17. *rank*] foul.
18. *rankling*] festering.
19–20.] i.e. like thunder and lightning that sever the clouds when the winds, belonging to the elements of air, do elemental combat with another of the four elements, the fire of lightning.
20. *Jove's stout champions*] In Du Bartas, 'le colere Autan et le Nort mutiné' (*Les Artifices*, 596), the angry South Wind and the Mutinous North Wind, for whom 'L'air des nues [the clouds]' (595) is 'la lice et le champ assiné [the tilting field and assigned ground]' (595) where they 'Se donnent la bataille, et fiers, jettent par terre / Maint bois qui, moytoien, veut esteindre leur guerre [Give each other battle and, fierce, throw to the earth / Many wooden lances, which, shivered, would extinguish their war]' (597–8). Marlowe presents a similar image in *1 Tamburlaine*: Auster and Aquilion, the north and south winds respectively, 'with wingèd steeds / All sweating, tilt about the watery heavens / With shivering spears enforcing thunderclaps, / And from their shields strike flames of lightning' (3.2.78–81).
21. *that*] he whom.
26–30.] See 2 Samuel, 16:8, where Shimei declares to David that 'The Lord hath brought upon thee all the blood of the house of Saul, in whose stead thou hast reigned: and the Lord hath delivered thy kingdom into the hand of Absalom thy son'. See also 1 Samuel, 18–31.
28. *baseness*] (a) low social origins and (b) moral turpitude.
31. *wreak ... Saul*] i.e. avenge the wrongs David committed against Saul while Saul was yet King of Israel.

Even as thy sin hath still importuned heaven,
So shall thy murders and adultery
Be punished in the sight of Israel,
As thou deserv'st, with blood, with death, and hell.   35
Hence, murderer, hence!

He [throws] at him.

Abishai. Why doth this dead dog curse my lord the King?
    Let me alone to take away his head.
David. Why meddleth thus the son of Zeruiah
    To interrupt the action of our God?   40
    Shimei useth me with this reproach
    Because the Lord hath sent him to reprove
    The sins of David, printed in his brows
    With blood that blusheth for his conscience' guilt.
    Who dares, then, ask him why he curseth me?   45
Shimei. If, then, thy conscience tell thee thou hast sinned
    And that thy life is odious to the world,
    Command thy followers to shun thy face,
    And by thyself here make away thy soul,
    That I may stand and glory in thy shame.   50

36.] *Hawkins (subst); Hence murtherer, hence, he threw at him. Q.*
36.1. SD] *aligned right in Q. throws] this edn; threw Q.* 37. SH *Abishai]*
this edn; Abis. Q; Abisai. Hawkins (subst). 37. this] *Hawkins (subst);* his *Q.*
39. SH *David] Hawkins (subst); Da. Q.* 42. Lord] *Q (subst).* 44. conscience' guilt] *Dyce 2 (subst);* conscience guilt *Q.*

32. *importuned*] troubled, begged, solicited (*OED*, v., 1, 3, 4).
36.] Q mistakenly prints this obvious half-line of speech in italics as a
stage direction on the same line as and immediately preceding the stage
direction *he threw at him.*
37. *dead dog*] i.e. worthless wretch. Blistein observes that 'in all sixteenth-
century versions of the Bible 2 Samuel, 16:9 reads, "this dead dog"' (274).
38.] i.e. Leave it to me to behead him.
39. *the son of Zeruiah*] Abishai is thus identified in 2 Samuel, 16:9–10.
44. *conscience' guilt*] Q's 'conscience' clearly is possessive here, but to add
an s after the apostrophe would alter the line's metre.
46–61.] Peele expands 2 Samuel, 16:13, which reports simply that, after
David has urged his followers to allow Shimei to pronounce his just curses
on David, 'Shimei went by the side of the mountain over against him and
cursed as he went, and threw stones against him, and cast dust'.
46–50.] i.e. If you, David, know that you have sinned and are hated for
your sin, then dismiss your followers and commit suicide, from which I,
Shimei, will obtain great satisfaction.

David. I am not desperate, Shimei, like thyself,
          But trust unto the covenant of my God,
          Founded on mercy, with repentance built,
          And finished with the glory of my soul.
Shimei. A murderer, and hope for mercy in thy end?   55
          Hate and destruction sit upon thy brows
          To watch the issue of thy damnèd ghost,
          Which with thy latest gasp they'll take and tear,
          Hurling in every pain of hell a piece!
          Hence, murderer, thou shame to Israel,   60
          Foul lecher, drunkard, plague to heaven and earth!

                    He throws at him.

Joab. What, is it piety in David's thoughts
          So to abhor from laws of policy
          In this extremity of his distress
          To give his subjects cause of carelessness?   65
          Send hence the dog with sorrow to his grave.

---

51. SH *David*] *Hawkins (subst); Da. Q.*   61.1. SD] *aligned right in Q.*

51–4.] Numerous psalms express similar confidence in God's mercy and David's election. In Psalm 89:20–8, for example, God declares, 'I have found David my servant: with mine holy oil have I anointed him ... My truth also and my mercy shall be with him, and in my Name shall his horn be exalted ... He shall cry unto me, Thou art my Father, my God and the rock of my salvation ... My mercy will I keep for him forevermore, and my covenant shall stand fast with him.'

51. *desperate*] without hope of God's mercy. At the beginning of 2.1 of *Doctor Faustus*, Faustus asks, 'Now, Faustus, must thou needs be damned? / Canst thou not be saved?', and concludes, 'What boots it then to think on God or heaven? / Away with such vain fancies, and despair' (*B-Text*, 1–4).

56. *Hate*] May hate.

57. *the issue*] the issuing forth, departure.

58. *they'll*] Hate and destruction will.

59. *pain*] Blistein glosses as 'pane, meaning "a piece, portion, or side of anything"' (274). Peele, however, might be using 'pain' as a metonym for the location of the infliction of pain. Shimei would then be cursing David's soul with all the various tortures of hell simultaneously, not just one of them or all of them serially.

63. *abhor*] shrink, recoil (*OED*, v., 1a).

policy] political conduct; political expediency; government (*OED*, n.1, 2b, 5a).

65. *carelessness*] i.e. lack of proper concern for their king.

David. Why should the sons of Zeruiah seek to check
His spirit which the Lord hath thus inspired?
Behold, my son, which issued from my flesh,
With equal fury seeks to take my life.   70
How much more, then, the son of Jemini,
Chiefly since he doth naught but God's command?
It may be He will look on me this day
With gracious eyes, and for his cursing bless
The heart of David in his bitterness.   75
Shimei. What, dost thou fret my soul with sufferance?
Oh, that the souls of Ishbosheth and Abner,
Which thou sentst swimming to their graves in blood
With wounds fresh bleeding, gasping for revenge,
Were here to execute my burning hate!   80
But I will hunt thy foot with curses still.
Hence, monster, murderer, mirror of contempt!

He throws dust again.

---

68. Lord] *Q (subst).*   76. dost] *Hawkins (subst);* doest *Q.*   82.1. SD]
aligned right in Q.

67. *the sons of Zeruiah*] Abishai and Joab.
check] stop, hinder.
68. *His*] Shimei's.
71. *son of Jemini*] Shimei, who as member of the Israelite tribe of Benjamin
was a Benjamite or 'son of Jemini'.
72.] In 2 Samuel, 16:10 David states that Shimei 'curseth even because
the Lord hath bidden him curse David. Who dare then say, "Wherefore hast
thou done so?"'
73-5.] In 2 Samuel, 16:12 David tells Abishai that 'It may be that the
Lord will look on mine affliction, and do me good for his cursing this day'.
74. *his*] Shimei's.
76. *dost ... sufferance?*] i.e. do you increase my anger by raising the possibil-
ity that God might forgive and bless you, thus thwarting my desire for revenge?
fret] rub, chafe (*OED*, v.4).
sufferance] allowance, forgiveness.
77. *Ishbosheth and Abner*] Shimei is insinuating that David is responsible
for the assassinations of Saul's general Abner, whom Joab murders without
David's knowledge or approval in 2 Samuel, 3:27, and of Saul's son
Ishbosheth, who reigns as king of Israel for two years after Saul's death until
he is assassinated. When the assassins present David with Ishbosheth's head,
David commands them to be executed (2 Samuel, 4:8-12). See note to 8.18.
80. *execute*] carry out.
81. *foot*] footsteps.
82. *mirror*] monstrous example.

Enter AHIMAAZ *and* JONATHAN.

Ahimaaz. Long life to David, to his enemies death!
David. Welcome, Ahimaaz and Jonathan.
    What news sends Hushai to thy lord the King?   85
Ahimaaz. Hushai would wish my lord the King
    To pass the river Jordan presently
    Lest he and all his people perish here,
    For wise Ahithophel hath counselled Absalom
    To take advantage of your weary arms   90
    And come this night upon you in the fields.
    But yet the Lord hath made his counsel scorn
    And Hushai's policy with praise preferred,
    Which was to number every Israelite
    And so assault you in their pride of strength.   95
Jonathan. Abiathar besides entreats the King
    To send his men of war against his son
    And hazard not his person in the field.
David. Thanks to Abiathar, and to you both,
    And to my Hushai, whom the Lord requite,   100
    But ten times treble thanks to His soft hand
    Whose pleasant touch hath made my heart to dance
    And play Him praises in my zealous breast,

---

83. SH *Ahimaaz*] *this edn; Ahim. Q; Ahimaas. Hawkins (subst).*   84. SH
David] *Hawkins (subst); Da. Q.*   86. SH *Ahimaaz*] *this edn; Ahim. Q;
Ahimaas. Hawkins (subst).*   92. Lord] *Q (subst).*   96. SH *Jonathan*]
Hawkins (subst); Ionat. Q.   100. Lord] *Q (subst).*   101. His] *this edn;* his
Q.   103. Him] *this edn;* him *Q.*

    87. *presently*] immediately.
    90. *weary arms*] military weakness.
    92–3.] i.e. But God has seen to it that Ahithophel's sage counsel is
rejected in favour of Hushai's much-praised (but flawed) plan.
    94. *to number every Israelite*] i.e. to reckon up the strength of the Israelite
army.
    95. *their ... strength*] their full power.
    97. *his son*] Absalom.
    98. *his person*] David's own royal self.
    100. *requite*] reward, repay.
    103. *And ... praises*] and plays hymns of praise to God.

That turned the counsel of Ahithophel
After the prayers of His servant's lips.   105
Now will we pass the river all this night
And in the morning sound the voice of war,
The voice of bloody and unkindly war.
Joab. Then tell us how thou wilt divide thy men
And who shall have the special charge herein.   110
David. Joab, thyself shall for thy charge conduct
The first third part of all my valiant men.
The second shall Abishai's valour lead;
The third fair Ittai, which I most should grace
For comfort he hath done to David's woes;   115
And I myself will follow in the midst.
Ittai. That let not David, for, though we should fly,
Ten thousand of us were not half so much
Esteemed with David's enemies as himself.
Thy people, loving thee, deny thee this.   120
David. What seems them best, then that will David do.
But now, my lords and captains, hear his voice
That never yet pierced piteous heaven in vain;
Then let it not slip lightly through your ears:
For my sake spare the young man Absalom.   125
Joab, thyself didst once use friendly words
To reconcile my heart incensed to him.
If, then, thy love be to thy kinsman sound
And thou wilt prove a perfect Israelite,

---

105. His] *this edn;* his *Q.* 111. SH *David*] *Hawkins (subst); Dau. Q.*
117. SH *Ittai*] *this edn;* Ith. *Q; Ithay. Hawkins (subst).* 121. SH
David] *Hawkins (subst); Da. Q.*

104–5.] i.e. God, who saw to it that Ahithophel's advice to Absalom was
rejected, as we, God's loyal servants, had prayed would happen.
   108. *unkindly war*] civil war, which is unkind or against kind because it
pits kindred against each other, brother against brother in general and, in
this instance, father against son.
   111. *for thy charge*] i.e. as your particular responsibility.
   114. *which*] whom.
   117.] i.e. King David, do not assign yourself a place in the actual battle.
   120.] i.e. We your loyal subjects, insist on this.
   121. *them*] to them, to my subjects.

Friend him with deeds, and touch no hair of him,   130
Not that fair hair with which the wanton winds
Delight to play and love to make it curl,
Wherein the nightingales would build their nests
And make sweet bowers in every golden tress
To sing their lover every night asleep.   135
Oh, spoil not, Joab, Jove's fair ornaments,
Which He hath sent to solace David's soul.
The best ye see, my lords, are swift to sin;
To sin our feet are washed with milk of roes
And dried again with coals of lightening.   140
O Lord, Thou see'st the proudest sins, poor slave,
And with his bridle pullst him to the grave.
For my sake, then, spare lovely Absalom.
Ittai. We will, my lord, for thy sake favour him.

                                              Exeunt.

---

132. love] *Dyce 2 (subst);* loues *Q.*   137. He] *this edn;* he *Q.*   138. see, my
lords, are] *Hawkins (subst);* see (my lords) are *Q.*   141. Lord] *Q (subst).*
144. SH *Ittai*] *this edn; Ith. Q; Ithay. Hawkins (subst).*

---

130. *Friend him with deeds*] i.e. befriend him with your actions in battle.

131–2. *that fair hair ... curl*] These lines recall Menaphon's decription of
Tamburlaine's 'knot of amber hair / Wrappèd in curls, as fierce Achilles'
was, / On which the breath of heaven delights to play, / Making it dance
with wanton majesty' (*1 Tamburlaine*, 2.1.23–6).

136. *Jove's fair ornaments*] i.e. Absalom's physical beauty, typified in his
golden tresses of hair.

139–40.] i.e. to commit a sin our feet move as if anointed with roe's milk
then stop or are pained as if burnt by coals produced by lightning. The
images in these lines emphasise the haste with which we rush into sin, suggested in the roe's quickness, and the painfulness of repentance or the
consequences of sin, suggested in the burning intensity of the lightning's
coals. The swift-footed roe's passage is impeded or made painful (euphe-
mistically described as a drying of the feet) by burning ground underfoot
('coals') set ablaze by a stroke from the heavens. See the second Concubine's
allusion to 'the nimble-footed roe' in 11.29.

139. *To sin*] when we sin.

140. *lightening*] Original spelling retained to preserve the metre.

142.] i.e. God chastises us and brings us to obedience by the inescapable
fact that we must die.

[Sc. 13]

[*Enter*] AHITHOPHEL [*alone*] *with a halter.*

Ahithophel. Now hath Ahithophel ordered his house
    And taken leave of every pleasure there;
    Hereon depend Ahithophel's delights,
    And in this circle must his life be closed.
    The wise Ahithophel, whose counsel proved   5
    Ever as sound for fortunate success
    As if men asked the oracle of God,
    Is now used like the fool of Israel.
    Then set thy angry soul upon her wings,
    And let her fly into the shade of death,   10
    And for my death let heaven forever weep,
    Making huge floods upon the land I leave,
    To ravish them and all their fairest fruits.
    Let all the sighs I breathed for this disgrace
    Hang on my hedges like eternal mists,   15

Heading Sc. 13] *Greg (subst); not in Q;* SCENE XI. *Bullen (subst);* ACT III.
SCENE IV. *Morley (subst);* Act II. Scene VIII. *Manly (subst);* xi *Rabkin
(subst).* o.1. SD *Enter*] *Dyce 3 (subst); not in Q. alone*] *this edn; solus Q.*
1. SH *Ahithophel*] *this edn; Achi. Q; Achitophel. Hawkins (subst).*
3. depend] *Dyce 2 (subst);* depends *Q.*

[*Sc. 13*] Located in front of Ahithophel's residence in his home city. 2
Samuel, 17:23 relates that 'Now when Ahithophel saw that his counsel was
not followed, he saddled his ass, and arose, and he went home unto his
city, and put his household in order, and hanged himself, and died, and was
buried in his father's grave'.
    o.1. SD halter] noose.
    1. *ordered his house*] Compare 2 Samuel, 17:23 quoted above in headnote
to scene: 'and put his household in order'.
    4. *this circle*] i.e. the noose or halter that Ahithophel is holding.
    7. *the oracle of God*] 2 Samuel, 16:23 states that 'the counsel of Ahithophel
which he counselled in those days, was like as one had asked counsel at the
oracle of God'.
    9. *Then set*] Then, Ahithophel, set free.
    thy] Ahithophel's (he is addressing himself).
    9, 10. *her*] Ahithophel's soul's.
    15.] Clothing was often hung on hedges to dry. See Autolycus's first song
in *The Winter's Tale*, 4.3.5, 'The white sheet bleaching on the hedge', etc.,
and Falstaff in *1 Henry IV*, 4.2.46–7: 'they'll find linen enough on every
hedge'.

As mourning garments for their master's death!
Ope, earth, and take thy miserable son
Into the bowels of thy cursèd womb!
Once in a surfeit thou didst spew him forth;
Now for fell hunger suck him in again,   20
And be his body poison to thy veins.
And now, thou hellish instrument of heaven,
Once execute th'arrest of Jove's just doom
And stop his breast that curseth Israel!   *Exit.*

[Sc. 14]

       [Enter] ABSALOM, AMASA, *with all his train.*

Absalom. Now for the crown and throne of Israel
   To be confirmed with virtue of my sword
   And writ with David's blood upon the blade!

---

16. mourning] *Hawkins (subst);* monrning *Q.*   19. didst] *Hawkins (subst);* diddest *Q.*

Heading Sc. 14] *Greg (subst); not in Q;* SCENE XII. *Bullen (subst);* ACT III. SCENE V. *Morley (subst);* Act II. Scene IX. *Manly (subst).*   0.1. SD] *Enter*] *Hawkins (subst); not in Q.*   1. SH *Absalom*] *this edn; Abs. Q; Absalon. Hawkins (subst).*   3. blade;] *Hawkins (subst);* blade, *Q.*

---

19. *surfeit*] 'illness attributed to excessive eating or drinking' (*OED*, n., 4a).

20. *fell*] fierce, terrible, deadly (*OED*, adj., 1, 2).

21. *be his body*] may his body be.

veins] The earth was popularly supposed to be like a body, with veins.

23. *Once*] once for all, just (*OED*, adv., 4).

th'arrest] the decree, sentence, judgement (*OED*, n.1, 13).

24. *his breast that*] i.e. the breast (i.e. breath) of him, Ahithophel, who.

breast] Dyce, Keltie, Morley, Bullen, and Thorndike emend to 'breath'.

[*Sc. 14*] In the days preceding the battle with his father, Absalom pitched camp in Gilead (2 Samuel, 17:26), 'a mountainous area east of the Jordan' (Browning, 130). As Absalom's speech is an address to his troops immediately before the battle, however, the scene is most likely located in the environs of the battlefield, the woods of Ephraim, 'an area in the north of the kingdom [of Israel] and west of the Jordan' (Browning, 100). The biblical narrative does not include the speech Peele gives Absalom in this scene.

2. *virtue*] power, strength (*OED*, n., 3a, 5a).

Now, Jove, let forth the golden firmament
And look on him with all Thy fiery eyes,   5
Which Thou hast made to give their glories light!
To show Thou lovest the virtue of Thy hand,
Let fall a wreath of stars upon my head,
Whose influence may govern Israel
With state exceeding all her other kings!   10
Fight, lords and captains, that your sovereign's face
May shine in honour brighter than the sun
And with the virtue of my beauteous rays

5. Thy] *this edn;* thy *Q.*   6. Thou] *this edn;* thou *Q.*   light;] *Hawkins (subst);* light, *Q.*   7. Thou] *this edn;* thou *Q.*   Thy] *this edn;* thy *Q.*   12. than] *Hawkins (subst);* then *Q.*

4–6.] i.e. Now, God, open the heavens and with the stars as Your eyes behold him (i.e. me, Absalom) whom You made to give light to the stars' glory. As at 11.11–16, Absalom's boasting recalls Tamburlaine's. Absalom is here hyperbolically praising himself as the source of the star's splendour, just as Tamburlaine does when he mounts his throne using Bajazeth as a footstool: 'Now clear the triple region of the air / And let the majesty of heaven behold / Their scourge and terror tread on emperors', Tamburlaine declaims, 'Smile, stars that reigned at my nativity / And dim the brightness of their neighbour lamps – / Disdain to borrow light of Cynthia, / For I, the chiefest lamp of all the earth, / ... / Will send up fire to your turning spheres / And cause the sun to borrow light of you' (*1 Tamburlaine*, 4.2.30–6, 39–40). See also Absalom's contention in scene 11 that 'in his face' (57) he '[c]arries the final purpose of his God' (58) and that 'with my beauty is His lightning quenched; / I am the man He made to glory in' (64–5).
    4. *let ... firmament*] i.e. unveil the heavens.
    5. *him*] Absalom.
    fiery eyes] stars.
    6.] i.e. whom Thou, God, have made to give or add light to the splendour of the very stars themselves! Line 6 can also mean 'which stars You have made bright to illuminate their own glory'.
    Which] whom (i.e. Absalom).
    glories] beauties, magnificences (*OED,* n., 6).
    8. *upon my head*] to form a triumphal wreath around my brows.
    9. *influence*] i.e. astrological influence beamed down on humankind. See note to 11.11, 'aspects'.
    10. *state*] majesty.
    her] i.e. Israel's, to whom all other kingdoms in the Middle East owe allegiance.

Make this fair land as fruitful as the fields
That with sweet milk and honey overflowed!   15
God in the whissing of a pleasant wind
Shall march upon the tops of mulberry trees
To cool all breasts that burn with any griefs.
As whilom He was good to Moses' men,
By day the Lord shall sit within a cloud   20
To guide your footsteps to the fields of joy,
And in the night a pillar bright as fire
Shall go before you like a second sun,
Wherein the essence of His godhead is,
That day and night you may be brought to peace   25
And never swerve from that delightsome path
That leads your souls to perfect happiness.
This shall He do for joy when I am King.
Then fight, brave captains, that these joys may fly
Into your bosoms with sweet victory!   30
                                              Exeunt.

---

19. He] *this edn;* he *Q.*   20. Lord] *Q (subst).*   24. His] *this edn;* his *Q.*
28. He] *this edn;* he *Q.*   30.1. SD] *printed on 30, aligned right, in Q.*

14–15.] In Exodus, 3:8 God declares that 'I am come down to deliver
them [the children of Israel] out of the hand of the Egyptians, and to bring
them out of that land into a good land and a large, into a land that floweth
with milk and honey'.

16–17.] In 2 Samuel, 5:24 and 1 Chronicles, 14:15 God's signal for David
to attack the Philistines is 'the noise of one going in the tops of the mulberry
trees'.

16. *whissing*] whistling, hissing (*OED*, whiss, v., 1).

19–22.] When Moses led the children of Israel out of Egypt, 'the Lord
went before them by day in a pillar of a cloud to lead them the way, and by
night in a pillar of fire to give them light' (Exodus, 13:21).

19. *whilom*] formerly, in the past (*OED*, adv., 2a).

[Sc. 15]

> [*Enter* JOAB's *and* ABSALOM's *soldiers to*] *the battle,*
> *and* [*at the end*] ABSALOM *hangs by the hair.*

[*Absalom.*] What angry angel sitting in these shades
Hath laid his cruel hands upon my hair
And holds my body thus twixt heaven and earth?
Hath Absalom no soldier near his hand
That may untwine me this unpleasant curl   5
Or wound this tree that ravisheth his lord?
O God, behold the glory of Thy hand
And choicest fruit of nature's workmanship
Hang like a rotten branch upon this tree,
Fit for the axe and ready for the fire!   10
Since Thou withholdst all ordinary help
To loose my body from this bond of death,
Oh, let my beauty fill these senseless plants
With sense and power to loose me from this plague,

Heading Sc. 15] *Greg (subst); not in* Q; SCENE XIII. *Bullen (subst);* Act II.
Scene X. *Manly (subst);* xii *Rabkin (subst).*   0.1. SD *Enter* JOAB's *and* ABSA-
LOM's *soldiers to*] *this edn; not in* Q.   *at the end*] *this edn; not in* Q.   1. SH
Absalom] *Dyce 2 (subst); not in* Q.   7. Thy] *this edn;* thy Q.   11. Thou] *this*
edn; thou Q.   12. loose] Q (*lose*).   14. loose] Q (*lose*).

    [*Sc. 15*] Located in the woods of Ephraim (see note to scene 14 above),
the scene dramatises the events recounted in 2 Samuel, 18:9–17.
    0.2. SD *ABSALOM* hangs by the hair] 2 Samuel, 18:9 relates that 'Absalom
rode upon a mule, and the mule came under a great, thick oak, and his head
caught hold of the oak, and he was taken up between the heaven and the
earth'. In an undated entry between 3 October 1602 and 11 October 1602,
Philip Henslowe, owner of the Rose theatre and manager of the Lord
Admiral's Men, records payment of 14 pence 'for pulleys and workmanship
for to hang Absolome' (Foakes, 217; qtd Dyce 3, 481). Although the record
does not specify for which play this special property was constructed, no
other play from the period featuring a hanging of Absalom is recorded or
survives, so it seems likely that the record testifies to the continued performance or revival of Peele's play almost a decade after its entrance in the
Stationers' Register in 1594. The property, with the actor playing Absalom
suspended in it, could be pushed on to the stage through the central discovery space while the soldiers of both armies exit in order to leave Absalom
alone to deliver his scene-opening soliloquy.
    1–16.] Absalom's lament is Peele's addition to the biblical narrative.
    6. *ravisheth*] seizes, snatches away (*OED*, v., 3a).

And work some wonder to prevent his death   15
Whose life Thou mad'st a special miracle.

[*Enter*] JOAB[*, carrying three spears,*] *with another soldier.*

[*1*] *Soldier.* My lord, I saw the young prince Absalom
Hang by the hair upon a shady oak
And could by no means get himself unloosed.
Joab. Why slewst thou not the wicked Absalom,   20
That rebel to his father and to heaven,
That so I might have given thee for thy pains
Ten silver shekels and a golden waist?
[*1*] *Soldier.* Not for a thousand shekels would I slay
The son of David, whom his father charged   25
Nor thou, Abishai, nor the son of Gath
Should touch with stroke of deadly violence.
The charge was given in hearing of us all,
And, had I done it, then I know thyself,

---

16. Thou] *this edn;* thou *Q.*   16.1. SD *Enter*] *Hawkins (subst); not in Q.*
, carrying three spears,] *this edn; not in Q.*   17. SH *1*] *this edn; not in*
Q.   Soldier] *Hawkins (subst); Sould. Q.*   23. shekels] *Q (*sickles*).*   24. SH
1] *this edn; not in Q.   Soldier*] *Hawkins (subst); Sould. Q.*   24. shekels] *Q*
*(*sickles*).*

16.1. SD carrying three spears] Peele's play does not clearly specify that
Joab brings in three spears here. Following Craik, however, this stage direction is based on the judgement that the play follows the biblical narrative in
its staging of Absalom's death (78). According to 2 Samuel, 18:14, Joab 'took
three darts in his hand, and thrust them through Absalom, while he was yet
alive in the midst of the oak'. Although conceivably 'darts' might refer to
arrows, the New King James Version specifies spears: Joab 'took three spears
in his hand and thrust them through Absalom's heart' (2 Samuel, 18:14).
The stage directions at 59.1, 74.1, and 75.1 follow Craik's positioning of
Joab's thrusts to coincide with his 'Take that' (58), 'this' (74), and 'this' (75).
Peele's audience would doubtless have seen in this action a remembrance
of Christ's crucifixion, when a soldier 'with a spear pierced his side, and
forthwith came there out blood and water' (John, 19:34).
    23. *shekels*] units of weight and currency, each shekel weighing half an
ounce (Geneva gloss to 2 Samuel, 14:26).
    waist] girdle, belt.
    26. *Nor*] neither.
    son of Gath] Ittai.
    29. *know thyself*] know that you.

Before thou wouldst abide the King's rebuke,   30
Wouldst have accused me as a man of death.
Joab. I must not now stand trifling here with thee.
Absalom. Help, Joab, help, oh, help thy Absalom!
Let not thy angry thoughts be laid in blood,
In blood of him that sometimes nourished thee   35
And softened thy sweet heart with friendly love.
Oh, give me once again my father's sight,
My dearest father and my princely sovereign,
That, shedding tears of blood before his face,
The ground may witness and the heavens record   40
My last submission sound and full of ruth.
Joab. Rebel to nature, hate to heaven and earth,
Shall I give help to him that thirsts the soul
Of his dear father and my sovereign lord?
Now, see, the Lord hath tangled in a tree   45
The health and glory of thy stubborn heart
And made thy pride curbed with a senseless plant.
Now, Absalom, how doth the Lord regard
The beauty whereupon thy hope was built
And which thou thoughtst His grace did glory in?   50
Findst thou not now with fear of instant death
That God affects not any painted shape
Or goodly personage when the virtuous soul
Is stuffed with naught but pride and stubbornness?
But preach I to thee, while I should revenge   55

---

33. SH *Absalom*] *this edn; Abs. Q; Absalon. Hawkins (subst).*   45. Lord] *Q
(subst).*   48. Lord] *Q (subst).*   50. His] *this edn;* his *Q.*

---

30. *Before*] rather than.

34. *laid in*] appeased by, allayed with (*OED*, v.1, 3a).

37. *my father's sight*] a chance to see my father.

39. *tears of blood*] tears shed with such vehemence as if they were the heart's blood.

41. *sound*] utterly sincere.
ruth] sorrow, repentance, remorse; compassion (*OED*, n., 1a, 2).

43. *thirsts*] thirsts for.

46.] i.e. a tragic fate that conquers your stubborn pride, dooming the health and glory of your immortal soul.

47. *senseless*] insensate.

52. *affects*] likes, has affection for, shows preference for (*OED*, v.1, 4a).
painted shape] artificial appearance.

Thy cursèd sin that staineth Israel
And makes her fields blush with her children's blood?
Take that as part of thy deservèd plague,
Which worthily no torment can inflict!

    [*He thrusts a spear into* ABSALOM.]

Absalom. O Joab, Joab, cruel ruthless Joab,   60
    Herewith thou woundst thy kingly sovereign's heart,
    Whose heavenly temper hates his children's blood
    And will be sick, I know, for Absalom.
    O my dear father, that thy melting eyes
    Might pierce this thicket to behold thy son,   65
    Thy dearest son, gored with a mortal dart!
    Yet, Joab, pity me; pity my father, Joab,
    Pity his soul's distress that mourns my life
    And will be dead, I know, to hear my death.
Joab. If he were so remorseful of thy state,   70
    Why sent he me against thee with the sword?
    All Joab means to pleasure thee withal
    Is to dispatch thee quickly of thy pain.
    Hold, Absalom, Joab's pity is in this;

    [*He thrusts the second spear into* ABSALOM.]

In this, proud Absalom, is Joab's love.   75

    He [*thrusts the third spear into* ABSALOM]
    and goes out [*with* 1 Soldier].

59.1. SD *He thrusts a spear into* ABSALOM.] *this edn; not in* Q. 60. SH *Absalom*] *this edn; Abs.* Q; *Absalon. Hawkins (subst).* 74.1. SD *He thrusts the second spear into* ABSALOM.] *this edn; not in* Q. 75.1. SD] *thrusts the third spear into* ABSALOM] *this edn; not in* Q. *with* 1. Soldier] *Dyce 3 (subst); not in* Q.

59. *worthily*] adequately, fully to the deserved extent.
61–2. *thou ... blood*] you wound the heart of kingly David, whose sweet temperament hates the sight of his children's blood.
65. *this thicket*] i.e. the boughs of the 'great, thick oak' (2 Samuel, 18:9) where Absalom hangs.
68. *his soul's distress*] the distress of David.
69. *dead*] dead with grief.
hear] hear of.
72. *withal*] with (*OED*, prep., a).

Absalom. Such love, such pity Israel's God send thee,
    And for His love to David pity me!
    Ah, my dear father, see thy bowels bleed,
    See death assault thy dearest Absalom!
    See, pity, pardon, pray for Absalom!   80

             Enter five or six soldiers.

[*2 Soldier.*] See where the rebel in his glory hangs!
    Where is the virtue of thy beauty, Absalom?
    Will any of us here now fear thy looks
    Or be in love with that thy golden hair,
    Wherein was wrapped rebellion 'gainst thy sire   85
    And cords prepared to stop thy father's breath?
    Our captain Joab hath begun to us,
    And here's an end to thee and all thy sins!

        [*The soldiers stab* ABSALOM, *who dies.*]

    Come, let us take the beauteous rebel down
    And in some ditch amidst this darksome wood   90
    Bury his bulk beneath a heap of stones,
    Whose stony heart did hunt his father's death.

      [*The soldiers begin to cut* ABSALOM *down.*]

    Enter in triumph with drum and ensign JOAB, ABISHAI,
         and soldiers to ABSALOM.

Joab. Well done, tall soldiers. Take the traitor down
    And in this miry ditch inter his bones,
    Covering his hateful breast with heaps of stones.   95

76. SH *Absalom*] *this edn; Abs. Q; Absalon. Hawkins (subst).* 77. His] *this edn;* his *Q.* 81. SH *2 Soldier*] *this edn; not in Q.* 88.1. SD *The soldiers stab* ABSALOM, *who dies.*] *Dyce 3 (subst); not in Q.* 92.1. SD *The soldiers begin to cut* ABSALOM *down.*] *this edn; not in Q.*

76. *God send*] may God send.
87. *hath begun to us*] i.e. has started the killing of Absalom that is now our duty to finish.
90–1.] 2 Samuel, 18:17 reports that 'they took Ambsalom and cast him into a great pit in the wood, and laid a mighty great heap of stones upon him'.
93. *tall*] brave, strong; handsome (*OED*, adj., 2b, 3).

This shady thicket of dark Ephraim
Shall ever lour on his cursèd grave.
Night ravens and owls shall ring his fatal knell
And sit exclaiming on his damnèd soul;
There shall they heap their preys of carrion   100
Till all his grave be clad with stinking bones,
That it may loathe the sense of every man.
So shall his end breed horror to his name
And to his trait'rous fact eternal shame.

[*The soldiers finish cutting* ABSALOM *down.*]

[*Exeunt with* ABSALOM'*s body*].

[Chorus 2]

[*Enter* Chorus.]

Chorus. Oh, dreadful precedent of His just doom
Whose holy heart is never touched with ruth
Of fickle beauty or of glorious shapes,

---

96. Ephraim] *Hawkins (subst);* Ephrami *Q.*   104.1. SD *The soldiers finish*
cutting ABSALOM *down.*] *this edn; not in* Q.   104.2. SD] *printed on 104,*
aligned right, in Q.   Exeunt] *Hawkins (subst);* Exit *Q.*   with ABSALOM'*s*
body] *this edn; not in* Q.

Heading Chorus 2] *Greg (subst); not in* Q; [THIRD] CHORUS. *Bullen*
(subst); II Chorus *Rabkin (subst).*   0.1. SD *Enter* Chorus.] *Dyce 3 (subst);*
5.Chorus. *Q.*   1. SH *Chorus*] *Dyce 3 (subst); not in* Q.   1. precedent]
Hawkins (subst); president *Q.*   His] *this edn;* his *Q.*   1–2. doom /
Whose] *Manly (subst);* doome, / Whose *Q.*

---

96. *Ephraim*] 2 Samuel, 18:6 states that 'the battle was in the wood of
Ephraim'.
100. *preys of carrion*] carcasses.
101. *clad*] clothed, covered.
102. *loathe*] fill with loathing.
104. *fact*] deed.

1. *precedent*] example, pattern. Q's 'president' is used in the same sense
in 16.32. Manly, Blistein, Greg, and Rabkin retain the original spelling, and
Blistein glosses the noun as 'Deity, guardian, according to *OED*; hence, God'
(277). In this reading, the line's opening 'O' would be vocative, its third-
person singular pronoun 'his' would refer to Absalom, and the following
line's 'Whose' would be a non-restrictive relative pronoun whose antecedent
would be 'president'. It seems entirely appropriate to construe the Chorus's
opening lines as moral commentary upon God's just judgement upon the

But with the virtue of an upright soul
Humble and zealous in his inward thoughts,   5
Though in his person loathsome and deformed!
Now, since this story lends us other store
To make a third discourse of David's life,
Adding thereto his most renownèd death
And all their deaths that at his death he judged,   10
Here end we this, and what here wants to please
We will supply with treble willingness.   [*Exit* Chorus.]

---

12. SD *Exit* Chorus.] *Dyce 3 (subst); not in Q.*   12.] *Immediately following 12 in Q is the following fragment, which runs to the bottom of G4v, whose catchword is* Then: *Absalon with three or foure of his seruants or gentlemen.* | *Abs.* What boots it Absalon, vnhappie Absalon, / Sighing I say what boots it Absalon, / To haue disclos'd a farre more worthy wombe.

---

proud, given that they immediately follow the spectacular example of Absalom's death, but Blistein's reading is equally possible. Blistein himself comments that Peele 'may have been influenced by "The Fourth Part of the Homily Against Disobedience and Wilful Rebellion"' (267), which uses Absalom as an example of the consequences of rebellion. According to the homily, when 'most men were afraid to lay their hands upon' Absalom, 'a great tree stretching out his arm, as it were for that purpose, caught him by the great and long bush of his goodly hair ... and so hanged him up by the hair of his head in the air, to give an eternal document, that neither comeliness of personage, neither nobility, nor favour of the people, no nor the favour of the king himself, can save a rebel from due punishment' (sig. O01r; cited Blistein, 267).

2. *ruth*] pity.

4. *virtue*] moral virtue, goodness (in contrast to its primary meaning of power, strength in 14.2).

7–10.] These lines suggest that *David and Bathsheba* is the second play of a projected trilogy, the last play of which would conclude with David's death. 1 Kings, 2:1–10 recount David's final exhortation to Solomon, which includes the advice that he should put Joab and Shimei to death, and David's own death. If either the first or the third play was written, there is no record of it.

7. *store*] store of information.

11. *want*] fails.

12.] Absalom's three lines in the misplaced fragment immediately following Chorus 2 (see collation notes) echo Cain's angry musings on Abel in Du Bartas after God has accepted Abel's sacrifice and rejected Cain's: 'Que te sert-il, Caïn? ô Caïn, que te sert / (Dit-il en souspirant) d'avoir premier ouvert / Le fecond amarry de la premiere mere [What use is it, Cain? O Cain, what use is it / (He says sighing) to have first opened / The fertile womb of the first mother]' (*Les Artifices*, 267–9).

[Sc. 16]

> *Trumpets sound. Enter* JOAB, AHIMAAZ, HUSHAI, AMASA,
> *with all the rest.*

Joab. Soldiers of Israel and ye sons of Judah
That have contended in these irksome broils
And ripped old Israel's bowels with your swords,
The godless general of your stubborn arms
Is brought by Israel's Helper to the grave,   5
A grave of shame and scorn of all the tribes.
Now, then, to save your honours from the dust
And keep your bloods in temper by your bones,
Let Joab's ensign shroud your manly heads,
Direct your eyes, your weapons, and your hearts   10
To guard the life of David from his foes.
Error hath masked your much-too-forward minds,
And you have sinned against the chosen state,
Against his life for whom your lives are blessed,
And followed an usurper to the field,   15
In whose just death your deaths are threatenèd.

Heading Sc. 16] *Greg (subst); not in Q;* SCENE XIV. *Bullen (subst);* ACT
IV. SCENE I. *Morley (subst);* Act III. Scene I. *Manly (subst);* xiii *Rabkin
(subst).*   5. Helper] *this edn;* helper *Q.*

[*Sc. 16*] Located in or around the woods of Ephraim. The biblical narrative contains only the germ of the first part of this scene in its brief assertion
that Joab 'blew the trumpet' (2 Samuel, 18:16) to prevent his army from
completely slaughtering Absalom's forces. Peele expands the biblical narrative's hint into a brilliant dramatisation of Joab's disturbing combination
of brutal military might and religious zeal. In 2 Samuel, 20:9–14, however,
Joab kills Amasa to turn back to David the troops that Amasa has led in
another, later, rebellion on behalf of a man named Sheba. Ahimaaz's desire
to run as messenger concurrently with Hushai, dramatised in lines 38–52, is
recounted in 2 Samuel, 18:19–23.

1.] Joab is addressing the rebel soldiers who fought for Absalom, who 'was
by the trumpet's sound / Proclaimed through Hebron King of Israel'
(11.50–1) earlier in the play.

8.] i.e. prevent your blood from being spilled (therefore maintaining it in
its appropriate state 'by your bones', within the body).

9.] i.e. Let the banner under which I have fought cover your heads (in
order to recover you to loyalty to King David).

13. *chosen*] chosen of God.

state] throne; prince; nation (*OED*, n., 17, 22a, 25).

But Joab pities your disordered souls
And therefore offers pardon, peace, and love
To all that will be friendly reconciled
To Israel's weal, to David, and to heaven.   20
Amasa, thou art leader of the host
That under Absalom have raised their arms;
Then be a captain wise and politic,
Careful and loving for thy soldiers' lives,
And lead them to this honourable league.   25

Amasa. I will, at least I'll do my best,
And for the gracious offer thou hast made
I give thee thanks as much as for my head.
Then, you deceived poor souls of Israel,
Since now ye see the errors you incurred,   30
With thanks and due submission be appeased,
And, as ye see your captain's precedent,
Here cast we, then, our swords at Joab's feet,
Submitting with all zeal and reverence
Our goods and bodies to his gracious hands.   35

[AMASA *and his soldiers throw down their swords and kneel.*]

Joab. Stand up and take ye all your swords again;
David and Joab shall be blessed herein.

All stand up [and pick up their swords].

Ahimaaz. Now let me go inform my lord the King
How God hath freed him from his enemies.

---

32. precedent] *Hawkins (subst);* president *Q.*   33. we] *QP, BL 2, Hv, Il,
Bod, Tex, NLS, HC, VAM, WC, M (subst);* me *QBL 1, H, Fol.*   34. rever-
ence] *QP, BL 2, Hv, Il, Bod, Tex, NLS, HC, VAM, WC, M (subst);* residence
QBL 1, H, Fol.   35.1. SD AMASA *and his soldiers throw down their swords and
kneel.*] *this edn; not in Q.*   37.1. SD] *Manly (subst); 35.1 SD, aligned right,
in Q; 36 SD Dyce (subst).   and pick up their swords*] *this edn; not in Q.*   38. SH
Ahimaaz] *this edn; Ahim. QP, BL 2, Hv, Il, Bod, Tex, NLS, HC, VAM, WC,
M; Iona. QBL 1, H, Fol; Ahimaas. Hawkins (subst).*

20. *weal*] welfare, good.
23. *politic*] prudent, shrewd (*OED*, adj., 2b).
25. *league*] compact, covenant, confederation (*OED*, n.2, 1a).
28.] i.e. I give thanks on behalf of my soldiers and myself.

Joab. Another time, Ahimaaz, not now.   40
  But, Hushai, go thyself and tell the King
  The happy message of our good success.
Hushai. I will, my lord, and thank thee for thy grace.
                                        Exit HUSHAI.
Ahimaaz. What if thy servant should go too, my lord?
Joab. What news hast thou to bring, since he is gone?   45
Ahimaaz. Yet do Ahimaaz so much content
  That he may run about so sweet a charge.
Joab. Run if thou wilt, and peace be with thy steps.
                                        Exit [AHIMAAZ].
  [*To* AMASA *and his soldiers*] Now follow, that you may
    salute the King
  With humble hearts and reconcilèd souls.   50
Amasa. We follow Joab to our gracious King,
  And him our swords shall honour to our deaths.
                                        Exeunt.

43. SH *Hushai*] *this edn; Cus. Q; Cusay. Hawkins (subst).*   43. SD] *printed on 43.1, aligned right, in Q.*   44. SH *Ahimaaz*] *this edn; Ahim. QP, BL 2, Hv, Il, Bod, Tex, NLS, HC, VAM, WC, M; Iona. QBL 1, H, Fol; Ahimaas. Hawkins (subst).*   44. too,] *Hawkins (subst);* to *Q.*   46. SH *Ahimaaz*] *this edn; Ahim. QP, BL 2, Hv, Il, Bod, Tex, NLS, HC, VAM, WC, M; Iona. QBL 1, H, Fol; Ahimaas. Hawkins (subst).*   48. steps.] *Dyce 2 (subst);* steps, *QBL 1, H, Fol;* steps: *QP, BL 2, Hv, Il, Bod, Tex, NLS, HC, VAM, WC, M.*   48.1. SD] *Hawkins (subst); 47 SD, aligned right, in Q.* AHIMAAZ] *Hawkins (subst); not in Q.*   49. SD *To* AMASA *and his soldiers*] *this edn; not in Q.*   51. SH *Amasa*] *Hawkins (subst); Ama. Q.*

44. *thy servant*] i.e. I myself.

too, my lord?] Although the immediate context, in which Joab has chosen Hushai rather than Ahimaaz as messenger, strongly suggests that Q's 'to' means 'too' or 'also', it is also possible to read 'to' as a preposition, which would render the editorial addition of a comma between 'to[o]' and 'my lord' unnecessary. Hawkins, Dyce, Keltie, Morley, Bullen, Thorndike, and Rabkin emend to 'too' and add the comma; Manly retains the original 'to' but adds the comma.

47. *run ... charge*] busy himself in discharging so pleasant a duty.
52. *to our deaths*] until the day we die.

[Sc. 17]

[*Enter*] DAVID, BATHSHEBA, SOLOMON, NATHAN,
ADONIJAH, CHILEAB, *with their train.*

Bathsheba. What means my lord, the lamp of Israel,
From whose bright eyes all eyes receive their light,
To dim the glory of his sweet aspects
And paint his countenance with his heart's distress?
Why should his thoughts retain a sad conceit   5
When every pleasure kneels before his throne
And sues for sweet acceptance with His Grace?
Take but your lute and make the mountains dance,
Retrieve the sun's sphere and restrain the clouds,
Give ears to trees, make savage lions tame,   10

Heading Sc. 17] *Greg (subst); not in Q;* SCENE XV. *Bullen (subst);* ACT
IV. SCENE II. *Morley (subst);* Act III. Scene II. *Manly (subst);* xiv *Rabkin
(subst).* 0.1. SD *Enter*] *Dyce 3 (subst); not in Q.* SOLOMON] *Q (Salomon).*
Modernised silently throughout. 1. SH *Bathsheba*] *this edn; Beth. Q; Bethsabe.
Hawkins (subst).*

[*Sc. 17*] Lines 141–280 dramatise 2 Samuel, 18:24–19:8, the events of
which take place around the gates of the city of Mahanaim. David has yet
to return to Jerusalem. Lines 1–140 dramatise 1 Kings, 1:1–31, in which
Adonijah proclaims himself King of Israel and the dying David replies
by naming Solomon as his heir. These events take place in and around
Jerusalem. Given that at the beginning of the scene David has yet to learn
the news of his army's victory that would permit him to return to Jerusalem,
however, it seems most plausible to locate the scene before the gates of the
city of Mahanaim. The conversation between David and Solomon in lines
1–140 is heavily indebted to the conversation between Adam and Seth in *Les
Artifices*, the fourth book of the first day of Du Bartas's *La Seconde Semaine*.
    1. *the lamp of Israel*] David. In *1 Tamburlaine*, 4.2.36, Tamburlaine calls
himself 'the chiefest lamp of all the earth'.
    5. *conceit*] thought, idea, notion.
    7. *sues*] petitions.
    8–12.] These lines translate Du Bartas's description of the first musician
Jubal's 'luth harmonieux, / Qui meine au bal les monts, retrograde les cieux,
/ Oreille les forests, les lyons dessauvage, / Impose aux vents silence, et
sereine l'orage [harmonious lute, / Which leads the mountains to dance,
retrogrades the heavens, / Gives ears to the forests, removes the savagery
from lions, / Imposes on the winds silence, and calms the storm]' (*Les
Artifices*, 503–6).
    9. *Retrieve*] 'cause (something) to return, esp. *into* or *to* a former place or
state' (*OED*, v., 3b, citing this line as its earliest example).

Impose still silence to the loudest winds,
And fill the fairest day with foulest storms!
Then why should passions of much meaner power
Bear head against the heart of Israel?
David. Fair Bathsheba, thou mightst increase the strength   15
Of these thy arguments drawn from my skill
By urging thy sweet sight to my conceits,
Whose virtue ever served for sacred balm
To cheer my pinings past all earthly joys.
But, Bathsheba, the daughter of the Highest,   20
Whose beauty builds the towers of Israel,
She that in chains of pearl and unicorn
Leads at her train the ancient golden world,
The world that Adam held in Paradise,
Whose breath refineth all infectious airs   25
And makes the meadows smile at her repair,

---

15. SH *David*] *Hawkins (subst); Da. Q.*   16. arguments drawn] *QBL 1, H, Fol (subst);* arguments, drawne *QP, BL 2, Hv, Il, Bod, Tex, NLS, HC, VAM, WC, M.*   18. served] *Morley (subst);* serud *QBL 1, H, Fol;* seru'd *QP, BL 2, Hv, Il, Bod, Tex, NLS, HC, VAM, WC, M.*   20. Highest] *Dyce 3 (subst);* highest *Q.*

11–12.] Bathsheba's point is that David can turn anything into its opposite: noise into silence and, conversely, silence into noise. The antithesis is reinforced by the lines' parallel images: David can silence 'the loudest winds' and raise 'the foulest storms'.

13. *of much meaner power*] i.e. of such a distressing and melancholic spirit.

14.] i.e. rain suffering on the heart of Israel's king.

17.] i.e. by urging me to think of thy beauty.

20. *daughter of the Highest*] Peace, so named in line 28 below. Du Bartas's *Les Artifices* opens with the poet's address to 'Saincte fille du Ciel [holy daughter of Heaven]' (1), who is 'Paix, heureuse Paix [Peace, happy Peace]' (6).

22–6.] In the opening lines of *Les Artifices*, Du Bartas describes peace as 'deese qui ramenes / L'antique siecle d'or, qui, belle, r'asserenes / L'air trouble des François: qui fait rire nos chams [goddess who leads back again / The antique Golden Age, who, beautiful, calms again / The troubled air of the French: who makes our fields smile]' (1–3).

22. *chains of pearl and unicorn*] i.e. necklaces (not shackles) made of pearl and unicorn horn, rare and highly valued (and mythical in the case of unicorn horn) natural substances.

23. *at her train*] at the head of her retinue.

25. *refineth*] purifies, cleanses (*OED*, v., 1a).

26. *repair*] visit, return (*OED* n.1, 4a).

She, she, my dearest Bathsheba,
Fair Peace, the goddess of our graces here,
Is fled the streets of fair Jerusalem,
The fields of Israel, and the heart of David,   30
Leading my comforts in her golden chains
Linked to the life and soul of Absalom.
Bathsheba. Then is the pleasure of my sovereign's heart
So wrapped within the bosom of that son
That Solomon, whom Israel's God affects   35
And gave the name unto him for His love,
Should be no salve to comfort David's soul?
David. Solomon, my love, is David's lord;
Our God hath named him lord of Israel.
In him (for that, and since he is thy son)   40
Must David needs be pleasèd at the heart,
And he shall surely sit upon my throne.
But Absalom, the beauty of my bones,

---

27. She, she,] *Hawkins (subst)*; Shee, Shee, *QP, BL 2, Hv, Il, Bod, Tex, NLS, HC, VAM, WC, M;* Shee, Shee *QBL1, H, Fol.*   33. SH *Bathsheba*] *this edn; Beth. Q; Bethsabe. Hawkins (subst).*   36. His] *this edn;* his *Q.*   38. SH *David*] *Hawkins (subst); Dau. Q.*   38. Solomon, my love, is] *Hawkins (subst);* Salomon (my loue) is *Q.*   39. Our] *QP, BL 2, Hv, Il, Bod, Tex, NLS, HC, VAM, WC, M (subst);* Or *QBL 1, H, Fol.*   Israel.] *Rabkin (subst);* Israel *QBL 1, H, Fol;* Israel: *QP, BL 2, Hv, Il, Bod, Tex, NLS, HC, VAM, WC, M.*

31–2.] i.e. depriving me of all comfort because of the death of Absalom.
35. *Solomon*] David and Bathsheba's son, first mentioned here in the play. This episode has no counterpart in 2 Samuel; Bathsheba's intercession on behalf of her son takes place much later, when David is 'old and stricken in years' (1 Kings, 1:1). It serves here to accentuate the importance of a male heir to the throne in place of Absalom – a theme of intense relevance in England in the 1580s and 1590s.
affects] loves, holds in his affection.
36.] 2 Samuel, 12:24–5 relates that, after Bathsheba has given birth to her and David's second child, David 'called his name Salomon: also the Lord loved him. / For the Lord had sent by Nathan the Prophet: therefore he called his name Jedidiah, because the Lord loved him.' Smith translates Jedidiah as 'darling of Jehovah' (269). (Actually, it is the name 'David' that means 'beloved' in Hebrew. 'Solomon' means 'peace'.)
37. *salve*] medicated ointment.
41. *Must David needs be*] David must necessarily be.

Fair Absalom, the counterfeit of love,
Sweet Absalom, the image of content,   45
Must claim a portion in his father's care
And be in life and death King David's son.
Nathan. Yet, as my lord hath said, let Solomon reign,
Whom God in naming hath anointed King.
Now is he apt to learn th'eternal laws,   50
Whose knowledge, being rooted in his youth,
Will beautify his age with glorious fruits,
While Absalom, incensed with graceless pride,
Usurps and stains the kingdom with his sin.
Let Solomon be made thy staff of age,   55
Fair Israel's rest, and honour of thy race.
David. Tell me, my Solomon, wilt thou embrace
Thy father's precepts gravèd in thy heart
And satisfy my zeal to thy renown
With practice of such sacred principles   60
As shall concern the state of Israel?
Solomon. My royal father, if the heavenly zeal

---

48. SH *Nathan*] *Hawkins (subst); Nat. Q.*   48. reign] *Q (*raigne*).*   57. SH
David] *Hawkins (subst); Da. Q.*   62. SH *Solomon*] *this edn; Sal. Q; Salomon.
Hawkins (subst).*

---

44. *counterfeit*] image, pattern, double (*OED*, n., 3). In *1 Tamburlaine*,
Zenocrate's passion for Tamburlaine renders her 'the ghastly counterfeit of
death' (3.2.17).
50. *apt*] fit, ready, inclined (*OED*, adj., 2b, 4c).
53. *incensed*] aroused.
55–6.] These lines echo Du Bartas's description of Seth, Adam's son, 'qui
tient de sainct Abel la place, / Baston de sa viellesse, et gloire de sa race
[who holds of holy Abel the place, / Staff of his [Adam's] old age, and glory
of his race]' (*Les Artifices*, 517–18).
56. *rest*] peace and security.
57–61.] In 1 Kings, 2:2–3 the dying David exhorts Solomon to 'be strong
therefore, and show thyself a man, / And take heed to the charge of the Lord
thy God, to walk in his ways, and keep his statutes, and his commandments,
and his judgements, and his testimonies, as it is written in the Law of Moses,
that thou mayest prosper in all that thou doest'.
58. *gravèd*] engraved; buried (*OED*, graved, adj.).
59.] and satisfy my eagerness that you achieve a noble renown.
62–77.] Solomon's reply to David amplifies Seth's reply to Adam in Du
Bartas's *Les Artifices*, lines 537–45. See the Appendix for the complete
passage and translation.

Which for my welfare feeds upon your soul
Were not sustained with virtue of mine own,
If the sweet accents of your cheerful voice 65
Should not each hour beat upon mine ears
As sweetly as the breath of heaven to him
That gaspeth scorchèd with the summer's sun,
I should be guilty of unpardoned sin,
Fearing the plague of heaven and shame of earth. 70
But, since I vow myself to learn the skill
And holy secrets of His mighty hand
Whose cunning tunes the music of my soul,
It would content me, father, first to learn
How th'Eternal framed the firmament: 75
Which bodies lead their influence by fire,
And which are filled with hoary winter's ice;
What sign is rainy, and what star is fair;

---

72. His] *this edn;* his *Q.*   74. me, father, first] *Hawkins (subst);* me (father) first *Q.*   75. Eternal] *Dyce 3 (subst);* eternall *Q.*   76. lead] *Q (subst);* lend *Dyce 3 (subst).*

73. *cunning*] skill, wisdom (*OED*, n., 2, 3a).

75. *framed*] constructed.

76–81.] These lines follow closely Du Bartas's description of Adam's lessons to Seth. Adam teaches Seth 'comme le Ciel se meut, comme son juste cours / L'an divise en ses mois, et le mois en ses jours, / Quel astre fait l'hyver, quel feu l'esté rameine, / Quel signe est pluvieux, quelle estoille est sereine [how the Heaven moves, how its proper course / The year divides into its months, and the month into its days, / Which star causes winter, which leads back fire, / Which sign is rainy, which star is fair]' (*Les Artifices*, 523–6).

76. *bodies*] heavenly bodies such as stars and planets.

lead] transmit. Dyce 3, Keltie, Morley, Bullen, and Thorndike emend to 'lend', but 'lead' follows Du Bartas's 'rameine' (*Les Artifices*, 525).

78. *sign*] sign of the zodiac, used by astrologers and almanack makers to prognosticate the weather. In his *Almanacke and Prognostication for x. yeeres, beginning at the yeere of our Lorde 1581 … Wherein is set downe … the iudgement of the weather* (1581), William Bourne writes that 'those that write the judgements astrological, have made long observation from age unto age, and accordingly unto the aspects of the planets, the one with the other of them, and the planets with the fixed stars, and how that they have been angled in the houses of the heavens, and also the nature of the signs … have found how the weather hath followed' (sig. A4v).

fair] good, of a benevolent influence, prognosticating good (as opposed to 'rainy') weather.

Why by the rules of true proportion
The year is still divided into months,   80
The months to days, the days to certain hours;
What fruitful race shall fill the future world,
Or for what time shall this round building stand;
What magistrates, what kings, shall keep in awe
Men's minds with bridles of th'eternal law.   85
David. Wade not too far, my boy, in waves too deep.
The feeble eyes of our aspiring thoughts
Behold things present and record things past,

---

86. SH *David*] *Hawkins (subst); Da. Q.*

79. *rules of true proportion*] According to Dionis Gray in *The store-house of Breuitie in woorkes of Arithmetike* (1577), the 'Golden Rule' of mathematics is the 'Rule of Proportion', which stipulates that 'the fourth and unknown number found by the work, shall bear such proportion unto the third of the known numbers, as the second beareth to the first' (sig. I6v). 'How of the world the time doth pass, / To make true computation', Gray declares in his prefatory poem, 'By number is dilated, / For knowledge universal' (sig. A4v–5r).

82–5.] In Du Bartas, Seth concludes his reply to Adam by expressing his desire to know 'quelle race feconde / Doit peupler l'univers, que deviendra le monde, / Combien doit-il durer, quels magistrats, quels rois / Tiendront serfs les humains sous la bride des lois [what fecund race / Must populate the universe, what will the world become, / How long must it endure, what magistrates, what kings / Will hold humans servile under the bridle of laws]' (*Les Artifices*, 549–52). Lines 551–2 of Du Bartas suggest that kings are tyrants who use the law to render their subjects servile ('serfs'). Peele's rendition, in contrast, implies that authority is ultimately good: magistrates and monarchs enforce 'eternal law' (85) in order not to debase their subjects but to maintain in their minds the proper reverence or 'awe' (84).

83.] i.e. or for how long a time this world will endure. In the early modern period, the date of the end of the world was a subject of considerable speculation, often fuelled by the belief that the Protestant Reformation had ushered the world into the apocalyptic time cryptically depicted in the biblical Book of Revelation and other biblical apocalyptic texts (Firth, 69–241). This speculation ran counter to the biblical assertion of that date's unknowability. 'Heaven and earth shall pass away', Jesus states, 'But of the day and hour knoweth no man, no not the angels of heaven, but my father only' (Matthew, 24:35, 36), to which the Geneva gloss adds, 'It is sufficient for us to know that God hath appointed a latter day for the restoring of all things, but when it shall be, it is hidden from us all, for our profit, that we may be so much the more watchful'.

87–115.] David's response to Solomon in these lines translates Adam's response to Seth's questioning in Du Bartas's *Les Artifices*, lines 553–72. See the Appendix for the complete passage and translation.

But things to come exceed our human reach
And are not painted yet in angels' eyes.   90
For those, submit thy sense and say, 'Thou Power
That now art framing of the future world,
Knowst all to come, not by the course of heaven,
By frail conjectures of inferior signs,
By monstrous floods, by flights and flocks of birds,   95
By bowels of a sacrificèd beast,
Or by the figures of some hidden art,
But by a true and natural presage,
Laying the ground and perfect architect

91. Power] *Manly (subst);* power *Q.*

87–98.] David's expression of the limits of human thought in these lines contrasts starkly with Tamburlaine's praise in *1 Tamburlaine* of 'aspiring minds' (2.7.20) that seek to 'comprehend / The wondrous architecture of the world / And measure every wand'ring planet's course, / Still climbing after knowledge infinite' (21–4).

87–9.] These lines are reproduced in Robert Allott's verse anthology *England's Parnassus* (1600), under the heading 'Thoughts'.

90. *painted*] depicted, observed, understood.

91. *submit thy sense*] i.e. submit your human perceptions to the realisation of their limitations.

92. *framing of*] designing and creating.

93. *the course of heaven*] the motion and trajectory of the stars and planets (as astrologically interpreted).

94. *inferior signs*] signs, like those listed in lines 95 and 96, that originate in the earthly rather than the heavenly realm.

97. *figures*] characters, diagrams, images (*OED*, n., 9a, 13, 14, 18).

hidden art] necromancy, for example, whose purported power, 'promised to the studious artisan', was based on occult 'Lines, circles, signs, letters, and characters' (*Doctor Faustus, A-Text*, 1.1.57, 53).

98. *presage*] divine foreshadowing, sign, prognostication (*OED*, n., 1b, 2a).

99. *perfect*] flawless; complete (*OED*, adj., 1a, 2b).

architect] architecture. The use of the word in this sense is unrecorded in the *OED*, but the primary senses of the noun as given in the *OED*, 'master-builder' or simply 'builder', do not fit in this context. 'Thou Power / That now art framing of the future world' (91–2) is the master-builder before whose sight is laid 'the ground and perfect architect / Of all our actions' (99–100). Dyce 3's emendation to 'archetype' addresses the initial semantic difficulty but is unnecessary if Blistein's contention that ' "Architect" must be Peele's form of "architecture" ' (278) is accepted. As far as I am aware Peele does not use the word in this sense elsewhere in his work, and in *Descensus Astraeae* the presenter urges that 'heaven's great Architect be praised for all' (59).

Of all our actions now before Thine eyes   100
From Adam to the end of Adam's seed.
O Heaven, protect my weakness with Thy strength!
So look on me that I may view Thy face
And see these secrets written in Thy brows.
O Sun, come dart Thy rays upon my moon,   105
That now mine eyes eclipsèd to the earth
May brightly be refined and shine to heaven.
Transform me from this flesh, that I may live
Before my death regenerate with Thee.
O Thou great God, ravish my earthly sprite,   110
That for the time a more than human skill
May feed the organons of all my sense,
That, when I think, Thy thoughts may be my guide
And, when I speak, I may be made by choice
The perfect echo of Thy heavenly voice.'   115
Thus say, my son, and thou shalt learn them all.

---

100. Thine] *this edn;* thine *Q.*   102. Heaven] *Manly (subst);* heauen
Q.   Thy] *this edn;* thy *Q.*   103. Thy] *this edn;* thy *Q.*   104. Thy] *this edn;*
thy *Q.*   105. Sun] *Manly (subst);* sun *Q.*   Thy] *this edn;* thy *Q.*   109. Thee]
this edn; thee *Q.*   110. Thou] *this edn;* thou *Q.*   111. than] *Hawkins
(subst);* then *Q.*   113. Thy] *this edn;* thy *Q.*   115. Thy] *this edn;* thy *Q.*

---

101. *seed*] progeny.
105. *my moon*] i.e. my inferior knowledge, entirely dependent on divine
revelation.
106. *eclipsèd to the earth*] confined to earthly perception.
107. *refined*] purified, cleansed (*OED*, v.1, 1a).
109.] i.e. before I am regenerated by you in my death.
110. *ravish*] transport in spirit, enrapture, fill with ecstasy (*OED*, v., 4a,
b).
   sprite] spirit.
111. *for the time*] while I live.
112. *organons*] 'bodily organ[s], esp. as an instrument of the soul or mind'
(*OED*, n., 1a, citing *2 Tamburlaine*, in which a physician tells Tamburlaine
that he will die because his arteries and veins are dry and, consequently, 'the
soul, / Wanting those organons by which it moves, / Cannot endure'
(5.3.95–7)).
115. *Thy heavenly voice*] The quotation begins at line 91 above; it is what
David wishes Solomon to pray for.
116. *them*] i.e. 'Thy thoughts' (line 113), God's ideas.

Solomon. A secret fury ravisheth my soul,
   Lifting my mind above her human bounds,
   And, as the eagle rousèd from her stand
   With violent hunger, towering in the air,   120
   Seizeth her feathered prey and thinks to feed,
   But, seeing then a cloud beneath her feet,
   Lets fall the fowl and is emboldenèd
   With eyes intentive to bedare the sun,
   And stieth close unto his stately sphere,   125
   So Solomon, mounted on the burning wings
   Of zeal divine, lets fall his mortal food
   And cheers his senses with celestial air,
   Treads in the golden starry labyrinth,
   And holds his eyes fixed on Jehovah's brows.   130
   Good father, teach me further what to do.

---

117. SH *Solomon*] *this edn; Salo. Q; Salomon. Hawkins (subst).*   120. hunger,
towering in the air,] *Dyce 3 (subst); hunger (towring in the aire) Q.*

117–30.] These lines echo Du Bartas's *Les Artifices*, lines 573–88. See
the Appendix for the complete passage and translation. The eagle's ability
to stare directly into the sun was a commonplace of classical and medieval
animal lore (see Pliny, *Natural History*, 10.3). In Christian writings, it is
used as the basis of metaphors equating the eagle and the soul. St Antony
of Padua, for example, writes that 'In the eagle the subtle intelligence of
saints and their sublime contemplation is set forth; for they turn towards
the aspect of the true Sun, to the light of wisdom' (235).
   119. *stand*] perch.
   124. *intentive*] intently directed (*OED*, adj., 2).
   bedare] stare defiantly at, stare down.
   125.] i.e. and ascends close to the highest point of the sun's majestic orb.
   stieth] 'ascends, rises or climbs to a higher level, soars' (*OED*, v.1).
   sphere] orb, globe; a heavenly body's spherically defined region of motion
and influence. In ancient Greek and medieval cosmology, God inhabits the
ninth sphere of the heavens and is the source of the motion of all the other
spheres, which are contained within the ninth sphere like concentric circles.
The eighth sphere is the sphere of the fixed stars. The first through seventh
spheres are the planetary spheres of the Moon, Mercury, Venus, the Sun,
Mars, Jupiter, and Saturn respectively. The earth is at the centre of the
spheres (Lindberg, 248–51). *The Compost of Ptholomeus* calls the spheres
'skies' and notes that some astronomers posit the existence of a number of
immobile 'skies' beyond the ninth (which they consider completely empty):
'There [have] been some astrologians say that above these nine skies one is
immobile, for it turneth not, and above it is one of crystal, over the which
is the sky imperial, in the which is the throne of God' (sig. E1v).
   127. *lets fall*] puts aside.

Nathan. See, David, how his haughty spirit mounts
       Even now of height to wield a diadem.
       Then make him promise that he may succeed,
       And rest old Israel's bones from broils of war.   135
David. Nathan, thou prophet, sprung from Jesse's root,
       I promise thee and lovely Bathsheba,
       My Solomon shall govern after me.
Bathsheba. He that hath touched thee with this righteous
              thought
       Preserve the harbour of thy thoughts in peace!   140

                    Enter Messenger.

Messenger. My lord, thy servants of the watch have seen
       One running hitherward from forth the wars.
David. If he be come alone, he bringeth news.
Messenger. Another hath thy servant seen, my lord,
       Whose running much resembles Zadok's son.   145
David. He is a good man and good tidings brings.

                    Enter AHIMAAZ.

---

132. SH *Nathan*] *Hawkins (subst); Nath. Q.*   139. SH *Bathsheba*] *this edn;*
Beth. Q; Bethsabe. Hawkins (subst).   140.1. SD Messenger] *Hawkins*
(subst); Mess Q.   141. SH *Messenger*] *Hawkins (subst); Mess. Q.*   141. the
watch] *QP, BL 2, Hv, Il, Bod, Tex, NLS, HC, VAM, WC, M (subst);* thy
watch *QBL 1, H, Fol.*   144. SH *Messenger*] *Hawkins (subst); Mess.*
Q.   146. SH *David*] *Hawkins (subst); Da. Q.*

---

132. *his*] Solomon's.
haughty] exalted, elevated, lofty (*OED*, adj., 2).
133. *of height*] to a sufficient height.
135. *rest ... bones*] give old Israel's bones respite.
136. *sprung ... root*] descended from Jesse, David's father (1 Chronicles,
10:14).
140-1.] i.e. may God preserve and give peace to the mind that protects
and gives utterance to these noble thoughts!
143.] Compare 2 Samuel, 18:25: 'And the king said, If he be alone, he
bringeth tidings.' (Only a messenger would come unattended.)
144-5.] 2 Samuel, 18:26-7 clarifies: 'the watchman saw another man
running ... And the watchman said, Me thinketh the running of the foremost
is like the running of Ahimaaz the son of Zadok.' Ahimaaz is unable (or
unwilling) to let King David know that Absalom is dead.
145. Zadok's son] Ahimaaz.
146.] Compare 2 Samuel, 18:27: 'He is a good man, and cometh with
good tidings.'

Ahimaaz. Peace and content be with my lord the King,
    Whom Israel's God hath blessed with victory!
David. Tell me, Ahimaaz, lives my Absalom?
Ahimaaz. I saw a troop of soldiers gatherèd   150
    But know not what the tumult might import.
David. Stand by until some other may inform
    The heart of David with a happy truth.

                Enter HUSHAI.

Hushai. Happiness and honour live with David's soul,
    Whom God hath blessed with conquest of his foes!   155
David. But, Hushai, lives the young man Absalom?
Hushai. The stubborn enemies to David's peace
    And all that cast their darts against his crown
    Fare ever like the young man Absalom,
    For, as he rid the woods of Ephraim,   160
    Which fought for thee as much as all thy men,
    His hair was tangled in a shady oak,

---

147. SH *Ahimaaz*] *this edn; Ahim. Q; Ahimaas. Hawkins (subst).*   149. SH
David] *Hawkins (subst); Da. Q.*   150. SH *Ahimaaz*] *this edn; Ahim. Q;
Ahimaas. Hawkins (subst).*   152. SH *David*] *Hawkins (subst); Dau. Q.*
157. SH *Hushai*] *this edn; Cus. Q; Cusay. Hawkins (subst).*   160–1. Ephraim,
/ Which] *Hawkins (subst);* Ephraim / (Which *Q.*   161. men,] *Hawkins
(subst);* men) *Q.*

150–1.] Compare 2 Samuel, 18:29: 'and me thy servant, I saw a great
tumult, but I knew not what.'
    151. *import*] mean, signify, portend (*OED*, v., 5b, d).
    152. *Stand by*] Compare 2 Samuel, 18:30: 'And the King said unto him,
Turn aside, and stand here.'
    154–5.] Compare 2 Samuel, 18:31: 'And behold, Cushi came, and Cushi
said, Tidings, my lord the King: for the Lord hath delivered thee this day
out of the hand of all that rose against thee.'
    156–64.] The account in 2 Samuel, 18:32 is more brief: 'Then the King
said unto Cushi, Is the young man Absalom safe? And Cushi answered, The
enemies of my lord the King, and all that rise against thee to do thee hurt,
be as that young man is.'
    159. *Fare*] may they fare.
    160. *rid*] rode through.
    161.] According to 2 Samuel, 18:8, during the battle in the woods of
Ephraim, 'the wood devoured much more people that day than did the
sword.' Hushai's more particular point is that the woods aided King David
by entrapping Absalom and thus delivering him to his enemies.

And, hanging there, by Joab and his men
Sustained the stroke of well-deservèd death.
David. Hath Absalom sustained the stroke of death?   165
Die, David, for the death of Absalom,
And make these cursèd news the bloody darts
That through his bowels rip thy wretched breast!
Hence, David, walk the solitary woods
And, in some cedar's shade the thunder slew   170
And fire from heaven hath made his branches black,
Sit mourning the decease of Absalom;
Against the body of that blasted plant
In thousand shivers break thy ivory lute,
Hanging thy stringless harp upon his boughs,   175
And through the hollow sapless-sounding trunk
Bellow the torments that perplex thy soul.
There let the winds sit sighing till they burst!
Let tempest muffled with a cloud of pitch
Threaten the forests with her hellish face   180
And, mounted fiercely on her iron wings,
Rend up the wretched engine by the roots
That held my dearest Absalom to death.
Then let them toss my broken lute to heaven,

---

163. there, by] *Hawkins (subst);* there (by *Q.*   men] *Dyce 3 (subst);* men)
Q.   170. shade the] *QBL 1, H, Fol (subst);* shade (the *QP, BL 2, Hv,
Il, Bod, Tex, NLS, HC, VAM, WC, M.*   171. black,] *Hawkins (subst);*
blacke *QBL 1, H, Fol;* blacke) *QP, BL 2, Hv, Il, Bod, Tex, NLS, HC,
VAM, WC, M.*   181. And, mounted] *Hawkins (subst);* And (mounted *Q.*
wings,] *Hawkins (subst);* wings) *Q.*

170–1. *the thunder ... black*] i.e. which lightning attacked and burned.
173. *that blasted plant*] that tree burned by lightning. (With suggestion of
the tree on which Absalom died. Peele here coalesces two images, that of a
burned thicket where David wishes to grieve, and the other the place where
Absalom died. The image calls to mind again the iconography of Christ's
crucifixion. 'Blasted' then has the suggestion of 'damned'.)
175. *his*] its.
176. *sapless-sounding*] both sapless and resounding in its hollowness.
177. *perplex*] torment; confuse (*OED*, v., 1a, b).
180, 181. *her*] the tempest's.
182. *engine*] trap, snare (*OED*, n., 2, 4c), i.e., the tree.
184. *them*] the winds and the tempest.

Even to His hands that beats me with the strings,   185
To show how sadly his poor shepherd sings.

He goes to his pavilion and sits close awhile.

Bathsheba. Die, Bathsheba, to see thy David mourn,
To hear his tunes of anguish and of hell!
Oh, help, my David, help thy Bathsheba,

She kneels down.

Whose heart is piercèd with thy breathy swords   190
And bursts with burden of ten thousand griefs!
Now sits thy sorrows sucking of my blood.
Oh, that it might be poison to their powers
And that their lips might draw my bosom dry!
So David's love might ease him, though she die.   195
Nathan. These violent passions come not from above.
David and Bathsheba offend the Highest
To mourn in this immeasurable sort.

---

185. His] *this edn;* his *Q.* 187. SH *Bathsheba*] *this edn; Beth. Q; Bethsabe.*
Hawkins (subst). 189.1. SD] *aligned right in Q.* 196. SH *Nathan*] *Hawkins*
(subst); Nat. Q. 197. Highest] *Hawkins (subst);* highest *Q.*

185–6.] i.e. even into the hands of God, who beats me with the strings of
my broken lute, in order to signify how mournfully I, David, God's 'poor
shepherd', sing now Absalom is dead.

186.1. SD pavilion] royal tent. If a movable stage property, like the booth
that might have been used as Bathsheba's bower in scene 1 or as the tower
in scene 2, were here used as David's royal pavilion, it would need to have
been on stage since the scene's beginning. The discovery space in the
tiring-house façade could be used equally well, however. In *Edward I*, the
bishop and others present Edward with his newly christened son while he
is sitting in his pavilion. The stage direction reads: '*Then all pass in their*
order to the king's pavilion, the king sits in his tent with his pages about him'
(1932.1–2 SD).

close] enclosed.

190. *breathy swords*] words and sighs. Blistein glosses as 'sharp sighs'
(280). 'Swords' could be a typographical error for 'words'.

193. *it*] Bathsheba's blood.

to their powers] i.e. matched to the power of David's blood-sucking
sorrows, or, to the greatest extent of sorrow's powers.

195. *she*] I myself.

David. O Absalom, Absalom, O my son, my son!
 Would God that I had died for Absalom!   200
 But he is dead, ah dead, Absalom is dead,
 And David lives to die for Absalom.

   He looks forth and at the end sits close again.

   Enter JOAB, ABISHAI, ITTAI, *with their train.*

Joab. Why lies the Queen so prostrate on the ground?
 Why is this company so tragic-hued?
 Why is the King now absent from his men   205
 And marcheth not in triumph through the gates?

   He unfolds the pavilion.

 David, awake, if sleep have shut thine eyes,
 Sleep of affection, that thou canst not see
 The honour offered to the victor's head.
 Joab brings conquest piercèd on his spear   210
 And joy from all the tribes of Israel.
David. Thou man of blood, thou sepulchre of death,
 Whose marble breast entombs my bowels quick,
 Did I not charge thee, nay, entreat thy hand,
 Even for my sake to spare my Absalom?   215

---

199. SH *David*] *Hawkins (subst);* Dau. *Q.*   204. tragic-hued] *Hawkins (subst);* Tragicke hew'd *Q.*   206.1. SD] *aligned right in Q.*   213. entombs] *Hawkins (subst);* intombe *Q.*

199–200.] 2 Samuel, 18:33 offers one of the most moving verses in all scripture: 'O my son Absalom, my son, my son Absalom: would God I had died for thee, O Absalom, my son, my son.'
 202.1. SD close] enclosed.
 206. *gates*] city gates.
 206.1. SD unfolds] opens.
 208. *affection*] emotion; 'abnormal bodily state; a disease' (*OED*, n.1, 1b, 7).
 210. *conquest … spear*] In 5.0.31–2 of *Henry V*, the Chorus anticipates Essex 'from Ireland coming, / Bringing rebellion broachèd on his sword' (Campbell, 259, n.1; cited Blistein, 280).
 213.] i.e. whose hardheartedness is as a tomb for my body that is still barely alive.
 214. *charge*] order.

And hast thou now, in spite of David's health
And scorn to do my heart some happiness,
Given him the sword and spilt his purple soul?
Joab. What? Irks it David that he victor breathes,
That Judah and the fields of Israel   220
Should cleanse their faces from their children's blood?
What, art thou weary of thy royal rule?
Is Israel's throne a serpent in thine eyes
And He that set thee there so far from thanks
That thou must curse His servant for His sake?   225
Hast thou not said that as the morning light,
The cloudless morning, so should be thine house,
And not as flowers by the brightest rain,
Which grow up quickly and as quickly fade?
Hast thou not said, the wicked are as thorns,   230

---

224. He] *this edn;* he *Q.*   225. His servant] *this edn;* his servant *Q.*   His
sake] *this edn;* his sake *Q.*   229. grow] *Hawkins (subst);* growes *Q.*
fade] *Hawkins (subst);* fades *Q.*

216. *in spite of*] to the detriment of.
218.] i.e. slain him with your sword and spilled his royal and purple-
coloured blood, the blood that kept body and soul together.
purple] *fig.* royal; splendid; bloody; penitent. The colour's connotations
of royalty, splendour, and penitence are derived from clothing: Roman
emperors and senators wore purple, and in the Church purple was worn on
Good Friday and other occasions of mourning and penitence (*OED*, adj.,
1a, b, 2b, c, 3). The colour assumes a range of meanings in Peele's work:
earlier in the play, David declares that 'Sin with his sevenfold crown and
purple robe / Begins his triumphs in my guilty throne' (4.78–9) after learning
of Tamar's rape; in *The Praise of Chastity*, however, the person who is able
to resist lust is to be crowned 'with laurel, for his victory, / Clad him in
purple, and in scarlet dye' (89–90).
224. *from thanks*] from being thanked by you.
225.] i.e. that you feel you must curse me, Joab, God's loyal servant, for
doing the Lord's work. Compare 2 Samuel, 19:5: 'And Joab came into the
house to the king, and said, Thou hast shamed this day the faces of all thy
servants, which this day have saved thy life.'
226–34.] Joab is recalling words that in the biblical narrative are recorded
as part of 'the last words of David … the sweet singer of Israel' (2 Samuel,
23:1): 'Even as the morning light when the sun riseth, the morning, I say,
without clouds, so shall mine house be, and not as the grass of the earth is
by the bright rain ['Which groweth quickly and fadeth soon' (Geneva gloss)]
… But the wicked shall be every one as thorns thrust away, because they
cannot be taken with hands. / But the man shall touch them, must be
defensed with iron, or with the shaft of a spear' (2 Samuel, 23:4, 6–7).

That cannot be preservèd with the hand,
And that the man shall touch them must be armed
With coats of iron and garments made of steel
Or with the shaft of a defencèd spear?
And art thou angry he is now cut off   235
That led the guiltless swarming to their deaths
And was more wicked than an host of men?
Advance thee from thy melancholy den,
And deck thy body with thy blissful robes,
Or by the Lord that sways the heaven I swear   240
I'll lead thine armies to another king
Shall cheer them for their princely chivalry
And not sit daunted, frowning in the dark,
When his fair looks, with oil and wine refreshed,
Should dart into their bosoms gladsome beams   245
And fill their stomachs with triumphant feasts,
That, when elsewhere stern war shall sound his trump
And call another battle to the field,
Fame still may bring thy valiant soldiers home
And for their service happily confess   250
She wanted worthy trumps to sound their prowess.
Take thou this course and live; refuse, and die.

236. led] *Q* (*lead*).   237. than] *Hawkins (subst);* then *Q.*   240. Lord] *Q*
(subst).

231. *preservèd*] defended against. Peele's use of the word here is idiosyn-
cratic and ultimately opposite its normal early modern and modern meaning.
232. *shall*] who shall.
234. *defencèd spear*] spear used in self-protection (*OED*). Blistein calls the
adjective's use here 'strange' (280) but observes that Peele picked the adjective up from 2 Samuel, 23:7 (see note to 226–34).
235. *he*] Absalom.
236. *the guiltless*] Absalom's army, whom Joab regards as not personally
blameworthy but as led by a bad ruler.
242. *Shall*] who will.
244. *his*] the 'another king' of line 241.
247. *That*] so that.
251.] i.e. that she, Fame, lacked enough trumpets to sound a fanfare
worthy of celebrating those soldiers' prowess in battle.
    trumps] trumpets. In Renaissance literature and art, Fame is commonly
represented with a trumpet. Thus, the emblem of Geffrey Whitney's 'To
Edwarde Dier *Esquier*' depicts a winged Fame blowing her trumpet, and its
poem announces that 'fame with trump, that mounts unto the sky: / ... /
Here hovereth at your will' (197).

Abishai. Come, brother, let him sit there till he sink.
Some other shall advance the name of Joab.

        Offers to go out [with JOAB].

Bathsheba. [*Rises*] Oh, stay, my lords, stay! David mourns no
    more   255
    But riseth to give honour to your acts.

        [JOAB and ABISHAI] *stay.*

        He [DAVID] *riseth up.*

David. Then happy art thou, David's fairest son,
    That, freed from the yoke of earthly toils
    And sequestered from sense of human sins,
    Thy soul shall joy the sacred cabinet   260
    Of those divine Ideas that present

254.1. SD] *aligned right in Q. with* JOAB] *Dyce 3 (subst); not in Q.* 255. SH
Bathsheba] *this edn; Beth. Q; Bethsabe. Hawkins (subst).* 255. SD *Rises*]
Dyce 3 (subst); not in Q. 256.1. SD] *printed on 256, aligned right, in Q.* JOAB
and ABISHAI] *this edn; not in Q.* 256.2. SD] *aligned right in Q.* DAVID] *this
edn; not in Q.*

    254.1. SD Offers to] Is about to.
    257. *David's fairest son*] Absalom. David's elegiac apostrophe to his dead
son continues to line 276.
    258–76.] David's farewell to Absalom closely follows Du Bartas's descrip-
tion of Enoch, whom God took to heaven before he died (Genesis, 5:24).
See the Appendix for the complete passage and translation. Enoch's translation from earth to heaven is his reward for a virtuous existence; significantly,
Peele adapts Du Bartas to create for Absalom a spiritual *telos* not of reward
but of redemption that does not bypass mortality but renders it irrelevant.
    259. *sequestered*] accented on first and third syllables (as it sometimes was
in early modern English poetry).
    260. *joy*] enjoy.
    sacred cabinet] sacred enclosed space containing thought.
    261. *divine Ideas*] thoughts of God. In Neoplatonism, the ideas that
subsist in God are the archetypes of all being. Additionally, here divine Ideas
and the 'sacred cabinet' (260) in which they are contained could be interpreted as metaphorical extensions of the ark of the covenant and its contents,
the stone tablets engraved with the Ten Commandments, into an image of
heaven.

Thy changèd spirit with a heaven of bliss.
Then thou art gone–ah, thou art gone, my son!
To heaven I hope my Absalom is gone.
Thy soul, there placed in honour of the saints   265
Or angels clad with immortality,
Shall reap a sevenfold grace for all thy griefs;
Thy eyes, now no more eyes but shining stars,
Shall deck the flaming heavens with novel lamps;
There shalt thou taste the drink of seraphim   270
And cheer thy feelings with archangels' food;
Thy day of rest, thy holy Sabbath day,
Shall be eternal, and, the curtain drawn,
Thou shalt behold thy Sovereign face to face
With wonder knit in triple unity,   275

---

274. Sovereign] *this edn;* soueraigne *Q.*

267. *for*] in exchange for.
268–9.] These lines translate Du Bartas's 'tes yeux, non-plus yeux, /
Decorent flamboyans d'astres nouveaux les cieux [your eyes, no longer eyes,
/ With their flames ornament the heavens with new stars]' (*Les Artifices,*
671–2), but also echo the beginning of Heironimo's lament for his murdered
son, Horatio, in 3.2 of Thomas Kyd's *The Spanish Tragedy*: 'O eyes, no eyes,
but fountains fraught with tears' (1). Kyd's line is itself an imitation of line
4 of Petrarch's sonnet 161, 'O my eyes, not eyes but fountains'. Campbell
(259, n.2; cited Blistein, 281) compares lines 268–9 to *Romeo and Juliet,*
2.2.15–17: 'Two of the fairest stars in all the heaven, / Having some business,
do entreat her eyes / To twinkle in their spheres till they return.'
269. *novel*] new.
270. *seraphim*] angels. In Isaiah, 6:2–3 the seraphim stand before God's
throne and 'every one had six wings: with twain he covered his face, and
with twain he covered his feet, and with twain he did fly. / And one cried to
another and said, Holy, holy, holy is the Lord of hosts: the whole world is
full of his glory.'
272. *holy Sabbath day*] 'the weekly seventh day of rest, fundamental in
Israelite life, sanctioned by God's rest from the work of creation (*Genesis,*
2:1–3) and accepted as such in all parts of the OT' (Browning, 318).
273. *the curtain drawn*] i.e. when you die.
275. *triple unity*] the Trinity, in whom, according to Christian doctrine,
are unified the three persons of God the Father, God the Son, and God the
Holy Spirit.

Unity infinite and innumerable.
Courage, brave captains! Joab's tale hath stirred
And made the suit of Israel preferred.
Joab. Bravely resolved, and spoken like a king!
Now may old Israel and his daughters sing.   280

Exeunt.

FINIS.

280.1. SD] *printed on 280, aligned right, in Q.*

278.] i.e. and has prompted me to accept and act upon the petition Joab has made on behalf of Israel, that I join in battle against God's enemies.

279.] Henry IV uses a similar formula in the anonymous Queen's Men play *The Famous Victories of Henry V* when he cheers his son's emphatic defiance of anyone seeking to take the crown from him: 'Nobly spoken, and like a king!' (8.62).

Bravely] valiantly; splendidly; worthily (*OED*, adv., 1, 2, 3).

APPENDIX
Extended Passages from Du Bartas

17.62–77 Solomon's reply to David amplifies Seth's reply to Adam in Du Bartas's *Les Artifices*, lines 537–45. 'O Pere, si le zele / Qui te ronge pour moy d'une ardeur eternelle / Ne m'estoit point cognu; si tu ne me couvois / D'un oeil sans fin veillant; si ta prudente vois / Ne battait nuit et jour mon oreille aprentice; / Je craindroy d'encourir d'un importun le vice, / Et me contenteroy d'avoir appris comment / L'Eternel sur ce Tout vouta le firmament, / Quels corps sont pleins de feu, quels corps sont pleins de glace [O father, if the zeal / That gnaws you for me of an eternal ardour / Were not at all by me known; if you did not cover me / With an eye without end waking; if your wise voice / Did not beat night and day upon my apprentice ear; / I would fear to incur the sin of one who is importunate, / And I will content myself with having learned how the Eternal upon this All vaulted the heavens, / Which bodies are full of fire, which bodies are full of ice]' (*Les Artifices*, 537–45).

17.87–115 David's response to Solomon in these lines translates Adam's response to Seth's questioning in Du Bartas: 'Mon fils (repond Adam), l'oeil de nostre pensee / Voit la chose presente et revoit la passee, / Nous cele qui nous suit, si, rendu plus qu'humain, / Il ne la lit au front du Trois-fois-souverain. / Toy donq, qui seul cognois toutes choses futures, / Non-fondé, comme nous, sur foibles conjectures, / Et cherchant à tastons la saincte Verité / Qui, parente, se tient chés ton Eternité, / Ains d'une prescience et certaine et parfaite, / Comme estant du futur l'agent et le profete, / Davant qui les trois tems coulent ensemblement, / A qui l'Eternité dure moins qu'un moment; / O Dieu, regarde-moy, à fin que je regarde / Le miroir de ta face. O Soleil, vient, et darde / Tes rais dessus ma lune, à fin qu'ore mes yeux / Eclipsent vers la terre et luisent vers les cieux. / Retire-moy du corps, à fin qu'heureux je vive / Au ciel avant ma mort. O ma vie, r'avive / Pour un temps mon esprit, et fay qu'à ceste fois / Je soy comme l'echo de ta celeste vois [My son (Adam responds), the eye of our thought / Sees the thing present and reviews the past, / From us conceals what follows us, unless, ren-

169

dered more than human, / It reads it on the forehead of the Thrice-Sovereign. / You, then, who alone knows all future things, not founded, like us, on feeble conjectures, / And searching blindly for the holy Truth / That, cousin to you, holds itself in your Eternity, / But from a foreknowledge certain and perfect, / As being both agent and prophet of the future, / Before whom the three times flow together, / For whom Eternity endures less than a moment, / O God, regard me, so that I may regard the mirror of your face. O Sun, come, and dart / Your rays below my moon, so that now my eyes / May eclipse towards the earth and shine towards the heavens. / Draw me from my body, so that I may happily live / In heaven before my death. O my life, revive / For a time my spirit, and make that at this time / I may be as the echo of thy celestial voice]' (*Les Artifices*, 553–72).

17.117–30 In Du Bartas, after Adam has instructed him how to pray, Seth 'est soudain poussé d'une fureur secrete [is suddenly possessed by a secret fury]' (*Les Artifices*, 573) that is 'non comme le Menade [not like the Bacchant]' (574) or 'le daemon' (578). Rather, 'comme l'aigle perd sa branche accoustumee, / Et ramant par les airs d'une gasche emplumee, / Voit sous ses pieds la nue, et fait, audacieux, / D'un oeil ferme cligner du clair soleil les yeux. / Le prophete guindé sur les ardentes ailes / Du seraphique amour, perd les choses mortelles, / Se paist du doux aether, fend les ronds estoillez, / Et tient dessus le front de Dieu ses yeux collez [as the eagle loses his accustomed branch and, soaring through the air from a squandered feathered prey, / Sees under its feet the clouds and, audacious, / Blinks with firm eye into the bright sun, / The prophet erect upon the burning wings / Of seraphic love loses mortal things, / Grazes upon sweet aether, cleaves through the starry rounds, / And holds his eyes fixed before the forehead of God]' (581–8).

17.258–76 David's farewell to Absalom closely follows Du Bartas's description of Enoch, whom God took to heaven before he died (Genesis, 5:24): 'Comme libre du joug des corporelles lois, / Et sequestré des sens, il vole quelquefois / Dans le sainct cabinet des idees plus belles, / Ayant la foy, le jeusne, et l'oraison pour ailes; / Comme à certains moments, bien qu'hoste de ce lieu, / Sainct il possede tout, sent tout, voit tout en Dieu; / Comme pour quelque temps montant de forme en forme, / En la forme de Dieu, heureux, il se transforme. / Voy comme le Tout beau qui, brulant d'amitié / Pour ses rares beautez, le veut non par moitié, / Ains tout, et pour tousjours dresse à son Tout l'eschelle / Qui conduit d'ici bas à la gloire eternelle. / C'est donq fait, tu t'en vas? tu t'en vas donq à Dieu? / Adieu mon fils Henoc, adieu, mon fils, adieu. / Vy là-haut bien heureux. Jà ton corps qui se change / En nature d'esprit, ou bien en forme d'ange, / Vest l'immortalité. Jà tes yeux, non-plus yeux, / Decorent flamboyans d'astres nouveaux les cieux. / Tu humes à longs traicts la boisson nectaree, / Ton Sabat est sans fin. La courtine tiree, / Tu vois Dieu front à front; et sainctment uni / Au Bien triplement-un, tu vis en l'infini [Liberated from the yoke of corporeal laws, / And sequestered from sense, he sometimes flies / In the holy cabinet of most beautiful ideas, / Having faith, fasting, and prayer for wings; / At certain moments, although guest in this place, / Holy, he possesses all, senses all, sees all in God; / Sometimes climbing from form to form, / Into the form of God, happy, he transforms himself. / See how the All Beautiful who, burning of love / For his rare beauties, wants not half of him, / But all and for always, prepares the ladder to his All / Which leads from here below to eternal glory. / So it's done, you are gone? You are, then, gone to God? / Adieu, my son Enoch, adieu, my son, adieu. / Live above most happily. Already your body that is changed / Into the nature of a spirit or even into the form of an angel / Wears immortality. Already your eyes, no longer eyes, / With their flames ornament the heavens with new stars. / You scent at length the nectared drink, / Your Sabbath is without end. The curtain drawn back, / You see God face to face, and holily united / To the triune Good, you live in the infinite]' (*Les Artifices*, 655–76).

Index

Absalom 19, 33, 43, 45, 79, 98,
105–9, 118, 137–9
beauty of 11, 53, 110, 122, 135
death of 11, 13–14, 19, 110,
140–6, 152, 159–62, 164
murder of Amnon 19–20, 27–8,
40, 45, 79, 105, 107–9, 146
as rapist 25, 30–1, 34, 119–21
rebellion 5, 9–11, 13, 22, 24,
27–8, 30–2, 36–7, 104, 112,
121–3, 125–6, 143
Tamburlaine 19, 119, 126, 135,
138
Admiral's Men 4–5, 42–3
Allott, Robert: *Englands Parnassus*
4, 39, 44, 59, 88, 156
Amnon 70, 78–9, 98
death of 19–20, 27, 40, 105,
107
as rapist 7, 25, 27–8, 40, 71–4,
99
astrology 63, 117, 119, 138, 154,
156, 158

Bathsheba 7–8, 20–2, 58–9, 61,
87, 89–90
beauty of 5–6, 10–12, 29, 33,
39, 55–6, 63, 151
coercion of 6, 25, 28–9, 31–3,
36, 55, 63
death of child 20, 29, 33–4, 64,
89, 94–7

Christ 8–9, 113, 141

David 39–41, 117, 124
adultery and, 5–8, 20–2, 29, 55,
59, 74, 87
as anointed king 6–7, 13–14, 16,
21–3, 28–32, 47, 52, 80,
114, 118, 128, 131, 147
grief for Absalom 19, 115, 143,
161–4

as penitent 8–10, 22–3, 41, 47,
91, 94, 135
as poet 10–13, 47, 52, 54, 89
as shepherd 17–18, 66, 128, 162
as sinner 5–10, 14, 16, 19–23,
29–33, 47, 50, 64, 88, 92,
103, 121, 128–32, 135, 146
punishment of 6–7, 10, 25,
30, 37, 59, 94, 129
Tamburlaine 16–21, 23, 47, 150,
156
despair 10, 22–3, 115, 131
Du Bartas, Guilliaume: *Divine
Weeks* 7, 38–40, 56–8, 75
see also Peele, George: *David and
Bathsheba*, sources

Eden 39–40, 56–8, 60, 75
Elizabeth I 2, 23–4

Hanun 31, 64–7, 81, 101
crown of 18, 103–4
Henslowe, Philip 4, 41, 140
hypermasculinity 16, 19–21

Joab 10, 19, 21–2, 31, 52, 55, 80,
102, 107–9, 120, 132, 146,
149
defeat of Absalom 14, 141–4,
164–5, 167
siege of Rabbah and 60, 64, 66,
81–3, 86, 101, 103

Lucretia 25–6, 30, 32

Marlowe, Christopher 2, 14–15
Doctor Faustus 10, 113, 126,
131, 156
Edward II 55
Jew of Malta 43, 88
Tamburlaine plays 4, 7, 14–21,
43, 53, 65, 119, 126, 128–9,
135, 138, 153, 156–7

mercy, divine 9–10, 23, 53, 97,
    131
murder 9, 16, 20, 23, 31–2, 54,
    132, 167
    see also Absalom, murder of
    Amnon

Peele, George 1–5, 15
    Anglorum Feriae 3, 24, 96
    Arraignment of Paris 4, 113
    Battle of Alcazar 4, 15
    David and Bathsheba 4–7, 13–14,
        43–4, 146
        abridgement of 45–6, 70,
            107
        chronology of 36–8, 74, 101,
            107–8, 152
        sources, classical 10–11, 25,
            27
        sources, Du Bartas 38–41,
            56–8, 60, 75, 88, 129,
            150–1, 153–5, 158, 166–7
        staging of 16, 55–6, 60, 66–8,
            75–6, 94, 103, 105, 140–1,
            159–60
    Edward I 4–5, 119
    Tale of Troy 2, 54, 105,
    Troublesome Reign 4–5, 15, 18

Queen's Men 5, 168

rape *see* sexual violence
rebellion 5, 22, 117
    see also Absalom, rebellion

Saul 13–14, 20, 24, 30, 66–7, 93,
    102, 115, 132
sexual violence 23–34
    coercion 6, 25, 28–9, 31–3, 36,
        47, 55
    patriarchy and 7, 25, 27–30, 47,
        72–5, 78
    rape 20–1, 24–32, 34, 78, 119
        sovereignty and 7, 25–34, 47,
            73–4, 78

    of Tamar 7, 20, 25, 27–8, 32,
        37, 40, 45, 71–4, 78–9, 99,
        101, 164
    women's agency and 29, 32–4,
        47, 64, 120
Shakespeare, William 5, 14–15
    1H4 136
    1H6 68
    3H6 126,
    Ant. 85, *H5* 163
    MM 113
    'Rape of Lucrece' 26, 32
    Rom. 166
    Tit. (with George Peele) 5, 25–6,
        32
    WT 136
shame 10, 23, 27, 31, 33, 90,
    119–21, 164
Sidney, Philip 11–12, 38, 52
sin 78, 92, 94, 99, 135, 169
    see also David, as sinner
Solomon 12, 89, 95, 97, 152, 157
    as anointed king 14, 153, 155,
        158
    as heir 27, 33, 36–7, 41, 47,
        146, 150, 159
    as Seth 40–1, 150, 153–5
Spenser, Edmund 3, 10, 104
succession crisis 24, 152
suicide 10, 33, 76, 130, 136

Tamar 7, 20, 27–8, 32, 37, 40, 45,
    70–5, 79, 89, 99, 101
Tamburlaine 16–21, 23, 119, 138
    see also Marlowe, Christopher
tyranny 13, 16, 19–22, 28, 79,
    103, 128, 165

Uriah 20, 27, 37, 61, 64, 69, 74, 80

vengeance 64, 107, 129
    divine 6–7, 28, 94, 104, 109,
        112, 142, 145–6
    for rape 26–8, 31, 33–4, 69, 99,
        111

Milton Keynes UK
Ingram Content Group UK Ltd.
UKHW021322250823
427489UK00028B/319

9 781526 163981